GEORGIA AND STATE RIGHTS

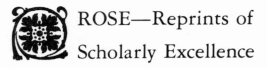

ROSE—Reprints of
Scholarly Excellence

Certain good books should be, like the rose, not only hardy perennials in their intrinsic worth and usefulness, but also perennial in their availability. The purpose of the ROSE series is to make available such choice books from the past that are not otherwise available.

ROSE is intended primarily to meet the needs of the university classroom. Volumes are included in the series upon the recommendation of professors in the classroom who indicate a need for a currently out-of-print text. When investigation indicates that a reprint is warranted and available, ROSE reprints the text in an attractive and durable, yet affordable, format—equal or even superior to the original quality.

Roses come in many varieties. So do books in the ROSE series. ROSE is not restricted to any one subject area but will reprint classics from any and all classes—the humanities, the sciences, the arts. But each is a "rose" of a reprint—preeminent among its kind, rare, of scholarly excellence.

GEORGIA AND STATE RIGHTS

by
Ulrich Bonnell Phillips, A.M., Ph.D.

introduction by
John Herbert Roper

Mercer University / ROSE
MP Press
Macon, Ga. 31207

ISBN 0-86554-103-5

Georgia and State Rights, by Ulrich Bonnell Phillips,
originally was published by
Washington: Government Printing Office, in 1902.
The ROSE edition is © 1984 by
Mercer University Press, Macon, GA 31207.
All Rights Reserved.
Printed in the United States of America.
MUP/ROSE
September 1983
Photomechanically reproduced from the original pages
by Omnipress of Macon, Inc., Macon GA
Margaret Jordan Brown, Associate Designer, MUP
Janet Middlebrooks, Data Entry Manager, MUP
All Mercer University Press books are produced
on acid-free paper that exceeds the minimum standards set
by the National Historical Publications and Records Commission.

Library of Congress Cataloging in Publication Data

Phillips, Ulrich Bonnell, 1877-1934.
   Georgia and state rights.

   (ROSE ; no. 7)
   Reprint. Originally published: Washington : G.P.O., 1902.
   Bibliography: 211.
   1. Georgia—Politics and government—1775-1865.
2. State rights. I. Title. II. Series.
F290.P56   1983   975.8'03   83-19635
ISBN 0-86554-103-5 (alk. paper)

TABLE OF CONTENTS

———

INTRODUCTION
BY JOHN HERBERT ROPER

Georgia and State Rights is a significant book, valuable not only for the wealth of information it imparts, but also for what it teaches us about the process of writing history. Its author, Ulrich Bonnell Phillips, long ago earned a place of importance among Southern historians—indeed among historians of the entire nation—and is a notable example of being a product of his environment. This Georgian who wrote so evocatively about the South made his career outside the region, teaching to great acclaim at the University of Michigan for eighteen years (1911-1929), and to even greater notoriety at Yale University during a period of exciting growth at the New Haven campus.Thoroughness, logical organization, clean narrative, and graceful expression were the distinguishing characteristics of this craftsman; so, too, was a genteel racism that drew criticism to his work, especially in the 1960s and 1970s.

While recognizing that all history is a compilation of concrete facts, we have come to understand the process of collecting these facts as interpretive action by historians who have their own points of view—sometimes useful, sometimes sheer bigotry. As Phillips had a good deal of both, he shows us much more of history—a history of an actual people. Understanding a little about how such a historian and his era developed such characteristics can help us to use not just this volume profitably, but history books in general. With this new understanding, it is not suprising that in the 1980s students who in no way share Phillips's racial attitudes have begun to express a renewed respect for the body of historical knowledge that Phillips's books still offer; other students of his era have noted that the general context of racism in which Phillips lived makes him seem mild by comparison.

With this book, actually a combination of his master's thesis from the University of Georgia (chapters one and two) and his doctoral thesis from Columbia University, Phillips created in 1902 a small revolution in the way that Southern history was written. In that day, most of the nation's historians emphasized legalistic and institutional history, concentrating on constitutional issues such as struggles between central and local authority or contests between president and court. The reigning mentality was that of Leopold von Ranke, Herbert Baxter Adams, and William Archibald Dunning, and the buzz word of the era was "scientific." Ranke used this term to describe meticulous attention to political detail revealed in primary sources with a minimum of editorial interpretation: the Scientific historian "let the facts tell the story." For Southerners, those gravitating to Dunning's superb "graduate seminaries" at Columbia University in New York or to Adams's at The Johns Hopkins University in Baltimore, the natural subject of study was Civil War/Reconstruction, for the still-provocative social issues of the war and its aftermath could be "safely" discussed through Rankean Scientific systems. The early Southern pioneers, Phillips's peers, included Walter Lynwood Fleming, Joseph Gregoire de Roulhac Hamilton, and William Watson Davis, who called themselves part of the "Dunning School" and Scientific historians. These men defended unreconstructed racial attitudes by selective quoting from contemporaneous sources to let the facts tell the story of white supremacy and, in a period of extreme racism, they won widespread acceptance.

In a way, Phillips was a part of that tradition, too. His preface includes the standard affirmation of Scientific theory and his study has a Dunning title, being about state rights. Certainly, he agreed with his fellow Southern historians that blacks were inferior and that Reconstruction was a mistake. However, he deliberately avoided the issues of Civil War and Reconstruction, cutting the narrative short for the period normally studied by Dunning's Southerners. Further, he employed a means of analysis quite different from the Scientists. As he states in the preface, while in Chicago he had "heard a suggestive lecture" by Frederick Jackson Turner, (then at the University of Wisconsin) that had inspired this book. Turner, in the process of creating Progressivism, was studying class structure and sectional and local politics, emphasizing economic conflict. Moved by the speech, Phillips studied with Turner one summer, corresponded with him, planned with Turner a program of study, and hoped to do graduate work with him. However, Turner recommended that he instead seek training with Dunning at the prestigious school in Morningside Heights; Phillips took this advice.

By writing about the antebellum South without much regard to the Civil War, and writing about class structure, class loyalty, regional variations in economic needs, and sectional politics, Phillips was doing something unusual for a Southerner—writing about the South; yet it was not unusual for a Midwesterner to write about that region. In this book, Phillips was bringing Turner to the South and was starting a movement toward a full-blown Progressive interpretation of the South that would culminate in William E. Dodd, who described the South as an agrarian elite experimenting with white democracy while steadfastly resisting encroaching bourgeois capitalism with its Northern patterns of industrialization, commercialism, and urbanization (*The Cotton Kingdom*, Yale University, 1919).

THE CONTRIBUTING ENVIRONMENT

Ulysses Bonnell Phillips entered this world 4 November 1877, only months after the last Federal troops had marched out of the South ending Reconstruction. Born in the western sector of Georgia, this baby represented the union of Southern elite and Southern yeomanry. His mother, née Jesse Elizabeth Young, came from a slaveholding planter family of some standing prior to the Civil War; his father, Alonzo Rabun Phillips, hailed from a family of obscure "plain folk."[1]

LaGrange, near the Alabama line, claimed Phillips, the baby, as its own years after Phillips, the man, had achieved prominence. At the time of his birth, considerably fewer people cared what happened in the Alonzo Phillips household. In this small town, Alonzo managed to rear his family, but what the head of the household did for a living has never been clear. The censuses for 1880 and 1890 suggest that he performed a variety of odd jobs, perhaps as a handyman of minor talents. Money was scarce for the family and a surviving photograph of the supposed home shows a modest, two-story, wooden-frame structure. As the Farmers' Alliance and the Populists would make known to all the world, times were bad economically for Southerners of this generation, so considering the time and the place,

---

[1]James C. Bonner to John Herbert Roper, 24 June 1976, with enclosure on genealogical data. Letter in possession of author.

Alonzo Phillips and family were existing in a fairly normal state of plain living, straitened but not impoverished.[2]

Because the family finances were marginal, all hands had to work to stay solvent. Jesse Phillips labored as a seamstress, bringing in precious dollars, and the boy tilled the neighboring cotton fields when he reached his teens. By wise management of this income, and luck, the family found the money to educate, as well as feed and clothe, U. B. [3]

Beyond these paltry facts, the available data by which a historian could understand U. B. Phillips's past are sadly lacking. The Georgia historian did say some very definite things about his early life, statements of a thinly masked autobiographical nature in his historical works. These general values, combined with particular judgments explicitly made, cast a revealing light on the things Phillips did not say, namely, his deliberate silence about his father.

In later years, Phillips spoke highly of his mother as a true lady, a matron both dedicated to her appointed role and willing to shoulder additional, then masculine, burdens of money-making, if not money-handling. Her image preserved on photographer's paper was of a poised, proud, erect brunette woman. For the boy and for the man, she stood in that line of women to whose work "no prosing pen can do justice."[4]

The essential nature of his mother's labor was childrearing, or socialization. As he said, the plantation "made more men that it made fortunes" and Jesse Phillips was of the plantation. He gave her credit for his character traits of patience, industry, kindness and, above all, a deep and impressive reserve, a quiet fortitude notable in the face of crisis. Since no particulars of this socialization process have been available, one must accept Phillips's word that he learned his manners and mores from his mother. If that supposition is a fair one, then the feminine side of such books as *Life and Labor in the Old South* describes in a general way Jesse Phillips. Should this be accurate, she would have been a charming, gracious lady dedicated to

---

[2]Ibid. Interviews, Mabel Phillips Parker, 12-14 July 1974, 12-15 March 1975. Mabel Phillips Parker is the surviving daughter of Ulrich Phillips. Unless otherwise noted, all interviews cited are filed with the Southern Historical Collection, Library of the University of North Carolina, Chapel Hill.

[3]Ibid.

[4]Ulrich Bonnell Phillips, *History of Transportation in the Eastern Cotton Belt to 1860* (New York: Columbia University, 1908) v.

the education of young men as leaders. A woman willing to follow worthy men, Jesse Phillips must have instilled in her boys unforgettable notions about masculine roles, about the duty of men. Certainly Phillips perceived the family as an ordered, hierarchical entity with a definite set of rules and specific functions for each member. As ladies, women exemplified the highest good in humanity. This feminine duty, a difficult and demanding one, required a certain freedom from the worries of wage-earning: it was enough that a woman raise her children, for she thus imparted the ethical sense that the grown adult must practice.[5]

Since the A. R. Phillips home could not offer the matron of the family this freedom, Jesse Phillips could not have fulfilled this role to her intimated capabilities. What Phillips told in *Life and Labor* represented a type, a model, his perception of what she tried to do, an ideal instructive of her potential as he envisioned it. Without undue speculation it is clear that the main lessons Phillips learned were control, discipline, and poise, all of which suggest a rather strict upbringing.[6]

Of A. R. Phillips, evidence incredibly slight and uninstructive endured. His son wanted it that way. Whether one blamed the circumstances of Georgia life in the third quarter of the nineteenth century or whether one blamed the man, A. R. Phillips could not provide, could not perform the appointed masculine role in the family. A Milledgeville newspaper discovered A. R. Phillips when his son became important to the city and the state in the 1920s. That newspaper printed a picture of a medium-sized man with a rather wispy moustache standing amidst the flowers of his garden. Bernice B. McCullar, the editor, used the occasion to sermonize the importance of meekness and generosity, for A. R. Phillips presented flowers to children of the town.[7]

Out of that garden stared an enigma all but lost in the mists of time and memory. Was he a shiftless ne'er-do-well who ought to have done better by Jesse Phillips? U. B. Phillips was too much the

[5]Bonner to Roper, 24 June 1976. Phillips, *Life and Labor in the Old South* (Boston: Little-Brown, 1929) passim.

[6]Walter E. Houghton, *Victorian Frame of Mind* (New Haven: Yale University, 1957). Interviews, Mabel Phillips Parker, 12-19 July 1974, 12-15 March 1975; Robert A. Warner, 13 February 1976; Norman D. Palmer, 6 May 1974.

[7]Bernice Brown McCullar, "Flowers for the Living," *Times* (Milledgeville) 19 November 1918, clipping in scrapbook, Ulrich Bonnell Phillips

gentleman and too much the devoted son of Jesse Phillips to castigate her husband in that language. Was he a hardworking, sturdy yeoman misunderstood by a son who demanded a Robert Toombs in a place and time where there was no room for such leadership? Phillips the historian had too much integrity, too much grace, and too much good sense to accept such an explanation. But Phillips the private man strove to be a strong father and a complete man, strove to fill the perceived role; at heart he must have demanded the same things of his father and gradually have been disappointed.[8]

In this maddeningly foggy area, so crucial to the child's personality development, from which the man grows, one can glean only these hard facts: Phillips consciously took his behavioral cues from his mother and not from his father; he glorified her both in specific remarks and in general eulogizing of female Southern plantation leadership; his father, he ignored purposely in specific remarks but indicted by implication. In general his early life, on reflection, came considerably short of his ideal, a failure only partly due to the strained economic circumstances surrounding that family life.[9]

If socialized to fill a definite role that his situation could not support, the growing boy still found sufficient room for happiness and for joy. His self-control and intelligence gave him a sharp wit and his laugther, when it came, was mellifluous and infectious. With time he grew tall, over six feet, and strong, an erect, athletic teenager. Like other boys in the region, U. B. was conscious of his Southernness, of the Civil War, and of the loss of that contest to the Yankees from the North. As Phillips related to friends later, his name, Ulysses, came from the doctor who delivered him. But in Georgia, in the late 1880s the name Ulysses conjured up no imagery of a brilliant Greek warrior; in Georgia it stood without mistake for Ulysses S. Grant, supposedly a drunken, cruel Yankee general during the war, and a drunken, foolish panderer to corrupt carpetbaggers and ignorant "darkies" after the war. Approaching his mother, U. B. requested a new name, one more fitting a devoted Georgian. She readily consented on condition that he select a name beginning with "U" so

Papers, Manuscript Division, Sterling Memorial Library, Yale University; hereafter cited as Phillips Papers, Yale.

[8]These are the author's speculations; both Bonner and Mabel Phillips Parker emphasize how little Phillips talked about his father.

[9]Again, these are the author's speculations. Cf. Houghton, *Victorian Frame of Mind*, passim, and Erik Homburger Erikson, *Childhood and Society* (New York: W. W. Norton, 1963): 15-108, 209-325.

that he could still be called "U. B." The boy found the Germanic "Ulrich" for his new, more fitting identity.[10]

The young Ulrich was marked for scholarship and in 1891 his mother arranged for him to attend Tulane Preparatory School, a precollege institution associated with the New Orleans university. The cost of $80 for nine-months' instruction, "payable in installments of $20 at the beginning of each quarter session," was a relatively high fee for the family, after just having moved to Milledgeville.[11]

How the selection of the preparatory school was made, whether it was by Jesse Phillips, young U. B., or someone else, is unclear. It was designed specifically to form an easy transition from high school into Tulane University; several of the university faculty instructed in the lower school and consciously gauged class demands by expectations for the future. Not surprisingly, all but five of Phillips's 192 classmates were from Louisiana and Mississippi and a good number of them did find their way into Tulane's college classrooms. Although it seems improbable that the boy could afford to attend the private college for four years, the preparation was well suited for the liberal arts colleges of the South: a rigorous daily schedule of training in the classics with emphasis on Latin, Greek, and mathematics. Also taught was gentlemanly behavior.[12]

Academic standards aside, the preparation for life was a strict one: the boys rose to attend classes by seven o'clock and remained there until four in the afternoon. Integral parts of the training were penmanship and drawing, skills developed under persistent coaching. In later life Phillips reflected this training with his meticulous, neat cursive notes and his disdain for the clumsy mechanics of the typewriter. Otherwise the curriculum made slight impact on the man; drilling in the classics did not produce a notable scholar at Tulane High, nor did the accomplished professor show a great affinity for literature, drama, language, or other such aspects of Greco-Roman culture.[13]

---

[10]Fred Landon, "Ulrich Bonnell Phillips: Historian of the South," *Journal of Southern History* 5 (Summer 1939): 365-72. Interview, Mabel Phillips Parker, 14-19 July 1974.

[11]"Tulane High School," in *Tulane University of Louisiana Catalogues*, 1891-1892, 1892-1893, University Archives, Tulane University Library, New Orleans.

[12]Ibid.

[13]Ibid.

While the schoolboy of the classroom was not discernible in the man's personality, the schoolboy as a young gentleman stood in direct line between Jesse Phillips's childrearing and the mannered academic. Tulane prepsters were prompt and courteous, orderly and respectful, reserved and well disciplined in a gentleman's sense; the school, in short, exercised the powerful paternalism that A. R. Phillips could not, which may well have been the school's attraction for Jesse, far more than the course work.[14]

There were other lessons, lessons from the city of New Orleans, that impressed the young man. He loved the big, dirty center of commerce and culture. New Orleans was also a town in turmoil, a battleground in the racial and class wars of the 1890s.[15] Although the most vicious political fighting came after the latter half of the 1890s, the battle lines were clearly taking shape while the boy was in school. There were Populists who would link the arm of city labor into the arm of rural labor, uniting in the process black and white races in a common cause. There were Bourbons who would resist that cause with all their vigor, who would and did do anything to turn that Populist tide. In addition, there were many men conscious of racial competition for labor, political office, and social station; there were whites who would annihilate the "uppity niggers" and tolerate the other blacks only on conditions severely limiting personal freedom. There were, finally, blacks in great numbers, in all colors, occupying all ranges in the societal spectrum, including a sizable and cohesive mulatto group.[16]

The boiling waters of race and class rose nearly to overflowing in New Orleans while the alert, impressionable, inquisitive youth attended his classes. When he went back to Georgia in 1893 for college, the lid literally blew with the overwhelming defeat of the Populists. When both Bourbon and Populist survivors turned to crush suffrage for blacks, and their perceived assertions of social

---

[14]Ibid.

[15]Phillips to Grace L. King, 5 June 1929, Ulrich Bonnell Phillips Papers, Southern Historical Collection, University of North Carolina Library, Chapel Hill; hereafter cited as Phillips Papers, Southern Historical Collection.

[16]Roger W. Shugg, *Origins of Class Struggle in Louisiana—a Social History of White Farmers and Laborers, During Slavery and After* (Baton Rouge: Louisiana State University, 1939).

equality, Phillips as a college student was deeply interested in his region's travail.[17]

When Phillips entered the University of Georgia, the state's liberal arts and agricultural education center, the school clearly reflected the hard times found at the turn of the century. The campus needed repairs and instruction was not of the highest caliber.[18]

Georgians had been the first Americans to charter a state university, the general assembly of 1785 establishing the site in the northeastern city of Athens. North Carolina, however, built and initiated classes at Chapel Hill first, while construction languished to the south. The antebellum University of Georgia never attained the level of the University of North Carolina or the South Carolina College, much less the national eminence of the University of Virginia or the College of William and Mary. Before Phillips arrived, the university had withstood the Civil War, the confusion of Reconstruction, the Southern agricultural recession, and the severe economic depression in which the whole nation suffered. When Phillips set foot on campus, the University of Georgia was struggling upward against great pressures.[19]

In spite of the pressures, the University of Georgia did offer quality instruction in certain fields. History and political science, located in the Franklin College of Liberal Arts, were two of those fields. The preeminent historian in residence was John Hanson Thomas McPherson, a product of Herbert Baxter Adams's graduate "seminary" at The Johns Hopkins University who had previously taught at the University of Michigan. McPherson, as a loyal protégé of Adams, emphasized political history: history was "past politics and politics present history." At the University of Georgia, McPherson was an accepted fixture at the Franklin College by 1891.[20]

---

[17]Ibid.

[18]Interview, Ellis Merton Coulter, June 1976.

[19]Walter Barnard Hill to Harriet Wadsworth Terry, 30 May 1904, Walter Barnard Hill Collection, Special Collections, University of Georgia Library. Merle Curti and Vernon Carstensen, *The University of Wisconsin, 1848-1925; a History* (Madison: University of Wisconsin, 1949) 1:580. *The University Record* 2 (1898): 38, in North Carolina Collection of the University of North Carolina Library, Chapel Hill.

[20]Phillips, typescript from *Pandora*, 1899, in possession of Ellis Merton Coulter, used here with his permission. Wendell Holmes Stephenson, "Ulrich Bonnell Phillips: Georgia Historian," *Georgia Historical Quarterly* 41 (Summer 1957): 103-25.

Phillips, the undergraduate student, built an inconsistent academic record, improving greatly in his last two years. As he later told a friend, he had enjoyed himself too much for real study his freshman and sophomore years. A member of Alpha Tau Omega social fraternity, Ulrich Phillips spent those early years of college as most students did and do, reveling in the freedom and camaraderie of the campus. In addition to this social life, the young student was an athlete, and a letter-winner in track; he set a school record for the mile run.[21]

At midpoint in his undergraduate years, Phillips became a serious student of past politics. His hard work earned him the attention of McPherson and of other professors; their respect for him was such that he occasionally conducted their classes. Soon, however, the hard work and the honors brought with them a new problem: he damaged his eyes and had to leave school for a semester at doctor's orders. It was then that he experienced a real farm life, apparently on a neighbor's cotton farm back home. As would become obvious, those brief months of raising cotton, combined with subsequent periodic visits to plantations, bore for the man a strikingly vivid reality, remaining poignant in his thoughts.[22]

After returning for a successful senior year, Phillips won admission to the graduate department in 1897, serving as a part-time instructor. For a master's thesis he produced two craftsmanlike essays on local and state politics in antebellum Georgia. Through these essays, basically unchanged in *Georgia and State Rights*, he traced the evolution of politics in Georgia from factional, personality-dominated coalitions into the almost "true-party" system operating on the eve of the national war.[23]

Working on his thesis led Phillips to begin his most important academic friendship, that with Frederick Jackson Turner. It was in 1893 that Turner, then at the University of Wisconsin, had risen to

---

[21]James Walter Mason, et al., *The Class of 1897* (Atlanta: Higgins-McArthur, 1948), in possession of Ellis Merton Coulter, used here with his permission. *Centennial Alumni Catalogue*, 1901, Special Collections, University of Georgia Library.

[22]Landon, "Ulrich Bonnell Phillips."

[23]The A.M. thesis has been lost from the University of Georgia, but it is the first two chapters of this book, originally published as "Georgia and State Rights," American Historical Association *Annual Report*, 1902, vol. 2. See Anthony R. Dees to John Herbert Roper, 17 June 1976, in possession of author.

giant's stature with his magnificent production, "The Significance of the Frontier in American History." With that one insight, Turner had grasped the nation's intellect, explaining, or claiming to explain, at once the peculiar genius of the United States—which was its expanding frontier—and the country's unique crisis at century's end—the closing of that frontier. Following that tour de force, Turner gathered bricks and mortar to make real the huge, perhaps unworkable, structure that he had outlined. Stooping from his awesome panoramic view, he bent to the gathering of local history in full detail.[24]

Phillips, showing a special faith and pluck, wrote to the giant of American historical writing seeking advice. Turner, showing the best side of professionalism, responded with warmth and enthusiasm, offering to read Phillips's thesis essays and offer useful criticism. Turner grew to be a special friend of the graduate student, advising him on doctoral programs. Together the two made the choice most Southern boys made then: Phillips would study with William Archibald Dunning at Columbia University. That remarkable teacher, whose great powers exerted such a profound influence on a coterie of Southern academics, could only modify the direction already set by Turner's young protégé, whom he greeted in New York City in 1900.[25]

Phillips had a strange career in that big city. Almost immediately he was teased for his conspicuous Georgia accent, a common enough teasing, for Dunning had attracted a large number of Southern scholars, most of whom studied Reconstruction. But Phillips's pride would not allow him to be the butt of jokes not of his own making. He set out to contrive himself a language, disdaining to play the hick and defying the style of the Northern accent. Instead, he chose a certain British accent, then a standard pronunciation and inflection for the stage. He worked at his new style of speech until he mastered it, refining it into quite an impressive, and a very natural, tongue. Obviously, that kind of pride and attention to detail of style emanated from a very powerful will and suggested much about his character.[26]

---

[24]Ray Allen Billington, *Frederick Jackson Turner, Historian, Scholar, Teacher* (New York: Oxford University, 1973).

[25]See Phillips-Turner correspondence in Frederick Jackson Turner Papers, Huntington Memorial Library, San Marino CA; and Frederick Jackson Turner Papers, Department of History, University Archives, University of Wisconsin Library, Madison; hereafter cited as Turner Papers, Madison.

[26]Interview, Ralph Henry Gabriel, 13 March 1975.

It wasn't long before Phillips had again impressed his fellow students and superiors. Still, his was not an unqualified success. While the records are not available, he told students that he had once failed some examinations at Columbia and had to repeat them. Despite this obscure setback, he won election as president of the Federation of Graduate Clubs, a body composed of officers from schools across the country.[27]

In his writing and research, Phillips made his greatest strides, expanding his local-party studies into a surprisingly mature dissertation, "Georgia and State Rights." As he had before, he focused on elite politics but demonstrated a good feel for the complexities of Georgia government, noting the middle-class and poor voters and their activities. Already he was emphasizing race, for he showed with a series of hand-drawn maps that predominantly black, slave-holding counties easily formed a special coalition, often acting in specific, unified response to slave-related issues. Moreover, he offered the Turnerian, Progressive perspective and wording in describing a conflict between "factions and political parties which, though they underwent several changes of name and of policy, perceived a certain degree of continuity throughout the entire period."

This Progressive class analysis reflects his fundamental assumption that conflict was "due not only to tradition in families and localities, but very largely [to] inequalities in the economic conditions of the population." As his maps and his prose say, the original "Troup Party" was a coalition of the wealthy planters who owned the most black slaves and farmed the best land, while the original "Clarke Party" was composed of "newer men," without many slaves and farming on less productive soil in less populated, poorer counties. Later, the names changed, but the issues remained the same: the competing material interests of different classes.

One of the beauties of this monograph is Phillips's success in keeping track of these class distinctions between Troup and Clarke, between large-scale and small-scale planters, and later between Whigs and Democrats, without losing sight of the sectional issues, such as opposition to the Supreme Court rulings on the Indians' rights or opposition to high protective tariffs that otherwise united

---

[27]See letterhead of notes, "The Situation of the South in 1903," unpublished manuscript on microfilm, Phillips Papers, Yale. William Archibald Dunning to Frederick Jackson Turner, 20 April 1902, Turner Papers, Madison.

Georgians in national politics. As he points out, there was a uniformity and unification, a surface harmony, for Georgians that masked deep internal conflicts of interest that were escaping the notice of his Scientific peers. It was Phillips's gift to locate such issues and trace their development.[28]

"Georgia and State Rights" did not possess the full measure of grace and felicity achieved in his later works and is even slow in places. Many a proud horse is similarly uncoordinated and clumsy before maturity, so that comparison seems apt. Phillips, at this early date, had all the skills and determination, but lacked a certain coordination of effort. Still, he drafted enough good chapters out of an impressive amount of research to win the Justin Winsor Prize from the American Historical Association. The award meant many things: it capped his graduate career; it was published by the Government Printing Office in 1902; and, most important, it brought with it an appointment as instructor in history at the University of Wisconsin, the home of Turner, the giant.[29]

Dreams were bright in Madison in 1902. The state university, Robert LaFollette's showpiece for Progressivism, was just achieving greatness. Already there had been the accomplishments in agricultural science by Harry L. Russell and William A. Henry; and Frederick Jackson Turner was setting in motion important historical studies, studies that would rely on the excellent archival collection directed by Lyman Draper. Additionally, there was Richard T. Ely, beginning to direct with John R. Commons a major series of economic studies of the nation's development.[30]

The atmosphere inspired bold plans and the young instructor met the challenge, intending no less than the reform of the University of Georgia and of the Georgia Historical Society. He was certain that Athens could be more worthy of its name by emulating Madison; and the historical society at home could profit as well by modeling itself on the Midwestern society. Not a small part of this progress would be Phillips's own role, for he decided to return to direct the

---

[28]Phillips, "Georgia and State Rights," passim; chapters 1 and 2 in this reprint.

[29]Cf. correspondence between Turner, Dunning, and Phillips in Turner Papers, 1902, Madison.

[30]Curti and Carstensen, *The University of Wisconsin,* , 2:374-496.

Georgia Historical Society in the winter months, performing his professorial duties with Turner in the spring and summer.[31]

To attain these ends, the instructor entered an incredible schedule of classroom work, historical research and writing, and contemporary economic research and newspaper reporting for the *Atlanta Constitution*. With Ely and Commons, he set to work collecting and editing plantation documents for two volumes of the *Documentary History of American Industrial Society*. The state of such resource material in that day should not be forgotten: except for Draper's exceptional Wisconsin archives, libraries did not possess great holdings of manuscripts, nor was what they had well organized. The work of gathering resources that Phillips began at Madison was something he continued all his career, coaxing and cajoling from descendant owners antebellum correspondence, diaries, and other records.[32]

As Wendell Holmes Stephenson has shown, the Georgia Historical Society was not ready for what Phillips proposed and that aspect of his dreams faded. He did bring some order to its collection, filing two reports on it with the American Historical Association. And still other dreams faded: he quit writing for the *Constitution* when it began supporting Theodore Roosevelt in 1906. His grandest project, a study of transportation in the antebellum South, ran into competition when William E. Martin published a book that discussed railroads in the central South, leaving Phillips precious little geographic area to cover.[33]

The series of setbacks and the realization that he could not work happily in Georgia forced him to assess his position: as part-time instructor with no real chance for a full-time job at Madison and no part-time jobs to supplement his income. The year 1907, then, must have been a difficult one for Phillips. Since he was divorced from his earlier vigorous activities in Georgia and his book had become limited in scope, what now of the Turner dream of following the Georgia frontier, perhaps being a little Turner in Georgia? Was that

---

[31]Stephenson, "Ulrich B. Phillips: Georgia Historian," 103-25.

[32]File of newspaper clippings, 1902-1906, Phillips Papers, Yale. U. B. Phillips, *Plantation and Frontier Documents: 1649-1863, Illustrative of Industrial History in the Colonial & White Ante-bellum South*, vol. 1, and *Documentary History of American Industrial Society*, vol. 2, ed. Richard T. Ely and John R. Commons (Cleveland: A. H. Clark, 1909). Interviews, Ralph Henry Gabriel, 13 March 1975; Avery Odelle Craven, 11-12 November 1975; Bell Irvin Wiley, 13 September 1974.

[33]Stephenson, "Ulrich B. Phillips: Georgia Historian," 103-25.

not a cruel vision in the face of his actual station, temporary lecturer grinding out research on railroads in the eastern cotton belt?

While the discouraging side of the late Wisconsin years seems obvious and occasionally surfaces, as in a bitter letter to Clark Howell, the fact remains that Ulrich Phillips did not record his emotions. Rather, he persisted in the faith, producing several articles in Southern journals, including the new *South Atlantic Quarterly* and the *Gulf States Historical Review*. As he had with earlier writings, he remained the growing show horse stepping out awkwardly in his books but with grace and élan in the short runs of articles and lectures. His theme remained consistent: the commanding power of elite planters in the South, perceptible and even dominant in the abuses of the transportation network.[34]

GROWTH AND EXPANSION

With the disappointments of 1907 came compensation in 1908. Tulane University called the young professor to teach history and political science. Phillips returned to New Orleans, evidently with pleasure, to take his first full-time job and finish the work he had begun in the Midwest. While at Tulane he saw *History of Transportation in the Eastern Cotton Belt* (1908) published by Columbia University Press, as well as his two volumes in Ely and Common's *Documentary History*. It was also at Tulane that he wrote several crucial chapters in the ambitious multivolume, *History of the South in the Building of the Nation*.[35]

Here Phillips was at the height of his career as an economic historian. Active in the affairs of the Tulane Society of Economics, he had access to plantations in the vicinity and used the opportunity for firsthand observation of the labor force, still black and still less than free. Moreover, he continued to speak with the voice of reform; he decried backward agricultural practices, including poor treatment of and lack of training for farm labor.[36]

---

[34]See articles reprinted in Eugene D. Genovese, ed., *The Slave Economy of the Old South; Selected Essays in Economic and Social History* by Ulrich Bonnell Phillips (Baton Rouge: Louisiana State University, 1968).

[35]*The South in the Building of the Nation*, 12 vols. (Richmond: Southern Publications Society, 1909) 2:146-71; 4:191-241, 382-422; 5:121-29, 358-67, 435-41, 475-78; 6:305-16; 7:173-99.

[36]"Tulane Society of Economics," 1914, pamphlet in University Archives, Tulane University Library, New Orleans.

A speech before the Society of Economics illustrated his attitude. Speaking on "the decadence of the plantation," the newcomer urged multicrop cultivation, the use of modern planting techniques, better transportation, and other agricultural reforms within the broad context of economic diversification. There was in the speech a pregnant suggestion, foreshadowing his famed "central theme": black labor should work the fields; white labor belongs in the mills. While the labor forces of both races should each receive better treatment, the two must be segregated.[37]

Outside Louisiana this historian of the economy was making a name for himself, establishing standards of scholarship in the use of sources, and in publications and presentations as a part of the growing bank of specialists in Southern studies. It was at such a historical conference in New York City that he began the most important relationship of his life. There, in 1909, he met Lucie Mayo-Smith.[38]

Lucie was a thoroughbred from a family of New York State and New England aristocrats important in academia: members of the circle included Columbia University political economist Richmond Mayo-Smith, the Massachusetts historian Worthington Chauncey Ford, and Cornell University historian Preserved Smith. She had a handsome visage and proud carriage that, along with a seeming austerity induced by hearing problems, gave her a rather haughty air. She was possessed, too, of late Victorian assumptions about sex roles, assumptions that fell neatly into place with those of Jesse Phillips and her son. Lucie, accustomed to a scholar's work habits, expected to fill the role of professor's wife, rearing the children, performing (or directing) domestic labor, entertaining company, and generally setting the household to order.[39]

According to family legend these two met in the best tradition of Victorian romance: the tall, handsome lady who served punch at the convention attracted the attention of the tall, handsome professor. The next day the professor left his card at the Smiths' hoping to escort the lady that evening. Properly cautious, the Smiths chaperoned Ulrich and Lucie to a concert and permitted the courtship

---

[37]Ibid.

[38]Interview, Mabel Phillips Parker, 12-14 July 1974.

[39]Ibid.

gradually to develop. After a decent interval, Ulrich won Lucie's hand and the newlyweds set up housekeeping in New Orleans.[40]

Repeating a pattern from other parts of his life, the man's wife was an enigma, an enigma of power and depth whose presence, while hazy, completed his being. Her looks, her lineage, her breeding, her style, all fit the greatest of his expectations. Moreover, she knew the problems of a historian, understood the dual needs of support and independence, of closeness and distance, and the crucial timing, the ebb and flow, of those needs. Finally, there were the intangibles that elude us, the vital components of her personality that drew Ulrich to his love.[41]

Did he meet the greatest of her expectations? Certainly he was already a star on the rise, offering her the responsibilities and pleasures she wanted; certainly, too, he had in the present the dignity and the quality she wanted. Yet there were flaws. For one, he was very Georgian and she did not care for the South, nor for any region far from the long-settled Northeast. There were also problems of lineage. Even Jesse's family did not begin to match the stature of the Smiths, while the paternal side was almost an embarrassment. But she was hardly the reluctant lover or less than the devoted wife, concluding that the weight of her suitor's deficiencies was quite less than that of his attributes.[42]

Nor should we overlook the ironies of the marriage, ironies that did not detract from but rather deepened the relationship. The first was the unfortunate issue of money. There is little doubt that Lucie's considerable family wealth allowed the couple to live higher than a professor's salary warranted; the earlier publications and appointments simply did not pay very well. The role of the father was the second. Because of his heavy teaching and research schedule, the young scholar had little time for his children. So, for different reasons, Lucie Phillips became as strong a mother as Jesse Phillips, and Ulrich played a paternal role less than he would want.[43]

This new household had scarcely begun when Ulrich received an appointment to the University of Michigan in 1911. This was a

---

[40]Ibid.

[41]Ibid. Cf. interviews, Robert A. Warner, 13 February 1976; Norman D. Palmer, 18 April 1974; Thomas E. Drake, 12 June 1975.

[42]Ibid.

[43]Interviews, Bell Irvin Wiley, 13 September 1974; Robert A. Warner, 13 February 1976; Ralph Henry Gabriel, 13 March 1975.

period when Ann Arbor was on the move, as it would continue to be during Phillips's long stay. The school's president, Harry Burns Hutchins, was determined to build greatness in the Midwest, something to equal the universities of Chicago and Wisconsin. The Tulane import was a major acquisition in the quest of that goal; but Hutchins got more than he hoped—or else he hoped for more than we realize—for the sound scholar, the craftsman of the monography, became a significant book writer, a historian of larger scope. To select two words among many, he grew, but it was hardly so simple: the show horse, after a clumsy beginning, achieved maturity and moved with prized style. A huge factor in that welcomed growth was Phillips's change, about the time of the first World War, from a Progressive analyst of class struggle to a more astute social analyst: The change, like the larger one still going on in American historiography, was not complete; it fell short of greatness, but it was, most definitely, a change.[44]

It began slowly. In many ways it was a wonder that it came at all. Lucie, not only a strong mother but also a strong wife, was bound in determination that her husband should enjoy the freedom necessary for scholarship; but that scholarship she presumed would be economic analysis. Willingly, and with the enthusiasm of one with energy denied other outlets, she set to order the house and its entertainment, entertainment that symbolized the unity of scholarship and friendship in the academic community. Lucie had seen such entertaining early in life, knew the vital spirit of its function, and mastered it. To help her along, she occasionally had her mother come to assist her; but, in general, Lucie did the job alone, making art of a maze of details, the sheer size and variegation of which would crush most people. She, however, loved the intricate patterns she created, and the Phillips's home came to be a center for graduate and faculty social life. That labor she carried through assuming Phillips would remain a scholar of the economy, not terribly unlike those among the Smiths and the Mayo-Smiths.[45]

---

[44]Howard H. Peckham, *The Making of the University of Michigan, 1817-1967* (Ann Arbor: University of Michigan, 1967) 69-138.

[45]Interview, Mabel Phillips Parker, 12-14 July 1974, including access to some personal correspondence between Lucie Mayo-Smith Phillips and her academic family, letters in possession of Mabel Phillips Parker.

Nor was Phillips inclined to make any great change in those first years at Ann Arbor; he was just beginning to sense an ownership of what he wanted: tenure, status, library and human resources, all the more meaningful because of his permanent station. It was the ideal time to be a little Turner, another in the line of Progressive historians. In that vein he continued his studies of Georgia's elite groups, producing a biography of Robert Toombs and editing the correspondence of Toombs, Alexander Stephens, and Howell Cobb.[46]

He joined the new Agricultural Historical Society and became increasingly important in the American Historical Association, taking a reformist stance in those organizations that paralleled his moderate Progressive politics. His position was a complicated one, for the reform involved an effort to make the AHA assume a national, instead of a strictly Eastern, leadership. The growth to prominence of Wisconsin, Chicago, Michigan, Berkeley, and Stanford was not at that time accurately reflected at the top of the AHA, with an invidious result in publications, appointments, and other honors. Obviously, Phillips in Ann Arbor felt a personal need to change the AHA, but the old guard included his in-law, Worthington Ford. Finally, the reform leader, Frederic Bancroft, an expert on the slave trade, made a moral question out of what Phillips saw as, at best, a practical, early resolution of an inevitability: Bancroft decried bad men blocking a holy cause; Phillips decried only short-sighted, good men slowing a process of change. With such problems of perception, Bancroft's movement broke apart, but the AHA soon changed its bylaws anyway, prompting Ray Allen Billington to brand the whole episode as "the tempest in Clio's teapot."[47]

Phillips's role in the struggle typified his image that was beginning to grow nationally—cautious, astute, helpful, amenable to reform but never to rapid transformation, a careful planner. The image was an attractive one and students began coming to his offices in increasing numbers. Already with the established Claude H. Van Tyne, an authority on colonial history, Phillips was making the new graduate department one to watch. He was accumulating a large body of original manuscript resources that he threw open to his graduate

---

[46]U. B. Phillips, *The Life of Robert Tombs* (New York: Macmillan, 1913). Phillips, *The Correspondence of Robert Toombs, Alexander H. Stephens, and Howell Cobb*, American Historical Association *Report* 2 (1911).

[47]Billington, *Frederick Jackson Turner*, 338-43.

students in the absence of any archival collection of any substance. That research was turning him into a more interesting teacher, for he literally knew some things unknown and unknowable, except in his classes. Moreover, he appealed to students at several levels, challenging the gifted while entertaining the mediocre. While never a great lecturer day by day, he had several presentations in which he sang slave songs and showed slides that captivated any audience.[48]

This continuing research moved him beyond Progressivism into another interpretation more social. This shift seems most apparent in *American Negro Slavery* and is dated by the First World War, but one should note other changes in his life. The Phillipses had begun a family in 1912 when Lucie bore a son whom they named Ulrich Bonnell Phillips, Jr. He grew to be huge, over six-feet, eight-inches tall, and sturdily built. More of a fun-lover than either parent, he had a quick mind when he cared to use it. This son with his bright promise, the unfortunate death of another baby boy, the joys of status attained, the complications of combining parenting and career, the holocaust of war, all served to create in the historian new attitudes and, eventually, a new history.[49]

THE CHALLENGE OF WORLD WAR I

As the armies of Europe moved into a war of unimagined proportions, Ulrich Phillips patiently amassed still more documentation on the slave economy of the South. Being a nationalist, as well as a Southerner, he was anxious to heal the ruptures of civil war and forge a powerful republican unity. He understood one of the ways of nations is war and did not shirk the challenge of a world war. The continued stability of mother England lay under a severe physical challenge; the continued growth of the republic lay under severe moral challenge. With resolution, Ulrich greeted the declaration of war in April of 1917. Nearing forty, with one child and a pregnant wife, he was unsuited for combat but he gladly served in other capacities.[50]

---

[48]See correspondence between Phillips and Van Tyne, 1911-1928, Claude Halstead Van Tyne Papers, Michigan Historical Collection, Bentley Historical Library, University of Michigan. Landon, "Ulrich Bonnell Phillips: Historian of the South," 365-72. Ray Allen Billington to John Herbert Roper, 27 January 1976, in possession of author. Interview, Thomas E. Drake, 12 June 1975.

[49]Interview, Mabel Phillips Parker, 12-14 July 1974.

[50]See wartime correspondence between Phillips and Van Tyne, 1917-1919, Van Tyne Papers, University of Michigan. Interview, Mabel Phillips Parker, 12-14 July 1974.

Initially he did volunteer work with the Young Men's Christian Association. This work involved a return to Georgia and Camp Gordon, then located near Atlanta. He took Lucie and his son, a bundle of notes, and an uncompleted manuscript on slavery. There were ironies redolent of another struggle: young Ulrich, like his father, young Ulysses before him, could not bear the Germanness of his Christian name, and he changed it to the Scandinavian "Ulric," and dropped the "Junior." After their daughter, Mabel, was born into the household, Lucie wearied of Atlanta and returned with the children to the Midwest.[51]

Back in his homeland Ulrich thrived: he entered a full schedule of research and writing and doing a thousand favors for the troops passing through Gordon, then a major transportation junction. The *Atlanta Constitution* reported a scene at the train station: a tall, ruddy-faced man brought postal cards and stamps to a mob of eager, apprehensive troopers after the clerk had closed the office; dramatically he delivered himself of the last cards as the train pulled from Atlanta heading to the coast and shipment to war. The talents of that man seemed too large for the "Y" Corps and soon the Regular Army accepted him in Intelligence with the rank of captain.[52]

Fascinated with the soldiers and the crusade, he observed closely the life of Camp Gordon. With his manuscript on slavery completed, the captain came to a conclusion—army life was much like that on a plantation, blacks made good soldiers because they had made good slaves. The special quality of his racism must be noted; he had lived through a time when Southern politicians Benjamin Ryan Tillman, James Kimble Vardamen, and Coleman Livingston Blease spoke in tones of near-genocidal racism: *kill the beast!* But Phillips recoiled from such butchery and held a different image, that of the child who could grow under supervision. Here, in his condescending view, were children, pure and good, "serio-comic" but responsible to intelligent white stewardship; the black was a ready ally in a war to save civilization. Others in the South were unhappy with black soldiery, fearing that they would find in service overseas a dignity beyond their "station" or "place": *how you gonna keep 'em down on the farm after they seen Pa-ree?* The Southern racism, and racists, that dominated the region was an intricate thing, a Janus-faced mask; and Phillips's images of the child capable of growth were from the smiling side of the visage, resistant to the howling other side whose

---

[51]Ibid.

[52]Newspaper clipping [1918?] in scrapbook, Phillips Papers, Yale.

adherents went into a paroxysm of lynching and other violent "retaliation" for the returning black veterans.[53]

At work in the South, Ulrich exhibited the definitive break with the Progressive interpretation of history. He explained his insight into the soldier-child in the introduction to his remarkable *American Negro Slavery*, the first such comprehensive study printed. He left no doubt of his position in the ongoing beast/child debate; nor did he leave any doubt about his distaste for racial equality. While many Progressives, even in the North, have agreed with his racial views, he had made still more changes away from the Progressive historians: the economic impetus for action, the class conflict, the Turner-Beard imagery was no longer his. Something social, something racial, informed the dynamics of the society he studied and he made that clear: "Plantation slavery had, in strictly business aspects, at least as many drawbacks as it had attractions. But in the large it was less a business than a life; it made fewer fortunes than it made men." And, lest someone make too rigid a sociology of that life, he concluded: "The government of slaves was for the ninety and nine by men, and only for the hundreth by law."[54]

The show horse had achieved maturity, stepping high and with spirit, yet showing control. *American Negro Slavery* is a book of passions restrained, of emotions tightly reined in; it is the promenade of a prize-winner. It did not win immediate and unqualified acceptance, but its success was remarkable. Except for some journalists and other intellectuals who objected to his sympathy with white supremacy, there were few demurrers. There was nothing like the book in depth and breadth of research—he claimed to have made a systematic study for over a decade—and nothing like it for scope— he wrote about black slavery from Nova Scotia to the Rio Grande, focusing on the Southern United States, but encompassing the entire hemisphere.[55]

The heart of the message is: the will to rule among white colonists made black slavery a special institution, full of complex

---

[53]Albert Dennis Kirwan, *Revolt of the Rednecks, Mississippi Politics: 1876-1925* (Lexington: University of Kentucky, 1951). Comer Vann Woodward, *Origins of the New South*, 1877-1913, vol. 9 of *History of the South*, ed. Ellis Merton Coulter and Wendell Holmes Stephenson (Baton Rouge: Louisiana State University, 1951).

[54]U. B. Phillips, *American Negro Slavery, a Survey of the Supply, Employment, and Control of Negro Labor as Determined by the Plantation Regime* (New York: D. Appleton, 1918) vii-ix, 514.

[55]Ibid., passim.

varieties including barbaric cruelties, but in the end it developed as good a regional culture as ever there was; and this accomplishment was achieved despite the economic failure of plantation monoculture. Another message, found in the preface and breathed in the spirit of every page, is the very antithesis of Progressive explanation: the racial system that powered the failed economy lived beyond that economy and powers the present one as well. In the South, race moved, and moves other things.[56]

Such proclamations one would expect to win acceptance in the South, where even the forces of Progressivism relied on segregation and belief in the inferiority of blacks. But acceptance beyond the former Confederacy was significant: historians as well as sociologists took *American Negro Slavery* as the secondary source from which to start investigation. At Chicago, the pioneer sociologist, Robert E. Park, found the book's conclusions compatible with his own schema of racial accommodation patterns. In time his black student, Charles S. Johnson, would rely with confidence on Phillips's work, even expressing public appreciation for him. Perhaps black authorities—and they were sadly few in number—had little choice but to acquiesce. Still, it was another decade before Carter G. Woodson and W. E. B. DuBois began to complain of Phillips in print.[57]

So Phillips stood near the top, within sight of greatness. He had a social explanation beyond economics that could probe the South before the Civil War. More important, he had the talent and the time to seek a grander explanation covering the ages and, conceivably, more geographic space. He began to attract more and better graduate students and more attention from peers: when he offered support for the then-independent Herbert Clark Hoover for president, it was big news in Ann Arbor; when he traveled by rail to conventions and turned to the topic of race, even the black porters—or, perhaps, especially they—paused to listen with care, if not with pleasure. He became a popular summer-school teacher at great centers on the East and West coasts with other schools trying to lure him away from Ann Arbor.[58]

Ever so supportive, Lucie persisted as the mother and the hostess extraordinaire. Their family grew. "Bonn" and Mabel were joined by

---

[56]Ibid., vii-ix and passim.

[57]August Meier to John Herbert Roper, 5 December 1975; Patrick J. Gilpin to Roper, 30 December 1975; Gilpin to Roper, 7 January 1976; letters in possession of author.

[58]"Hoover Club Is Organized," 26 March 1920, clipping in possession of Mabel Phillips Parker, used here with her permission. Landon,"Ulrich Bonnell Phillips: Historian of the South," 365-72.

Worthington Washington Phillips, equally as bright, tall, slighter of build than his siblings, but lacking his father's motivation. As before, this family frequently lost its *pater* as Phillips continued his extensive research and writing in his careful, methodical way. He was preparing still another, closer look at Southern antebellum society, this time embracing more than slavery. He continued his travels, building his personal manuscript collection, and performing his own kind of firsthand investigation of plantation life from California "bounty farms" to the Louisiana sugar bowl, to the Mississippi cotton delta.[59]

During this development, the University of Michigan, since 1920 under the direction of Marion L. Burton, grew spectacularly all around him. His colleague, Van Tyne, rose to the top in colonial interpretations, and Detroit trustee William L. Clements forced into being a great new library. The library accepted Phillips's words of inspiration for the building inscription: "In darkness dwells the people which knows its annals not."[60]

ON THE BRINK OF ACHIEVEMENT

By 1927 he was poised to establish a hold on greatness. In his study lay the manuscript to explain antebellum Southern society and another, more interpretative piece, to explain that society before and after the great schism of the war. The former he pushed along partially in anticipation of his first lucrative contract—the Little-Brown publishers proposed a $2,500 bounty for the best book in 1928. The latter was a speech of less than an hour, prepared for the alumni of the University of Georgia at the commencement of 1927.[61]

The speech was titled "The Central Theme in Southern History" and it was Phillips at his best. In it he described the one distinctive trait of the Southern region: race relations and, specifically, white supremacy. Before the Georgia audience he emphasized the essential presence of blacks as subordinate partners in Southern society. He emphasized segregation but insisted on white direction of the segregated blacks. Moveover, he stressed elite direction of both races, with

---

[59]Interview, Mabel Phillips Parker, 12-14 July 1974; Cecil Slaton Johnson, 28 February 1974.

[60]William L. Clements to Phillips, Phillips Papers, Southern Historical Collection.

[61]Herbert F. Jenkins to Phillips, 1 June 1929, Phillips Papers, Southern Historical Collection.

a white elite cooperating with the junior-partner black elite. For the training of these elites, he demanded the best education possible, namely, integrated university instruction at the finest schools of the country. Finally, he did not build a static model frozen in time: the South would grow and develop, race was the alpha but not the alpha and the omega of life, and there is no sympathy here for narrowly racial politics; progress must come in the context of the racial order, white over black, but progress must come.[62]

The "Central Theme" was uncharacteristically bold for Phillips and even radical in one perspective: it denied William E. Dodd's thesis of Southern white democracy and defied the nation's egalitarianism. It was elitist and white supremacist by frank avowal, both in describing what is and what ought to be. In the fall he produced a more polished, better-grounded version of the same paper before an audience of the AHA. At both places, and in between, he suffered attacks; but he had struck a telling blow and created a controversy for historians as teachers, researchers, or more important, as citizens or leaders.[63]

That winter, *Life and Labor in the Old South* won selection by the Little-Brown editors for publication and was awarded first prize. The book is by no means a significant departure from *American Negro Slavery*, although its discussion of racial inferiority seems milder. The "Central Theme" runs through both works and quite clearly so. What is different is the perspective of the study, in that Phillips tried to incorporate plain folk, industrial folk, town and business folk, and the labors that extended beyond the plantation. It is withal a lovely poem, with none of the prosaic passages found in *American Negro Slavery*, yet matching it in quality. It well deserved the Little-Brown award that it received and probably the Pulitzer Prize, which it did not.[64]

Life and Labor won two other honors for him. It moved Yale University to seek him out for its growth program, and it moved the Albert Kahn Foundation to give him its travel award, a year's sojourn around the world. Both honors he accepted with little hesitation: Yale's because it seemed to be advancing faster than anywhere else and Lucie pined for the well-settled East; and Kahn's as a matchless

---

[62]Phillips, "The Central Theme in Southern History," 30-43.

[63]Ibid.

[64]Bernard DeVoto, "The Pulitzer Prize in History," *Saturday Review of Literature* (13 March 1937): 3-14.

chance for Lucie and the children to see Europe and for him to observe blacks in Africa.[65]

In the midst of these honors came a problem, one he superficially dismissed as slight, but whose true weight one suspects he knew: a troubling throat condition that he refused to attend to before his trip. He set sail for Europe, thence Africa, happily collecting art curios and shipping them to his new home at Yale courtesy of a new friend, British historian Wallace Notestein. With rapt attention to detail he watched the Nilotic tribesmen and their British colonial overseers. Despite a brief, painful illness, perhaps complicated by the throat ailment, he kept up a vigorous physical pace, winning the admiration of his hosts, and earning a set of correspondents for the time when he returned to America.[66]

The family, apart from the busy scholar, flourished, with Lucie delighting in her trip, the children picking up the French language and other knowledge without having to take formal studies seriously. There was some disappointment with Bonn, who was to stand the Yale entrance examination in the fall of 1919. It became apparent that he would never make it and, when he did not, his parents selected the University of North Carolina as a nice place for him to learn about the South and about studying. At this time, too, Lucie came to the realization that she did not want public schools for her talented but reluctant scholars. It was decided to enroll Mabel and "Worthy" in Hopkins, a private New Haven school for faculty children.[67]

In their new home in New Haven, they joined in the ambitious rebuilding of Yale by President James R. Angell. There was a growth at Yale unmatched even by what Phillips had seen at Wisconsin and Michigan. First, there was sheer physical expansion: nine new college buildings, a new law school building, the massive Sterling Memorial Library, all done in what the caustic called "Girder Gothic"—a Gothic overlay on modern steel girders. The physical growth matched its mental growth, a conscious molting of the comfortable New England skin and an exposure to more universal influences. Talent from outside the Ivy League came, both in the

---

[65]Frank D. Fackenthall to Phillips, 27 April 1929, Phillips Papers, Michigan Historical Collection, Bentley Historical Library, University of Michigan.

[66]See Phillips-Notestein correspondence, 1928-1929, Wallace Notestein Papers, Manuscript Division, Sterling Memorial Library, Yale University.

[67]Interview, Mabel Phillips Parker, 12-14 July 1974.

person of new students and new faculty. Special attention went to the graduate department, which was greatly expanded in size and to a grand project, History, Arts, and Letters (HAL), an early attempt at interdisciplinary investigation that was later called American Studies.[68]

In the department of history there was Charles McLean Andrews, the eminent colonial scholar, and his successor, Leonard Woods Labaree; Ralph Henry Gabriel, intellectual historian, a leader of HAL; Notestein; Charles Seymour, diplomatic historian once close to the Wilson administration; and a group of young instructors led by Stanley Pargelis and George W. Pierson. Phillips was regarded as a key addition to this group, being expected to play a part in HAL, plus develop the graduate program. He was known to be working on Civil War causality, the completion of which study would form, with his earlier work, a holistic social thesis for Southern history.[69]

Thus great expectations arrived with the family at the substantial Victorian house on the hill at Canner Street. Arriving shortly thereafter were excellent graduate students: David Morris Potter, Bell Irvin Wiley, Gerald Mortimer Capers, Frontis W. Johnston, Thomas E. Drake, and others who would work with Phillips. The students came to the house where Lucie and Ulrich entertained them, breaking the often-stiff New England formality of some of the faculty; and each year the family selected one graduate student to live, free of charge, in their home. The opportunity was more than a nice gesture, for these were years of the Depression and students needed what help the professors could offer. Phillips gave them room and board, got them part-time jobs, and helped get them full-time jobs at graduation. Yet he presented them with more—his copious manuscripts, his living "oral" sources, and inspiration from his work, the previous as well as the ongoing.[70]

For all of these reasons and then some, he seemed particularly well suited for his next honor, being named the professor first

[68]George Wilson Pierson, *Yale: the University College, 1921-1937* (New Haven: Yale University, 1955) 103-22, 620-98.

[69]Ibid. Interviews, Ralph Henry Gabriel, 13 March 1975; Gerald Mortimer Capers, 1 June 1975; Thomas E. Drake, 12 June 1975; Leonard Wood Labaree, 14 March 1975.

[70]Interviews, Ralph Henry Gabriel, 13 March 1975; Gerald Mortimer Capers, 1 June 1975; Thomas E. Drake, 12 June 1975; Bell Irvin Wiley, 13 September 1974; Cecil Slaton Johnson, 28 February 1974; Norman D. Palmer, 6 May 1974.

attached to the new Jonathan Edwards College, the man to advise
students there, take meals there, and give direction to the dormitory
life there.[71]

Such promises shone as brightly as had those a generation before
at Madison. Again, as at Wisconsin, there would be disappointments,
more crushing this time because so final. The throat ailment developed into cancer, too far gone to cure by 1929, and the man of
promise would not live far into the New Deal of Franklin Delano
Roosevelt, a program of which he approved. Complication upon
complication filled his behavior in this regard, almost hopelessly
clouding one's ability to understand him. Never a simple man, his
attitudes toward possible death, and then toward inevitable death,
are peculiarly *sui generis* and perhaps closed forever to outsiders. He
quite possibly could have prevented the development of the cancer;
later he could have checked its growth, but he chose to do neither.
While he had so much to live for, occasionally voicing regrets to a
select few, he showed no real fear of dying. He pushed against the
limits of his physical endurance, teaching, at the finish in the winter
of 1933-1934, from his bed. This man, so sensitive to matters of style,
lived to the end an incredibly melodramatic life at Yale, the subject of
awesome inspiration to a host of students, younger faculty, and peer
faculty. They remember it still: the face reddened by treatment,
slipping from consciousness during a dull report, then suddenly
lighting with the fire of the savant to praise or condemn; the tall,
bent figure laboring up the hill to his house; the periods of recovery
and active physical play; the periods of relapse culminating with a
ghost of his former physique, whispering and coughing through a
seminar of slight content but of immeasurable impact on its
members.[72]

It wasn't because of his fatal illness that he fell short of greatness.
He simply could not explain the coming of the Civil War, failing to
bridge the chasm between his two assumptions: one, that the South
formed a disparate and distinct society whose very being abolitionism threatened; and two, that the war could have been prevented,
that it was, in fact, "the repressible conflict." Consequently, his last

----

[71]Charles Seymour to Phillips, 15 June 1932, Phillips Papers, Yale.

[72]Interviews, Leonard Wood Labaree, 14 March 1975; Mabel Phillips
Parker, 12-14 July 1974; Cecil Slaton Johnson, 28 February 1974; Ralph
Henry Gabriel, 17 July 1974. Paul B. McCready to Phillips, 15 December
1930, Phillips Papers, Southern Historical Collection.

book, *The Course of the South to Secession*, published posthumously and uncompleted, is characteristically enjoyable reading but lacks the sharp insights of *Georgia and State Rights*, *Life and Labor*, and "The Central Theme."[73]

He died in 1934. The students and faculty were both relieved and beset: relieved to end the palpable suffering; beset by the loss of his guidance. What lay unaccomplished, the unfilled promises, the hurt, whether because of his short, fifty-seven-year life span, or his Southernness, or some things not to be understood then or now, don't measure up to what he did accomplish. These achievements made the unfinished work an almost tangible thing: here was the beginning of a systematic study of the society of an entire region in the republic, a special region.

What he did and what he left undone are not things of the dead past because historians still struggle with his ideas. It is the fascination, sometimes the frustration, that impels one to examine in some detail the thought of this historian. So, too, is it a combination of fascination and frustration that impels one to examine this book.

Knowing this biography, the modern reader can read *Georgia and State Rights* with appreciation of its good qualities, an appreciation tinged, rather than drenched, with regret at its bad qualities. The education it provides about regional economics, Georgia history, Southern politics, race relations, and about Southern as well as national intellectual trends is invaluable.

---

[73]U. B. Phillips, *The Course of the South to Secession: an Interpretation*, ed. Ellis Merton Coulter (New York: D. Appleton-Century-Crofts, 1939).

GEORGIA AND STATE RIGHTS.

A STUDY OF THE POLITICAL HISTORY OF GEORGIA FROM THE REVOLUTION TO THE CIVIL WAR, WITH PARTICULAR REGARD TO FEDERAL RELATIONS.

BY

ULRICH BONNELL PHILLIPS, A. M., Ph. D.,

SOMETIME FELLOW IN COLUMBIA UNIVERSITY; SOMETIME FELLOW IN THE UNIVERSITY OF GEORGIA; INSTRUCTOR IN HISTORY IN THE UNIVERSITY OF WISCONSIN.

[The Justin Winsor Prize of the American Historical Association was awarded to the author for this monograph.]

GEORGIA AND STATE RIGHTS.

A STUDY OF THE POLITICAL HISTORY OF GEORGIA FROM THE REVOLUTION TO THE CIVIL WAR, WITH PARTICULAR REGARD TO FEDERAL RELATIONS.

By ULRICH BONNELL PHILLIPS, A. M., Ph. D.,

SOMETIME FELLOW IN COLUMBIA UNIVERSITY; SOMETIME FELLOW IN THE
UNIVERSITY OF GEORGIA; INSTRUCTOR IN HISTORY IN
THE UNIVERSITY OF WISCONSIN.

[The Justin Winsor Prize of the American Historical Association was awarded to the
author for this monograph.]

PREFACE.

As a result of listening to a very suggestive lecture by Dr.
F. J. Turner upon American sectionalism, I set to work some
years ago to study the effect of nullification upon Georgia
politics. The search for information in the Georgia newspapers of the nullification period quickly showed me that I
had to deal with numerous complexities in the local field
which to be understood needed more than a knowledge of
the main current of American politics. The conditions in
Georgia had been evolved through the influence of men and
events now long forgotten, and those local conditions were
destined to importance in shaping the history of the country
at large. The study of the whole situation with its recurring
changes has proved absorbing. My effort has been to seek
out the causes of things, and to follow developments to their
conclusion. The work has expanded, almost of itself, until it
has reached the present compass of a complete survey of the
antebellum period of the State's history. I have declined
to adopt the suggestion of several gentlemen who have
wished me to add the period of the Civil War and Reconstruction to my view, because the cataclysm of the sixties
is foreign to the sequence of my narrative. The discussion
of that decade would involve so many new influences and
complications that the unity of the monograph would be
destroyed.

It is not difficult for one whose native environment is the
Cotton Belt to orient himself into antebellum Georgia. I
have made little use, however, of the historical imagination.

The method is that of the investigator rather than the literary historian. The work is intended to be a thorough scientific treatment of its subject. No pains have been spared in obtaining exhaustive and accurate information. I have made research in person in every important library in America, and in several of those abroad, and have made use of a large amount of material which is in the possession of private individuals. The most useful collections of material for the work have been found in the University of Georgia Library, the Carnegie Library of Atlanta, the Congressional Library, and the libraries of the Historical Societies of Georgia, New York, and Wisconsin.

The two chapters dealing with the local parties in Georgia were submitted as a master's thesis at the University of Georgia in 1899. The monograph, as a whole, is my doctor's dissertation at Columbia University in 1902. For suggestions, criticism, and encouragement in the work, I am indebted to Dr. J. H. T. McPherson, of Athens, Ga., to Dr. F. J. Turner, of Madison, Wis., and especially to Dr. W. A. Dunning, of New York City. To these gentlemen I must express my sincere gratitude. To numerous librarians, and to persons possessing manuscripts, newspapers, or other material which I have used, I can at this time only render a sweeping expression of thanks for courtesies shown me.

ULRICH B. PHILLIPS.

Milledgeville, Georgia.

CONTENTS.

8

CHAPTER III.—THE EXPULSION OF THE CHEROKEES.

CHAPTER IV.—THE TROUP AND CLARKE PARTIES:

CHAPTER V.—THE STATE RIGHTS AND UNION PARTIES.

CHAPTER VI.—THE WHIGS AND THE DEMOCRATS: SLAVERY.

CHAPTER VII.—THE KANSAS-NEBRASKA STRUGGLE AND ITS RESULTS.

12

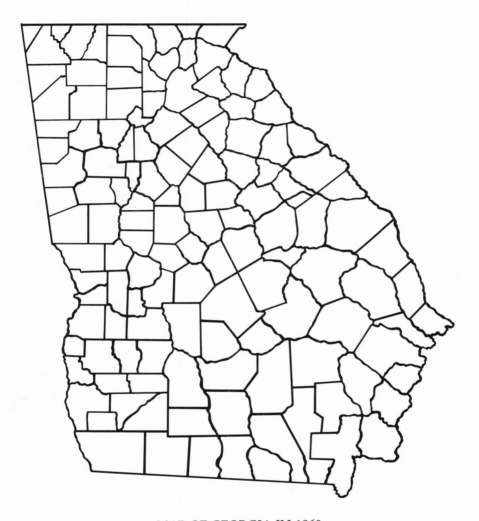

MAP OF GEORGIA IN 1860

GEORGIA AND STATE RIGHTS

CHAPTER I.—THE ADOPTION OF THE FEDERAL CONSTITUTION.

The close of the war for American independence found the little commonwealth of Georgia in a sadly disorganized condition so far as concerned finance and industry, but with a self-consciousness and an appreciation of its possibilities which had been brought into existence only by the stress of war times. The gain in public spirit far more than counterbalanced the loss of material goods. As a colony Georgia had been the most dependent of all the colonies; as a State she was destined for many years to struggle against tendencies which her citizens believed would bring about a greater tyranny than that from which they had escaped.

The course of events in the South during the Revolution developed certain strong opinions in Georgia which were subsequently of powerful influence. The dreadful warfare between Whig and Tory neighbors led to the conviction that while difference of opinion in public affairs is natural and wholesome, the commonwealth ought to be united when once a policy has been adopted, and especially when an outside power is involved. An attempt of South Carolina to destroy the political existence of Georgia by merging the two States into one aroused the indignation of Georgians and heightened their esteem for autonomy and independence.[a] The spread of a rumor, when the extreme South was in the hands of the British, that peace was about to be made on the basis of the retention of South Carolina and Georgia as colonies, while the independence of the other States was to be recognized, developed

[a] C. C. Jones, History of Georgia, vol. 2, p. 275. W. B. Stevens, History of Georgia, vol. 2, p. 302.

a lively anxiety for the preservation of the Union of the States.[a] The proximity of powerful Indian tribes, and the Spanish possession of Florida, after 1783, made Georgia an outpost against two powers which might become hostile, and thus tended to further strengthen the desire among the citizens for a permanent arrangement looking to mutual support among the States. For several reasons, then, the State was in favor of a strong central government in control of international affairs and matters of broad scope, while on the other hand it was not willing to make a complete surrender of its own political independence. A federal system of government, and none other, would meet the requirements.

The arrangements by which the United States carried on the war against Great Britain had been little more than an ill-defined league between independent powers. The Articles of Confederation, which secured adoption only a short while before the cessation of hostilities, were hardly an improvement upon the preceding provisional organization. Month by month the unsatisfactory nature of the Confederation became more patent and more distressing to all citizens who looked to a prosperous career for the American people under a stable government, yet large numbers of men were to be found in many of the States who were firmly opposed to any sacrifice of authority by the members of the Confederation. Jealousies among the commonwealths and real or fancied advantages which several of the States held over their neighbors increased the difficulty in reaching a solution.

By the summer of 1786 the inefficiency of the confederate government had become intolerable, but the problem of securing improvements remained most delicate and complicated. The fact that it was accomplished in a short time, and without great confusion, demonstrates the adroitness and ability of the statesmen of the time.

The convention which, upon the initiative of Virginia, assembled at Annapolis in 1786 to consider interstate questions of a commercial nature, was led by Alexander Hamilton to extend its view over the general field of American political

[a] Cf. "Observations upon the effects of certain late political suggestions: by the delegates of Georgia " in the Continental Congress. This pamphlet, originally printed in 1781, was reprinted in a limited edition in the Wormsloe series in 1847. The text may also be found in White's Historical Collections of Georgia, pp. 106 to 110.

conditions. The result was the adoption on September 14, of a recommendation to the Congress and to the legislatures of the several States represented at Annapolis that commissioners be appointed from each of the thirteen States to meet in Philadelphia in May of the next year "to devise such provisions as shall appear to them necessary to render the Constitution of the Federal Government adequate to the exigencies of the Union."[a] The Congress approved the plan and called the convention accordingly.

In response to the invitation which Georgia received, the assembly passed an ordinance February 10, 1787, appointing William Few, Abraham Baldwin, William Pierce, George Walton, William Houston, and Nathaniel Pendleton as commissioners for the convention.

The second Monday, or the 14th, of May, 1787, had been set for the assembling of the convention, but a quorum of States was not obtained until the 25th of the month, when the regular sittings were begun. On that day William Few was present from Georgia, but by the State ordinance two delegates were required to attend before the State could be officially represented. Georgia had no vote in the convention until the arrival of Mr. Pierce, on May 31. Mr. Houston reached Philadelphia on June 7 and Mr. Baldwin on June 11. Messrs. Walton and Pendleton are nowhere mentioned as having attended.

Soon after the assembling of the convention it was decided that in it, as was the rule in Congress during the Confederation, each State represented should have one vote. Georgia used her vote constantly in advocating the policy of strengthening the central government. This was to be done by depriving the State legislatures of some of their powers without removing all authority from them. Mr. Baldwin, the most influential member of the Georgia delegation, said in the convention on June 29: "It appears to be agreed that the government we should adopt ought to be energetic and formidable, yet I would guard against the danger of being too formidable." His colleague, Mr. Pierce, expressed the same opinion on the same day.

[a] Jonathan Elliot, Debates on the Federal Constitution, vol. 1, p. 118 (2d edition).

That the Georgia delegates acted in accord with public sentiment at home the following extracts from the columns of a contemporary Augusta newspaper will tend to show:

" We hear with great satisfaction that the convention for revising the confederation is now assembled and doing business at Philadelphia. Among the many important matters to be taken under consideration by that august body the following are said to be the principles: 1st. That the Thirteen states be divided into three distinct Republics, who ought to leak together for their common defense as so many separate governments independent of each other; 2ndly. If the Thirteen states remain as they are confederated, to lessen their sovereignty by abolishing their State Legislatures and leaving the whole laws to be made by the national congress, assembly, or parliament; 3rdly. The Thirteen states to remain as they are, except that their laws be revised by Congress so as to make the whole act in conformity as of one, and the executive powers of Congress enlarged. It is much to be wished that the latter may be adopted."[a]

When the debate began on the question as to whether representation in the National Assembly should be divided equally among the States or should be apportioned to the population, Georgia, in a measure, astonished the States of her own rank in strength and population by joining the side of the large States, seemingly against her own interests. This was accounted for by Luther Martin in his letter to the speaker of the house of delegates of Maryland:

" It may be thought surprising, sir, that Georgia, a State now small and comparatively trifling in the Union, should advocate this system of unequal representation, giving up her present equality in the Federal Government and sinking herself almost to total insignificance in the scale; but, sir, it must be considered that Georgia has the most extensive territory in the Union, being as large as the whole island of Great Britain and thirty times as large as Connecticut. This system being designed to preserve to the States their whole territory unbroken and to prevent the erection of new States within the territory of any of them, Georgia looked forward to when,

[a] Georgia State Gazette or Independent Register, July 21, 1787. This weekly newspaper was published at Augusta by John E. Smith, printer to the State. It afterwards became the Augusta Chronicle.

her population being increased in some measure proportional to her territory, she should rise in the scale and give law to the other States, and hence we found the delegation of Georgia warmly advocating the proposition of giving the States unequal representation."

The discussion of the method of election of Senators brought forth several speeches from the Georgia delegation. On June 6, Mr. Pierce spoke in favor of the election of the first branch of the National Legislature by the people and of the second by the States, in order that the citizens of the States might be represented individually and collectively. On June 29, Mr. Baldwin declared that the second branch ought to be the representation of property and that it ought not to be elected as the first.

When the question was put as to whether each State should have an equal vote in the Senate, there was an exciting scene in the convention. Five States had voted on either side of the issue, and when Georgia's turn arrived to cast her ballot her delegates had the deciding voice. Mr. Baldwin had already made known his opinion as siding with the larger States, but from the fear of disrupting the convention he abandoned his intention, divided the vote of his State, and thus caused the motion to be lost by a tie.[a]

In the apportionment of representation in the lower House South Carolina was given five seats and Georgia three. Both States made resolute efforts to increase their strength in the House, but were persistently voted down on every motion to that effect. The underlying reason for these attempts, which North Carolina and Virginia supported, was the desire to equalize the power of the South in the House with that of the North, which was given a slightly larger number of seats.

The principle of assignment of the seats was that each State should be entitled to one representative for every 30,000 of its inhabitants, according to the authoritative estimate, with slaves counted as five to three. It was known that on this basis Georgia should not be assigned three members, but the argument was accepted that the "unexampled celerity of its population" would cause the State to be entitled to that number before the Constitution could be put in effect.[b]

[a] Madison Papers (Gilpin), p. 807.　　　[b] Ib.. pp. 1054, 1060, 1076

When the question of legislating against the slave trade arose in the convention, South Carolina took an extreme position, with Georgia approving her contentions. The delegates of the two States threatened that if the importation of slaves were not allowed, their States would undoubtedly refuse to ratify the Constitution. Mr. Baldwin suggested that, if left to herself, Georgia would probably put a stop to the trade. From this prophecy, which was fulfilled in a decade, and from other sidelights on the subject, we have reason to doubt that the prohibitory clause would have led to the rejection of the Constitution by Georgia. The North was forced to yield to the stubbornness of South Carolina, supported by Georgia and North Carolina. A compromise was finally reached, which was embodied in Article I, section 9, of the Constitution: "The migration or importation of such persons as any of the States now existing shall think proper to admit shall not be prohibited by the Congress prior to the year eighteen hundred and eight, but a tax or duty may be imposed on such importation not exceeding ten dollars for each person."

The deliberations of the convention were brought to a close on September 17, 1787, and the engrossed Constitution was signed by delegates from each of the thirteen States except Rhode Island. The complete instrument was delivered to the Congress of the Confederation, which, on September 28, "Resolved unanimously that the said report, with the resolutions and letter accompanying the same, be transmitted to the several legislatures, in order to be submitted to a convention of delegates chosen in each State by the people thereof, in conformity to the resolves of the convention made and provided in that case."

A copy of the Constitution and accompanying resolutions reached Georgia in time for publication at Augusta, in the Gazette, October 13, and the resolution of the Congress to submit it to the States was published a week later. The State legislature happened to be in session at the time, and on October 25 it resolved that a convention be elected on the day of the next general election, to consist of not more than three members from each county, to meet at Augusta in December following, to consider the report and to reject or adopt any part or the whole thereof.

In the Georgia Gazette of December 15 there appears an article which states: "The following gentlemen are appointed in the convention for this State, and are the names only of those who have come to hand: For Green County, ——— Daniel, Robert Christmas, ——— Middleton; for Wilkes County, George Mathews, Florence Sullivan, ——— King; for Burke County, Edward Telfair, Dr. Todd, George Walton; for Glynn County, George Handley, Charles Hillery, John Milton."

In the issue of December 29 there appears under date of December 28: "Yesterday twenty-four members of the State convention met in this town and, being a quorum, proceeded to the choice of a president, when the Hon. John Wereat, esq., was elected to that important office. Mr. Isaac Briggs was appointed secretary. Members returned from Liberty County to serve in the convention: James Powell, John Elliott, James Maxwell, esqs.; for Effingham County, Jenkin Davis, Nathan Brown, Caleb Howell, esqs."

The Gazette of January 5, 1788, is quite disappointing, for it might naturally be expected to contain an account in detail of the debates and transactions of the convention. Instead, its only article relating to the subject reads: "We have the pleasure to announce to the public that on Wednesday last the convention of this State unanimously ratified the Federal Constitution in the words following," etc. The ratification bears all the names of the delegates above named, and also those of John Wereat, president and delegate for the county of Richmond, and Henry Osborne, James Seagrave, and Jacob Weed, of Camden County. The article in the Gazette closes with a statement that "as the last name was signed to the ratification a party of Colonel Armstrong's regiment, quartered in this town, proclaimed the joyful tidings opposite the statehouse by thirteen discharges of two pieces of artillery."

In point of the time which elapsed between the receipt of instructions from Congress and the ratification of the Constitution by the State, Georgia should be ranked second, if not first, indeed, for her delegates signed their resolutions only twenty-four days after Delaware had signified her approval, whereas very nearly a month was required for the transmission of news from Philadelphia to Georgia. But when dates are compared it is found that the ratifications by Delaware, Pennsylvania, and New Jersey preceded that by Georgia; and when the States are listed according to the dates at which their notifications of approval, reach the Congress, it is discovered that the news of ratification by two Eastern States had reached that body before Georgia's communication was received.

Delaware, New Jersey, and Georgia are the only States whose conventions were unanimous in their approval of the instrument. The citizens of Georgia had no objections to a closer form of union among the several States. Their representatives had obtained practically all that they had seen fit to ask. Certainty of law and order between the States, guarantees of support against the Spanish and Indians in the possible emergency of war, non-interference in the realm of local affairs and in the matter of slavery and the slave trade, and full representation in the legislature of the General Government left nothing to be desired in the Constitution.

Georgia was insignificant among the States, but her ratification of the Federal Constitution was very important. When it became known to the northward that a State with such intense Southern spirit had ratified so quickly and without an amendment or a dissenting voice, a thrill of encouragement was felt by the workers for the cause throughout the States, while the hearts of many anti-Federalists failed them.[a]

The Georgia State constitution, which was confessedly of a temporary character, had for some years been considered unsatisfactory. As soon as the activity of the State regarding the Federal Constitution came to an end, the matter of remodeling the State government was vigorously undertaken with the purpose of adapting it better to the Federal system. The general assembly on January 30, 1788, resolved to name three citizens from each county "to be convened after nine States have adopted the Federal Constitution, to take under their consideration the alterations and amendments that are necessary to be made in the constitution of this State." After receiving news of the ratification of New Hampshire, the ninth State, Governor Handley called this convention to meet on November 4. It formulated a new constitution, which was published

[a] Cf. J. B. McMaster, History of the People of the United States, vol. 1, p. 476.

in the State. Another convention was elected by the people early in December, with the function of offering amendments to the proposed document, and it met on January 4, 1789. By January 20 its work was finished and the second convention adjourned.

The instrument, as then offered for adoption and as finally adopted, differed from the one which it superseded in being much more systematic, and in containing several conservative but important new features. It established a bicameral legislature, and heightened the qualifications for members of the assembly. It is an interesting detail of these qualifications that, while only two years' residence in Georgia was required of a member of the lower house, he must have been a citizen of the United States for seven years; and for the senate, a similar requirement of three and nine years was made. This is the earliest instance where any such discrimination was made in a State constitution, and is indicative of the national spirit which existed among the people of Georgia at that time.

Regarding the adoption of this second State constitution by Georgia, the following self-explanatory item occurs in the Georgia Gazette for May 9, 1789: "On Monday last (May 4) the third convention met in the Town Hall to consider the alterations proposed by the convention of January last to the constitution formed by the convention of 1788; and on Wednesday they finally adopted and ratified the new form of government, to commence in October next. * * * The new form being an assimilation to the Federal constitution, its notification and deposit was announced to the town by a discharge of eleven cannon, in honor of the federated states; when his Honor, with the President and the members of the convention, and the President and the members of the council, repaired to the Government House and drank a glass of wine to its prosperity."

The eager ratification of the Federal Constitution in 1788 was undoubtedly a truthful expression of the will of the people of Georgia. But the people, in ratifying, understood that they did nothing more than was involved in the literal interpretation of their act. They adopted the Constitution in the capacity of the people of a sovereign State, delegating certain specified powers to the central government in order to increase its efficiency, but reserving to themselves and to their previously existing State government all rights and powers which were not expressly thus delegated in the instrument. The new Constitution for the United States was accepted and welcomed as a reform upon the old one, and not as a revolutionizing instrument. Evidence of this may be found in several issues which arose almost contemporaneously with the adoption of the Constitution. Of these we may deal first with the celebrated case of Chisolm v. Georgia before the Supreme Court of the United States.

At the August term of the Supreme Court in 1792 an action was brought by a Mr. Chisolm, of South Carolina, to recover a sum of money by suit against the State of Georgia.[a] Copies of the action were served by the United States marshal upon the governor and the attorney-general of the State of Georgia. On August 11, 1792, Mr. Randolph, the Attorney-General of the United States, as counsel for the plaintiff, moved " that unless the State of Georgia shall, after reasonable previous notice of this motion, cause an appearance to be entered in behalf of the said State on the fourth day of next term, or shall show cause to the contrary, judgment shall be entered against the said State, and a writ of inquiry of damages shall be awarded." But on motion of Mr. Randolph it was ordered by the court that the consideration of this motion be postponed to the February term, 1793. At that term a written remonstrance and protestation against the exercise of jurisdiction in the cause was presented to the court on behalf of the State. In consequence of positive instructions from the State government, the attorneys who presented its protest declined to take any part in arguing the question.

Mr. Randolph made an extensive argument on the nature of the American Government. He urged that the States were sovereignties, but that they might combine in government, and that they had so combined in the Articles of Confederation. When that system proved inefficient the Federal Constitution was established and produced a new order of things. " It derives it origin immediately from the people; and the people are individually, under certain limitations, subject to the legislative, executive, and judicial authorities thereby

[a] The case is reported in full in A. J. Dallas, U. S. Supreme Court Reports, vol. 2, pp. 419 to 480.

established. The States are in fact assemblages of these individuals who are liable to process." "I hold it, therefore, no derogation of sovereignty in the States to submit to the Supreme Judiciary of the United States." The majority of the court gave decisions favorable to the plaintiff, Chief Justice Jay and Justice Wilson making strong arguments for the national character of the system which was erected by the United States Constitution of 1787.

Justice Iredell gave the only dissenting opinion; and it is the one most interesting to us here, because it was in line with the convictions of the officials and of the people of Georgia. His argument was that the United States Supreme Court could not try a suit against a State by a citizen of another State. If such a case were within the general realm of the activity of the court the court would still be unable to try the action unless a Congressional act had established the appropriate procedure, whereas no such act had been passed. "Every State in the Union in every instance where its sovereignty has not been delegated to the United States I consider to be as completely sovereign," he said, "as the United States are in respect to the powers surrendered. The United States are sovereign as to all the powers actually surrendered; each State in the United States is sovereign as to all the powers reserved. It must necessarily be so, because the United States have no claim to any authority but such as the States have surrendered to them." The powers of the United States "require no aid from any State authority. That is the great distinction between the old Articles of Confederation and the present Constitution." The power to try suits against a State, he concluded, is not expressly given to the United States Supreme Court, and therefore the court does not possess that power.

As a result of the decision of the majority of the justices in favor of the plaintiff, it was ordered that notice be served upon the governor and attorney-general of Georgia, and in case the State should not appear in due form, or show cause to the contrary in the court by the first day of the next term, judgment by default should be entered against the State.

Judgment was accordingly rendered against the State of Georgia in the February term of 1794, and a writ of inquiry was awarded to the plaintiff. But it was evident that the

State would not obey the writ if an attempt should be made to execute it; and it was further evident that no means of executing a judgment against a State was known to administrative law. The judgment lay unenforced upon the court records until the eleventh amendment to the United States Constitution removed such questions from the cognizance of the court in 1798.

The fact that there were a series of similar cases pending in the same court against several other States rendered the issue in the suit of Chisolm v. Georgia of interest in all sections of the country. But we must now attend mainly the events in the narrower field of Georgia policy.

On December 14, 1792, during the first session of the general assembly after the first notification to the State that Chisolm's suit was pending, a resolution was introduced in the Georgia house of representatives declaring that the suit, "if acquiesced in by this State, would not only involve the same in numberless lawsuits for papers issued from the treasury thereof to supply the armies of the United States, but would effectually destroy the retained sovereignty of the States, and would actually tend in its operations to annihilate the very shadow of the State governments, and to render them but tributary corporations to the Government of the United States." The resolution went on to suggest an "explanatory amendment" to the constitution.[a] Apparently the motion was not carried, but it nevertheless outlined the policy which the State was to follow.

Shortly after the decision was rendered by the Supreme Court, in February, 1793, Governor Telfair was notified of the judgment by the United States marshal of the district. At the opening of the next session of the legislature, November 4, 1793, he discussed the subject in his annual message. That portion of the document reads: "A process from the Supreme Court of the United States at the instance of Chisolm, executor of Farquhar, has been served upon me and the attorney-general. I declined entering any appearance, as this would have introduced a precedent replete with danger to the Republic, and would have involved this State in complicated difficulties, abstracted from the infractions which it would

a Augusta Chronicle and Gazette of the State, Dec. 22, 1792. H. V. Ames, Sta s Documents on Federal Relations, p. 8.

have made in her retained sovereignty. The singular predicament to which she has been reduced by savage inroads has caused an emission of paper upward of £150,000 since the close of the late war, a considerable part of which is still outstanding, and which in good faith and upon constitutional principles is the debt of the United States. I say were action admissible under such grievous circumstances, an annihilation of her political existence must follow. To guard against civil discord as well as the impending danger, permit me most ardently to request your most serious attention to the measure of recommending to the legislatures of the several States that they effect a remedy in the premises by amendment to the Constitution; and that, to give further weight to this matter, the delegation of this State in Congress be requested to urge that body to propose an amendment to the several legislatures." [a]

The House of Representatives adopted a report for the preparation of an address to the legislatures of the several States, looking toward the amendment which all men had in mind. A bill which passed the same House soon afterwards showed a much more radical spirit than had previously been manifested.

The Journal of the House for November 19, 1793, records: "The House proceeded to resolve itself into a Committee of the Whole to take under consideration a bill to be entitled 'An act declaratory of certain parts of the retained sovereignty of the State of Georgia.' Mr. Speaker left the chair. Mr. McNeil took the chair of the committee, and some time being spent therein, Mr. Speaker resumed the chair, and Mr. McNeil, from the Committee of the Whole, reported that the committee had taken the bill under consideration, had gone through the same, and had made several amendments thereto, which he reported. And the bill as reported amended being read, a motion was made by Mr. Waldburger to strike the following section therein: 'And be it further enacted that any Federal marshal, attempting to levy on the territory of this State, or on the treasury, by virtue of an execution, by the authority of the Supreme Court of the United States, for the recovery of any claim against the said State of Georgia

[a] Augusta Chronicle, Nov. 9, 1793. Ames, State Documents on Federal Relations, p. 8.

shall be guilty of felony, and shall suffer death, without benefit of clergy, by being hanged.' On question to strike out—yeas, 8; nays, 19. Ordered that the bill be engrossed for a third reading."[a]

An item in the Journal of the same House for November 21, 1793, records that on that day the bill was finally passed and sent to the Senate. The State senate probably realized that matters elsewhere were progressing so nicely toward the amendment of the Constitution that any such violent act was uncalled for in Georgia. We find no record of the passage of the fire-eating bill through the upper House.

Immediately after the decision of the Supreme Court in the case of Chisolm v. Georgia, a Massachusetts Senator introduced a bill into Congress for a constitutional amendment. The legislatures of Massachusetts, Connecticut, and Virginia, each also proposed an amendment. The Congressional act for the change in the Constitution, or, as many preferred to call it, an explanatory clause, was sent to the States on March 5, 1794, and its ratification was announced by the President on January 8, 1798.[b]

The adoption of the eleventh amendment thus put an end to the controversy, which had caused much excitement. The whole matter was ill calculated to make the Georgians more national in spirit. Its chief value as an historical incident in this connection lies in the demonstration that the unanimous vote of the Georgia convention in 1788 was given in the understanding that the State remained in possession of all residuary rights and powers.

Other occasions for the expression by the State government of views on the intent of the Constitution arose in connection with the two subjects of Indian affairs and public lands. The history of Indian affairs may conveniently be postponed to subsequent chapters. The consideration of the developments concerning public lands and the Yazoo sale will lead us somewhat afield before the constitutional question reappears, and will demonstrate in the later stages that after some years a reaction set in against the decided State sovereignty views which prevailed in Georgia from 1789 to 1796.

[a] Augusta Chronicle, Nov. 23, 1793.

[b] H. V. Ames, Proposed Amendments to the U. S. Constitution, pp. 156, 157, and 322. McMaster, History of the People of the U. S., vol. 2, p. 182. Cf. Cohen v. Virginia, in 6 Wheaton, U. S. Reports, 406.

The treaty of Paris in 1783 left Georgia in nominal possession of a great expanse of territory stretching from the Savannah River to the Mississippi. But of this region only the small portion lying east of the Oconee River was actually settled and possessed by the citizens. The ownership over the western lands consisted in the right merely to take possession of them after extinguishing the Indian title. Even this contingent ownership, called the right of preemption, was not held by Georgia without contestation. The United States Government was inclined for a time to urge that it alone possessed the right of preemption to the district south of Tennessee, but in seeking to support the argument it was forced to concede that the only valid rebuttal of the claim of Spanish possession of the region lay in the documents which established Georgia's ownership.

Most of the States which possessed extensive claims to lands in the West ceded their claims to the United States about 1787. Georgia was not willing to make an unqualified gift of all her vacant territory, but in 1788 she offered to Congress a grant of a district 140 miles wide, and stretching from the Chattahoochee River to the Mississippi, a district which constituted the southern half of the territory lying beyond the line of the Chattahoochee. But conditions were included in the offer. The State was to be confirmed in its possession of the lands which it did not cede and was to receive a reimbursement in the amount of $171,428.45, which it had expended in quieting and resisting the Indians, and of which a large portion was then outstanding in the bills of credit of the State. Congress rejected the offer of Georgia, but resolved that it would accept a cession, if all the lands west of a line based on the Chattahoochee were offered, and if the conditions were suitably modified. [a]

The State government was not disposed to follow this suggestion of Congress. It was quite ready to keep possession of all the lands to which it had claim, but was at some loss as to the best method of gaining the benefit of them for the State. In 1789 the legislature passed a law, at the suggestion of would-be purchasers, enacting a sale of some 25,000,000 acres in the western district near the Yazoo River in three

[a] American State Papers, Public Lands, vol. 1, p. 100.

parcels, to as many companies, for a total sum of about $200,000.[a] It was distinctly declared that the State would not trouble itself in the matter of extinguishing the Indian title, or in adjusting disputes with previous settlers. The companies were required in the act to pay the full amount of the purchase money into the State treasury within two years. This stipulation was not fulfilled, and the agreement lapsed at the end of the period set.

The fever of land speculation was beginning to run wild among the people of the United States. The members of the Yazoo companies of 1789 were greatly disappointed when they realized the failure of their plans. But some of the original movers were determined to persevere in their schemes, and numerous other enterprising men were eager to participate in similar undertakings.

The legislature of Georgia was induced to pass an act, approved by the governor on January 7, 1795, which enacted the sale of the greater part of the territory now comprised in the States of Alabama and Mississippi, in four districts to four new companies, for a total consideration of $500,000.[b]

The corrupting influence which secured the passage of the act is not here in point. The important fact for our view is that the whole procedure was in open contravention of a law of the United States. Although the act was repudiated by the popular voice, those sections of it which deal with the theoretical power of the State in the premises may be taken as no great exaggeration of the convictions of the people. The act sets forth that although the United States had by enactment declared its control over cessions of the Indian lands and had guaranteed the Creek Indians in the possession of all their lands west of the Oconee River, the State of Georgia had in no way transferred its right of soil or pre-emption. The right of preemption and the fee simple to the western lands were declared to be in the State, together with the right of disposing of the said lands. Upon the basis of this assertion the act proceeds to declare the sale of some 35,000,000 acres of the lands in question.

[a] C. H. Haskins, The Yazoo Land Companies, p. 7. Stevens, Hist. of Ga., vol. 2, p. 464. Indian Affairs, vol. 1, p. 114. George Watkins, Compilation of the Laws of Ga., p. 387.

[b] American State Papers, Public Lands, vol. 1, pp. 144, 156, and 157. Stevens, Hist. of Ga., vol. 2, p. 467. White, Statistics of Ga., p. 50. A. H. Chappell, Miscellanies of Georgia, vol. 2, p. 87. J. Hodgson, Cradle of the Confederacy, p. 88.

As soon as information of the Yazoo sale reached President Washington he sent copies of the act to Congress, with a brief message to the effect that the matter involved was worthy of deep consideration. Before any further steps were taken at the capital the news arrived of important developments in Georgia, which rendered it advisable to postpone any Congressional action.

While the Yazoo bill was yet awaiting the governor's signature, a petition was presented by William H. Crawford and other citizens of Columbia County, demonstrating the bad policy of the bill and asking that it be given the executive veto. As the news of the act spread over the State, accompanied by rumors of bribery in the legislature, the indignation of the citizens became aroused. The sale of the lands was condemned on all sides and in the roundest of terms. James Jackson, then a member of the United States Senate, resigned his seat in order to accept a nomination to the State legislature and devote his whole energy to accomplish the nullification of the sale. A convention of the people of the State, in May, condemned the act of the legislature and directed the attention of the next assembly to the matter of its repeal.

In obedience to the clamorous popular demand, and under the powerful leadership of Jackson, the newly elected legislature passed an act in February, 1796, which rescinded the act of the previous year as being dishonorable to the State and repugnant to the constitution, in that it pretended to grant monopolies and to establish an aristocracy, which, if permitted, would overthrow the democratic form of government.

The framers of the rescinding act foresaw the struggle which would be made by the grantees under the act of 1795, and they took pains to discredit their claims by a declaration of their corrupt practices and to forestall their efforts by an assertion of State sovereignty. They stated in the act: "Whereas the free citizens of this State * * * are essentially the source of the sovereignty thereof * * *; and whereas the will or constitution of the good people of this State is the only existing legal authority derived from the essential source of sovereignty * * * ;" and whereas, for various reasons stated, the "usurped act" of the Yazoo sale was unconstitutional, "be it enacted that the said usurped act * * * is hereby declared null and void." All grants and claims arising from the act were declared of no effect, provision was made for the repayment of all moneys received at the treasury to those who had bought the lands, and direction was issued to the State authorities to assemble publicly in the near future to witness the expunging of all record of the "vile and fraudulent transaction" from the books of record of the State.[a]

But the speculators were determined not to relinquish their enterprise so long as any hope of success remained. After it had become clear that the State government could not be shaken in its utter denial of the validity of the sale, the owners of the Yazoo scrip made appeal to the Federal authorities.

The State government declared in the rescinding act of 1796 that no court existed in which an issue could be tried between a State and a citizen, and that if the contrary were true the dignity of the State would not allow it to appear where its own sovereignty was in question. A constitutional convention which assembled soon afterwards was made use of in order to give more authoritative utterance to the principles upon which the sale had been declared null. A section of the new constitution was made to read in part: "All the territory without the present temporary line and [east of the Mississippi River] is now, of right, the property of the free citizens of this State, and held by them in sovereignty inalienable but by their consent." The next section repeats the nullification of the Yazoo sale, and orders all moneys received for the lands to be returned to the purchasers or held indefinitely, awaiting their demand. The constitution containing these clauses was ratified in 1798, and continued to be the fundamental law of the State until 1861.

This was the final dictum of the State of Georgia in the Yazoo matter. The question of the binding effect of the sale came before the Central Government at a later time as an issue between the Federalist and Republican parties.

Meanwhile the widespread agitation over the Yazoo complication led Congress to inquire anew whether Georgia had indisputable right over the land in question. A special com-

a Public Lands, vol. 1, p. 156.

mittee of the Senate reported March 2, 1797, after an examination of documents. The royal proclamation of 1763 impressed the committee very strongly, because it reserved under the sovereignty of the King all lands lying westward of the sources of the rivers which flowed into the Atlantic. Hence they reported that Georgia could have no good claim to the western lands. But they neglected to observe that the King's instructions to Governor Wright, issued a year later than the proclamation of 1763, distinctly extended the limits of Georgia to the Mississippi River. The committee advised that commissioners be appointed to make an amicable agreement with Georgia, and that, after obtaining Georgia's consent, a Territorial government be established over the region.[a]

In April, 1798, Congress enacted a statute appointing the commissioners to confer with Georgia, and at the same time providing a government for the Mississippi Territory, without waiting to receive an expression of consent from the State authorities.[b] A Congressional act of June, 1800, confirmed that of 1798 and put the Territorial government into operation.[c] Each of these acts included clauses providing that they should not impair the right of Georgia to the jurisdiction or to the soil in the region; but it is difficult to see how the Territorial government could have had authority to perform its functions without impairing Georgia's jurisdiction.

During the session of the general assembly of Georgia which began toward the close of 1800 a resolution was adopted remonstrating against the two acts of Congress. The tone of this document is so mild and obsequious as to mark a new epoch in the Federal relations of the State. "The Legislature of the State of Georgia," it began, "approach the Legislature of the Union with that respect and veneration which the representative body of the nation ought ever to command. They approach it to lay the complaints of Georgia before it and to solicit a redress of the grievances which her citizens feel. The state does not wish a relinquishment of constitutional power by the Legislature of the Union, but she hopes that that high body, in return, does not wish an operation of its laws where constitutionality may be questioned, to the injury of the rights of Georgia." The grievances

a Public Lands, vol. 1, p. 79.   b U. S. Statutes at Large, vol. 1, p. 549.   c Ib.,vol. 2, p. 69.

of the State regarding its western territory were then set forth, its willingness to negotiate for amicable settlement was stated, and the hope was expressed that the whole disgraceful matter of the Yazoo sale might be concluded by a cession of the territory to the United States on acceptable terms and with reasonable boundaries. In conclusion: "With the most profound respect for the legislature of the United States, the legislature of Georgia assure them of their inviolable attachment to the constitution of their country and their inalienable fidelity to the United American Nation." [a]

The striking character of the change in the attitude of the Georgia government and people will be more fully shown in the chapter on Creek affairs. Its occurrence was due in part to a more sympathetic understanding with the Federal authorities and in part to the satisfactory conditions then existing in Indian affairs, while additional factors in bringing about the new frame of mind were a feeling of shame over the Yazoo corruption and a fear that hostilities would soon arise with the Spanish in Florida.

The remonstrance of Georgia was received by Congress in due time. The committee of the House to which it was referred reported on February 28, 1801, that since negotiations were well under way for the cession of the district in question, no action need be taken. [b]

The cession was finally made and ratified on April 24, 1802. The western boundary of the State was fixed in the terms of the agreement as it has remained to the present day. All lands which Georgia had claimed beyond that boundary she ceded to the United States. She stipulated that $1,250,000 should be paid her out of the proceeds of the sales of the lands, since that was approximately the amount which she had expended in connection with them. The lands were to be used for the common benefit of the States, with the exception of 5,000,000 acres, which might be devoted to the settlement of the Yazoo claims. A State was to be erected in the ceded territory and domestic slavery was to be permitted therein. [c]

[a] This "Address and remonstrance of the legislature of Georgia," approved December 6, 1800, was printed by the United States in pamphlet form in 1801.. A copy of it may be found in the Congressional Library and another in the library of Yale University. The document was reprinted in the Augusta Constitutionalist July 28, 1835.

[b] Public Lands, vol. 1, p. 112.

[c] Ib., vol. 1, p. 125.

For our view the fourth provision in the first article of the agreement should be kept clearly in mind. It stated that the United States were bound to extinguish, "at their own expense, for the use of Georgia, as soon as the same can be peaceably obtained on reasonable terms, the Indian title to the country of Tallassee" and other specified districts, "and that the United States shall in the same manner also extinguish the Indian title to all other lands within the State of Georgia." The second article, which was also important in later years, set forth that the United States "cede to the State of Georgia whatever claim, right, or title they may have to the jurisdiction or soil of any lands lying [within the limits of Georgia]."

The chief immediate effect of the cession of 1802 was to place within the sphere of the Federal authorities the whole problem of quieting the Yazoo claims. The solution of that problem proved difficult and tedious, on account of the differing opinions held by the three departments of the Government. The owners of claims to the Yazoo lands petitioned Congress again and again for the enforcement of their rights, or at least for an equitable compromise; but nearly a decade passed without any substantial progress toward a settlement. President Jefferson thought that the claims were not valid, but that it would be good policy to arrange a compromise in order to avoid troublesome litigation in equity. Many of the claimants were third parties, who had bought the lands from the Yazoo companies; there was no accusation of bad faith against them, and it was not clear that they deserved to be left without indemnity for their losses. As regards Congress, the complexion of the lower House is noteworthy. The Democrats had a clear majority, and the Southern wing of the party controlled the policy of the whole. John Randolph, vigorously supported by Troup, of Georgia, and other Southerners, took the ground that any interference by the central Government in the matter would constitute an infraction of the rights of the State of Georgia. By this line of argument and by copious vilification of the bribe-giving Yazoo speculators Randolph caused Congress to defer action year by year from 1804 to 1814.[a]

The judiciary remained as the only branch of the Government from which the claimants might obtain assistance. The

[a] Cf. Henry Adams, Hist. of the U. S., vol. 2, p. 212.

nationalist attitude of Chief Justice Marshall was well known, and his action could be foretold regarding the claims, if any litigation should bring them within his province. The holders of the Yazoo scrip at length saw the futility of their routine petitions to Congress, and adopted a scheme to obtain a declaration of the Supreme Court in favor of the validity of their claims. Accordingly they made up the case of Fletcher v. Peck, which was brought before the court in 1809.[a]

The declaration of the plaintiff in the suit was that he, Fletcher, had bought of Peck, for $3,000, the title to a tract of 15,000 acres of land, lying within the limits of Georgia. It stated that Peck had bought this tract of Phelps, who had bought it of Prime, who had bought it of Greenleaf, who had acquired it from the Georgia Company, to which the Georgia legislature had sold the land in 1795. It pleaded that this title which the plaintiff had acquired had been rendered faulty by the rescinding act of 1796, and that therefore he was entitled to reimbursement in the sum of $3,000.

The decision of the court was rendered by Chief Justice Marshall on February 16, 1810. It was to the effect that Peck's title to the land was valid, and that therefore Fletcher had no adequate ground for demanding reimbursement. Answering the arguments of the plaintiff's attorney, the court decided that the constitution of Georgia of 1789 established no restriction upon the legislature which inhibited the passage of the act of 1795, and that that act was of force. The court dealt with the validity of the rescinding act as a general question, having no special application to Georgia. It held that when a law is in its nature a contract, and when absolute rights have vested under that contract, a repeal of the law can not divest those rights. It further observed that the Constitution of the United States especially forbids the States to make laws which impair the obligation of contracts. "The validity of the rescinding act, then, might well be doubted, were Georgia a simple sovereign power. But Georgia can not be viewed as a single, unconnected, sovereign power, on whose legislature no other restrictions are imposed than may be found in its own constitution. She is a part of a large empire; she is a member of the American Union; and that

[a] W. Cranch, U. S. Supreme Court Reports, vol. 6, p. 87.

union has a constitution, the supremacy of which all acknowledge, and which imposes limits to the legislatures of the
several States which none can claim a right to pass."

Justice Johnson rendered a separate decision upon two
points involved, and in it he displayed a view of the actual
relations between the Central Government, the State governments, and the Indian tribes, which, if it had been pronounced
fifteen years before or after its actual date, would have led to
vigorous replies from Georgia. He held that the Indian
tribes to the west of Georgia possessed the general attributes
of nations and retained the absolute proprietorship of their
soil; that all the restrictions which Georgia had upon the
right of soil in the Indians amounted only to an exclusion of
other competitors from the purchase of their lands. He concluded, "And if this [right of Georgia to acquire the lands] was
even more than a mere possibility, it certainly was reduced
to that state when the State of Georgia ceded to the United
States, by the constitution, both the power of preemption
and of conquest, retaining for itself only a resulting right
dependent on a purchase or a conquest to be made by the
United States."

In view of the decision of the Supreme Court, Randolph's
majority in the House of Representatives diminished until,
in 1814, a Senate bill was concurred in which provided for
a compromise with the Yazoo claimants by appropriating
$5,000,000 from the Treasury.

The State rights adherents throughout the South were irritated and chagrined by the decision of the Supreme Court
and by the final act of Congress. But it was a relief to
everyone to be rid of the hated Yazoo business, which for
twenty years had been so troublesome. In the view of the
Georgia populace the corruption of the State government of
1795 was of more consequence than the later question of jurisdiction. A vote of thanks which the legislature gave to
Randolph in 1807 was awarded to the champion of Georgia's
honor rather than of her sovereign rights. The people felt,
indeed, that the Central Government had meddled where of
right it had no jurisdiction; but as early as 1802 the State
had shown that it was not absolutely opposed to the idea of a
compromise, by agreeing to the possible use of a portion of
the ceded lands for that very purpose.

At the period in which the decision was rendered in the case of Fletcher *v.* Peck the popular interest in internal questions of all kinds was largely replaced by engrossing attention to foreign affairs. The South was eager for strong measures to be taken by the United States to resent the indignities offered by England and France. But New England was resolved to foster peace and commerce and was inclined to go as far as the dissolution of the Union if its end could be achieved in no other way. This state of affairs caused a reaction from the particularist doctrines in the South and it led to the adoption of the principles of the so-called Federalist party by the whole body of the Democrats.

Georgia was eager to engage in the war of 1812, and her leaders condemned the lack of patriotism in all those who, living in other sections, held opposing views.

We have reached, then, a period coinciding roughly with the first two decades of the nineteenth century, where a distinct lull occurred in Georgia's contentions for the recognition of her sovereign rights.

CHAPTER II.--THE ACQUISITION OF THE CREEK LANDS.

In the period from 1764 to 1802, during which the Mississippi River was the legal western boundary of Georgia, her territory embraced the homes and hunting grounds of large portions of the four main tribes of Southern Indians. Of these the Chickasaws and Choctaws dwelt so far away to the west as never to come into contact with any settlements which acknowledged the jurisdiction of Georgia. The southern limit of the Cherokee lands was 200 miles distant from the original plantation at Savannah, and that tribe also was for a long time exempt from any great encroachment by Georgians. The Creek Indians were the aboriginal proprietors of the whole southeastern district, and as such were alone concerned in the early cessions of land to Georgia. The Creek tribe or nation, exclusive of the Seminoles, with whom we are not concerned, was a loose confederation of villages, in two main divisions, called lower and upper, or eastern and western. The homes of the Lower Creeks were chiefly within the present limits of Georgia, while the villages of the Upper Creeks were grouped near the Alabama River and its tributaries.

The colony of Georgia had found little difficulty in securing enough land from the Creeks to satisfy the reasonable wants of the settlers. By means of three treaties, dated, respectively, 1733, 1763, and 1773, the tribe had ceded its title to such districts as were considered most desirable by the immigrants. The result was that at the time of the Revolution, the commonwealth was in possession of a very long and narrow strip of land bordering the Atlantic Ocean and the Savannah River. This district probably embraced an eighth of the territory now owned by Georgia, or a twentieth of that within her chartered limits in that period.

During the war with Great Britain, both the Creeks and the Cherokees were guilty of numerous depredations. The

Cherokees were punished by a raiding party at the beginning of 1783, and were forced to make a treaty ceding their claims to certain lands about the sources of the Oconee River. Since this region had been held in joint possession by the Cherokees and the Creeks, Georgia needed to extinguish the Creek claim in order to perfect her title. A delegation of Creek chiefs made a treaty with the State authorities at Augusta in 1783, ceding the claim of their tribe to the lands demanded.[a] It soon afterwards appeared that a part of the Creeks were dissatisfied with the treaty and claimed that it was invalid; but the malcontents did not proceed to violence, and the new lands were occupied in peace by the incoming settlers.

The two treaties of 1783 were made and ratified by the State of Georgia without any participation by the Central Government of the Confederation, but in 1785 the Congress sent commissioners to the two southeastern tribes, with instructions to make definitive peace and to obtain further cessions of land, if practicable. Commissioners were also appointed by Georgia to attend the negotiations as representatives of the State. They were instructed to protest against any measures of the United States commissioners which should seem to exceed the powers given by the Articles of Confederation, and to report upon these matters to the State legislature. The Creeks were invited to a conference at Galphinton, in Georgia, but only a small delegation appeared at the appointed time. The representatives of the Congress declined to negotiate under such circumstances, and left Galphinton in order to keep an engagement with the Cherokees at Hopewell, in South Carolina. The Georgians, however, made a treaty with the chiefs on the spot, obtaining from them a cession, in the name of the whole Creek nation, of what was called the Tallassee country, comprising the district south and southwest of the Altamaha River.[b] The United States commissioners afterwards made a treaty with the Cherokees at Hopewell, which was of little benefit to Georgia. The Georgia commissioners reported to the legislature that the instructions which had been issued by the Congress for the negotiations involved an infringement upon the rights of the State. The State government, after ratifying the treaty of Galphinton

a Indian Affairs, vol. 1, p. 23. Pickett, Hist. of Ala., vol. 2, p. 59.
b Ib., vol. 1, p. 17.

and thanking its commissioners for their vigilance and patriotism, addressed to the Congress a memorial against the attempted infringement of State rights.[a] In the same spirit as at Galphinton, negotiations were held in October, 1786, at Shoulderbone Creek, between Georgia commissioners and a small delegation of Creek chiefs, who assumed authority to act for the whole nation. A treaty was made which extinguished the Creek title to all lands east of the Oconee River.[b]

A large number of Creeks showed hostility to the treaties which Georgia had recently made, and prepared to contest their validity. Alexander McGillivray, a half-breed chief of decided political ability and of great ambition, was the moving spirit of this unfriendly party, which plainly comprised a majority of all the Creeks. In the treaties of Augusta, Galphinton, and Shoulderbone, McGillivray saw the development on the part of Georgia of a firm policy to which he was resolved not to yield in any degree. He remonstrated with the Central Government, and at the same time directed his warriors to harass the Georgia frontier in order to compel speedy attention to his protest. After making a perfunctory investigation the Congress decided that the treaties of Galphinton and Shoulderbone had been made unlawfully, and that the cessions of land were invalid.

The ensuing condition of affairs was very disagreeable for all parties involved. The majority of the Creeks felt outraged by the scheming between Georgia and the treaty faction of their own tribe, and they probably made the minority feel the weight of their displeasure. The people of Georgia realized that the failure of the Congress to support the official and almost necessary policy of the State would afford McGillivray an opportunity to play off one government against the other to his own advantage and at the expense of the State.[c] The predicament of the Congress was no novelty for that body, for its powerlessness had become notorious. It probably felt that its decision in the case was the correct one, but it had no power to make Georgia abide by that decision. On

[a] For substance of instructions to the United States commissioners, stating that Congress was sovereign over all the country, and that Congress wanted none of the Indian lands, see Indian Affairs, vol. 1, p. 41. For resolution of the Georgia legislature, thanking the Georgia commissioners, see Indian Affairs, vol. 1, p. 17. Pickett, vol. 2, p. 67.

[b] Indian Affairs, vol. 1, pp. 18 to 23. Pickett, vol. 2, p. 71.

[c] Report of committee, Georgia House of Representatives, Indian Affairs, vol. 1, p. 24.

the other hand, the Confederation was so feeble that in case a war should arise with the Creeks a national force could hardly be put into the field.

Congress was strongly inclined to keep the peace at any cost, but neither Georgia nor the Creeks were so amicably. disposed. Desultory hostilities increased, and continued for several years. Several attempts at conciliation were made, but neither of the parties would yield upon any point.

The establishment of the new system of government in 1789 placed the United States authorities in a much better position to cope with the Indian troubles of the country; but immediate solution was not found for all the problems. President Washington was inclined to approve Georgia's contention in Creek affairs. He decided, however, to send a confidential agent to McGillivray with an invitation for the Creek chiefs to a conference at New York. The Creeks accepted, and at New York a treaty was made, August 7, 1790, without any consultation with the government of Georgia.[a] The Indians, for a monetary consideration, agreed to validate the treaty of Shoulderbone, which ceded the lands east of the Oconee. On the other hand they refused to recognize the treaty of Galphinton in any degree, but inserted an article in the new treaty reserving the Tallassee country to the Creek Nation.

A novel and striking feature of the new treaty was embodied in the fifth article, which reads: "The United States solemnly guarantees to the Creek Nation all lands within the limits of the United States to the westward and southward of the boundary described in the preceding article." The Georgians at once attacked this article as an unwarrantable stretch of the Federal power. James Jackson declared in Congress that the treaty was spreading alarm among the people of Georgia, and complained that it had ceded away a great region which was guaranteed to the State by the Federal Constitution.[b] The State legislature adopted a remonstrance to Congress declaring the fifth article of the treaty to be liable to censure because of the objectionable and innovating phrase

[a] Indian Affairs, vol. 1, p. 81. Pickett, vol. 2, p. 122. The text of this and all other treaties of the United States Government with the various tribes of Indians, between 1789 and 1825, may be found in a volume entitled "Indian Treaties," published by authority of the Department of War, 1825. The treaties ratified after 1789 may also be found in the United States Statutes at Large.

[b] Cf. McMaster, History of the People of the U. S., vol. 1, p. 604.

which it contained. The fear was expressed that the giving of a guaranty for their lands to the Creeks by the Central Government would lead to the conclusion that the sovereignty over such lands belonged to the United States; whereas, the legislature asserted, the said sovereignty appertained solely to the State of Georgia and had never been granted to the Union by any compact whatsoever.[a]

The discord over these unoccupied lands was due to opposing conceptions of the status of the Indian tribes. The theory of the colonial governments had been that these tribes were independent communities with the rights and powers of sovereign nations. During the Revolution and in the period of the Confederation the central government adhered to that theory. But public opinion, following the arguments of the State governments which were involved in Indian problems, reverted to the original European conception that the relations of the tribes to civilized nations were merely those of dependent communities without sovereignty and without any right to the soil but that of tenants at will. The reorganization of the Government in 1789 brought no change of Indian policy so far as concerned the central authorities. On the other hand, the State governments were growing more positive in their own views. Georgia was in the forefront of this development, but as in the case of the eleventh amendment, her doctrines were quickly accepted by States whose attention was being forcibly directed to the question by similar predicaments of their own.[b]

The conflict in policy was felt to be very unfortunate. The treaty of New York was regretted by Georgians because it tended to emphasize the lack of harmony and to show the Creeks that in a possible war with Georgia they would not have to fear the arms of the Union.[c] The frontier settlers did not stop with coldly disapproving the treaty. They hotly declared that they would permit no line to be marked out as a permanent boundary between Georgia and the Creek lands denied to her. Further trouble was made by a party of the Creeks dominated by Spanish influence. Frontier depreda-

a Indian Affairs, vol. 2, p. 791.

b Robert Weil, The Legal Status of the Indian, p. 17. Cf. charge of Judge Walton to a Georgia grand jury, Indian Affairs, vol. 1, p. 409. Cf. message of Governor Milledge, April 18, 1803, in MSS. journal of the senate of Georgia, 1803, p. 4.

c Indian Affairs, vol. 1, p. 24; report of committee, Georgia house of representatives.

tions began again and continued spasmodically for several years. The Georgians became highly incensed at the Indian outrages, the more so because of the impossibility of deciding where retaliation for the maraudings should be made. A large number of the Creeks were known to be peaceable and friendly, but exact knowledge of the attitude of each village could not be had.[a]

A period of comparative quiet at the beginning of 1793 was rudely disturbed in March by the raid of a party of Creeks upon Glynn and Camden counties on the extreme southern frontier of Georgia. The whole State was thrown into excitement. The disorderly Creeks along the whole border took the marauding fever to such an extent that Governor Telfair proposed to build a line of blockhouses reaching from North Carolina to Florida.[b] On May 8, the governor wrote to the President that the savages were making such havoc that retaliation by open war was the only resort. At the middle of June General Twiggs was dispatched with about 700 militia to invade the Creek country. He advanced as far as the Ocmulgee River, but there turned back because of the lack of supplies. During July and August the State authorities continued active preparation for warfare. Councils of war were held, and their recommendations for an offensive campaign were sent to the President for his approval. But Washington was strongly opposed to a Creek war. He replied that he utterly disapproved the plans, because the right of declaring war belonged to Congress alone, because a great portion of the Creeks were clearly desirous of peace, and because of considerations regarding Spain, and regarding the Cherokees.[c]

It soon became apparent that the great majority of the Creeks were very much troubled that the hostility had arisen. Their alarm at the threatening preparations of Georgia caused them to give information that the marauders belonged to a few specified towns on the Flint and Chattahoochee rivers, and to intimate the willingness of the tribe as a whole to make reparation for damages.[d] The overtures of the Creeks re-

[a] Pickett, vol. 2, p. 122. Indian Affairs, vol. 1, pp. 258, 327, 369, 392, and 409. Stevens, vol. 2, p. 445.
[b] Indian Affairs, vol. 1, p. 368.
[c] Ib., pp. 365, 369, and 370.
[d] Ib., pp. 327, 383, and 386.

moved all cause for war, much to the disappointment of Governor Telfair, who wanted a few battles which would tend to vindicate Georgia's policy and advance her contentions for the validity of the treaties of Galphinton and Shoulderbone. The sentiment for the rights and dignity of the State was at this time so radical that the governor was prompted to inform the Central Government on September 26, 1793, of certain "conditions that will be required on the part of the State of Georgia on the establishment of peace between the United States and the Creek Indians."[a]

The death of Alexander McGillivray, in February, 1793, left the Creeks so disorganized that very delicate handling was required before any treaty could be negotiated and ratified by what the United States Government considered the sovereign Creek Nation. James Seagrove took up residence in the midst of the tribe, as United States Indian agent, in the effort to restore tranquillity. His work encountered the opposition of the lawless element of the Creeks and of the self-sufficient, unruly whites on the frontier. In April, 1794, he was able to bring a delegation of the chiefs on a friendly visit to the governor of Georgia. All parties expressed themselves as anxious for peace, and the delegation went home well satisfied.[b] The work of conciliation was having effect among the Georgians as well as with the Indians. In August, Governor Matthews wrote the Creeks that the State wanted no more of their lands if they would desist from depredations.[c] The good faith of this statement may be questioned; but it is clear that Matthews was less aggressive than his predecessor in office, and that the general temper of the State was more moderate.

In December the Georgia legislature requested the Central Government to make arrangements for making a treaty with the object of extinguishing the Creek claim to the lands between the Oconee and the Ocmulgee. On June 25, 1795, Washington appointed three commissioners for the purpose. The negotiations were held at Coleraine, in southern Georgia, in June, 1796. When it was found that the Creeks would cede no lands, a treaty was made which ratified the treaty of New York and established peace.[d]

a Indian Affairs, vol. 1, p. 412.   b Ib., p. 472. Pickett, vol. 2, p. 154.
c Ib., vol. 1. p. 497.   d Ib., pp. 486 and 560.

Commissioners from Georgia were present during the negotiations at Coleraine, but they felt that their importance was not fully recognized. They drew up a protest against the proceedings of the United States commissioners and against the treaty as made.[a] A large part of the document consists of complaint about slights to the dignity of the Georgia commissioners. Only two points in the protest are worthy of note. The fifth article remonstrated against the cession by the Creeks to the United States of land in Georgia for the purpose of posts and trading houses without the consent of the State government. This point met the approval of the United States Senate, and the objectionable clause was stricken from the treaty. The sixth article repeated the complaint of Georgia against the power of the Central Government to repudiate the treaties of Galphinton and Shoulderbone and foretold disastrous consequences if such a policy should be continued. In accordance with this part of the protest a committee of the lower House of Congress reported that it failed to find reason for the relinquishment to the Creeks of the land obtained by Georgia through the treaty of Galphinton unless from general policy toward keeping the peace. It recommended that the United States make compensation to Georgia for the injury.[a] Mr. Pinckney of South Carolina was chairman of the committee, and Georgia realized that her claims found enough support in Congress to make any strong resolutions unnecessary on her part. The protest of the Georgia commissioners failed to rouse any great turmoil, for a more sympathetic understanding now prevailed. The Central Government was not inclined to support the unwarranted action of its commissioners, and, on the other hand, the people of Georgia probably thought that the representatives of the State, from the influence of personal pique, had overstated their case.

Throughout the remaining years of the century there was peace on the Creek frontier. Indeed, the hatchet was not again dug up until the time of the second war between the United States and Great Britain.

The general atmosphere of the Creek border at the end of the century is well indicated by an incident which occurred in

<hr>

a Indian Affairs, vol. 1, p. 613.   Stevens, vol. 2, p. 456.
b 1b,, vol. 2, p. 770.

1794, with Elijah Clarke[a] as its central figure. Clarke was a rough and fearless son of the backwoods, who sometimes with the best of intentions, thought that his own will should be the law of the land. When he saw the cabins of the settlers being built within sight of each other and contemplated the ever-swelling tide of immigration from Virginia and the Carolinas, he felt that the population of Georgia was about to become too dense. With an unconscious application of the doctrine of beneficent use, he decided that 20,000 Creeks could not actually need forty or fifty million acres of good tobacco and corn lands. His actions were governed accordingly. He had defeated the Indians as a general in the Continental Army, and had a contempt for their power in battle. As for interference from any other source, he expected Georgia to support his undertaking, and thought that a bold front would prevent trouble with the Federal authorities.

A number of home seekers fell in with the scheme of Clarke to take possession without ceremony of some of the unceded Creek lands. These men were not necessarily of desperate character. The clause in the treaty of New York, 1790, which guaranteed the title of the Creeks to all their lands not then ceded, justified the conduct of Clarke and his followers in the minds of many people in middle Georgia. Clarke launched his enterprise by establishing his band of pioneers on lands west of the Oconee and within the district guaranteed to the Indians. He built two little forts for protection, and began clearing the ground for cultivation.

Governor Matthews heard a rumor of the settlement in May, 1794, but did not obtain definite information until July. He then sent officers to command Clarke to move off the Creek lands. Upon receiving a refusal to obey, the governor issued a proclamation against the settlement and ordered the arrest of the leader. Clarke surrendered himself to the authorities of Wilkes County. Four justices of the peace sat upon the case, and with unanimous voice and in pompous terms declared him discharged from custody. The governor then wrote Washington for advice and assistance, meanwhile organizing a troop of horse to place Clarke's settlement in state of siege. The Indians had already complained to the

[a] Elijah Clarke sometimes wrote his name Clark. His sons nearly always used the longer form.

President.   Washington directed Governor Matthews to sup-
press the settlement with the use of the military, in case such
force were necessary.   Judge Walton, of the Georgia bench,
made occasion to condemn the settlement and to urge its
abandonment.   But Clarke and his men declared that they
would maintain their ground at the expense of their lives.
The governor pushed on his military preparations.   Federal
and State troops were hurried to the vicinity of the illegal
settlement, and artillery was ordered to the spot from Savannah.   It soon became evident that armed resistance on the
part of Clarke would be foolhardy.   At the end of September
he evacuated his forts with the honors of war, and thus closed
the episode.[a]

While many of the frontiersmen were disposed to ignore
the forms of the law, especially where the inferior race was
concerned, the State as a whole was inclined to emphasize the
observance of legal and constitutional restrictions by its own
citizens as well as by the United States Government.   The
incidents of the Yazoo sale demonstrated that the two governments were not entirely in accord upon all points; but at
the beginning of the new century there was no single dispute between them which was not smoothly approaching a
settlement.

The ratification of the articles of agreement and cession
between Georgia and the United States, in 1802, gave very
general satisfaction in the State.   The government of Georgia
was glad to extricate itself from the predicament in which
the Yazoo sale had placed it.   The lands ceded to the United
States were remote from the settled districts, and of little
practical value to the State at that time; while as a consideration for them the Central Government agreed to pay a sum
of money, yielded all claim to land or jurisdiction within
Georgia's limits east of the Chattahoochee line, and promised
to remove the Indians from the territory of the State as soon
it should become practicable.

Very soon after the signing of the agreement, commissioners of the United States entered upon successful negotiations
for a Creek cession.   The Indians, by the treaty of Fort Wil-
kinson, agreed to yield their title to a part of the Tallassee
country, lying south of the Altamaha, and to a part of the dis-

a Indian Affairs, vol. 1, pp. 495, ff. Stevens, vol. 2, p. 404. Pickett, vol. 2, p. 156. G. R. Gilmer, Georgians, pp. 190 to 194.

trict between the Oconee and the Ocomulgee. The Georgians had hoped to obtain greater cessions, but were contented for the time being with what was obtained for them. Some of the Western Creeks were disposed to make trouble over the encroachment upon the lands of their nation, but the very efficient Indian agent, Col. Benjamin Hawkins, proved equal to the occasion and pacified the malcontents.

The Georgia authorities were not disposed to let the United States Government forget the obligation assumed in 1802. Negotiations were held at the Creek Agency on the Flint River in 1804, in which the Indian title was extinguished over the remaining territory east of the Ocmulgee. Another treaty was made with the Creek chiefs at Washington, D. C., in 1805, but no further lands could then be secured for Georgia.[a] During the next decade the tremendous wars in Europe attracted attention everywhere at the expense of other matters. The probability that America would be involved, and the fact that Georgia was a frontier State, added to the consideration that there was no pressing need for more land, led to the avoidance of any policy tending to arouse the hostility of the Indians or the Spaniards in Florida. The Creeks were thus granted a respite from the theretofore incessant demands for territory.

Toward 1812 relations became strained between the United States and England. Anticipating the outbreak of war, British emissaries began the work of securing allies among the American Indians. The great chief Tecumseh readily fell in with the plans of the British and undertook to incite all the tribes between Canada and Florida to attack the frontier settlements. The Upper or Western Creeks were already ill disposed toward the whites, and their young warriors listened eagerly to the speeches of Tecumseh at Atauga and Coosada, on the Alabama River, in October, 1812. The older and more experienced chiefs shook their heads at the incendiary talking, but the bulk of the Western tribes put aside their advice as that of timid dotards.

The Creeks, like the Cherokees, were at this time in a transitional stage from savagery to semi-civilization. Their habits and disposition had formerly been those of huntsmen and warriors; but in imitation of their white neighbors, and

[a] For the three treaties, see Indian Affairs, vol. 1, pp. 669, 691, and 696.

H. Doc. 702, pt. 2——4

largely through the instruction of the United States Indian agents, they had begun to raise cattle and to cultivate the ground more extensively. The younger element, however, sighed for the barbaric life of their forefathers and resented the advance of the white settlements. As a rule the Eastern Creeks were decidedly peaceable, but among the tribes on the Alabama all the young men were anxious for battle. Their warlike spirit was fired the more by the urging of their prophets and medicine men, who foretold victory over the Americans, and long life in happy hunting grounds for the braves who fell in battle. A wide conspiracy was organized among the Western Creeks in the winter and spring of 1812–13, without the knowledge of the Americans or of the friendly Indians.

The older chiefs of the Upper Creeks finally discovered the trouble brewing, and in April, 1813, protested their good will to the United States in letters to Colonel Hawkins. Alexander Cornells, one of the older chiefs and sub-agent of the United States for the Upper Creeks, learned the details of the plot. He saw that the prophets of the Alabamas, who were enemies of the plan of civilization and advocates of the wild Indian mode of living, were the chief assistants of Tecumseh in preparing the outbreak which was just beginning. Cornells at once informed Hawkins of his discoveries and hurried in person to Milledgeville to get aid from the governor of Georgia. But neither Colonel Hawkins nor Governor Mitchell could be certain that the trouble among the Upper Creeks was anything more serious than a contest for power betwen rival groups of chiefs.[a]

Murders and depredations had already begun on the Tennessee frontier, which was nearer the Upper Creek villages than were the Georgia settlements. The hostile spirit was also encountered by the little colony of Americans near Mobile and by the settlers in Mississippi. The first skirmish was at Burnt Corn, in Southern Alabama, where the Creeks repulsed an attack of badly organized frontiersmen. On July 30 an outrage was perpetrated which aroused all the Southern people to the serious character of the uprising. This was the capture of Fort Mims, on the lower course of the Alabama

[a] Indian Affairs, vol. 1, pp. 813, 846, 848, and 898.

River, and the massacre of almost every man, woman, and child who had fled within its stockade for refuge.

Large numbers of Americans were at once put in readiness to invade the Alabama country. Gen. Andrew Jackson quickly organized a little army of Tennesseeans and crossed the boundary in October. He attacked and defeated the Creeks wherever he could find them, but the want of food and supplies hampered him and prevented a rapid campaign. Raids into the Creek country were made by General Cocke with an army from East Tennessee; by General Floyd with Georgia militia, and by General Claiborne with a force of Mississippians and Choctaws. Each of these achieved a victory, but from lack of supplies was compelled to make a hasty retreat to his respective basis of operations. At the beginning of 1814 both Jackson and Floyd met with reverses, due as much to the wildness of the country as to the bravery of the Indians. But in March Jackson advanced with strong reinforcements and won a decisive victory at the Horseshoe on the Tallapoosa River. All of the surviving hostile Creeks fled across the Florida boundary.[a] In August Jackson assembled at Fort Jackson the chiefs who remained in Alabama and dictated terms of peace to the Creek Nation.

This done, he threw diplomatic considerations to the winds and advanced with his army into Florida, then a colony of the neutral power, Spain. He expelled the British from Pensacola and drove the Creeks and Seminoles into the dense swamps; but his conduct in foreign territory had almost led to censure from the President, when he transferred his forces to New Orleans and won such a signal victory there that his popularity with the people led the Cabinet to drop its consideration of his former conduct. There were some further slight hostilities with the Creeks and Seminoles in 1815, but the final pacification in October simply established more firmly the treaty of Fort Jackson of August 9, 1814.

By this treaty or capitulation of Fort Jackson the Creeks were forced to give up a great quantity of land. The territory ceded lay in what is now central and southern Alabama and in southern Georgia. Jackson's object in requiring the particular cession that he demanded was a strategic one. He

[a] Indian Affairs, vol. 1, p. 813. Pickett, vol. 2, pp. 271 et sq. Henry Adams, Hist. U. S., vol. 7.

wished to isolate the Creeks as far as he could from other possible enemies of the United States. The cession of lands in the valley of the Alabama led to a strong settlement of whites between the Creeks on the east and the Chickasaws and Choctaws on the west, while the securing of a broad belt in southern Georgia cut off the Spaniards and Seminoles from all mischievous communication.[a]

At the time of holding the treaty Colonel Hawkins represented to General Jackson that Georgia was anxious to secure possession of her Creek lands as far as the Flint River; but in addition to the argument of strategic advisability the fact was clear that while the Western Creeks had been warring upon the United States the Eastern half of the nation had remained friendly, thus it would hardly be fair to require the Eastern Creeks to give up an unnecessary amount of their lands as punishment for what the Western Creeks had done.

The Georgia legislature in December addréssed a remonstrance to the President of the United States regarding the treaty of Fort Jackson. The citizens of Georgia, it said, had hoped that the United States would have taken advantage of the victory over the Creeks to carry out the agreement made with Georgia in 1802. But as a matter of fact, Georgia had obtained little or no benefit from the treaty. The territory acquired, it stated, was sterile and unprofitable. All the territory left to the Creeks lay in Georgia or very near its western boundary. The protest concluded with a request that further cessions be soon obtained.

Negotiations were set on foot to accomplish the wish of the Georgians, the result of which was a cession at the Creek Agency, January 22, 1818, of 1,500,000 acres of land in two parcels, the one lying about the headwaters of the Ocmulgee River, and the other consisting of a tongue of land lying between the Altamaha River and the northern boundary of the cession of 1814. This second district, which was the larger of the two, was not held in high esteem for agricultural purposes, and therefore the treaty of 1818 did not secure for the Creeks a long intermission from the importunities of Georgia.

President Monroe in a message to Congress, March 17, 1820,

---

[a] Pickett, vol. 2, p. 826. Indian Affairs, vol. 1, p. 838.

requested appropriations to extinguish by treaty the Indian title to all remaining lands in Georgia. As a result of this a treaty was made at Indian Spring, January 18, 1821, by which Georgia obtained from the Creeks their remaining lands east of the Flint River. Governor Clarke convened the legislature to distribute the ceded lands, and sent in a message which was characteristic of the attitude of Georgia. He stated that the Federal authorities showed themselves ready to abide by the agreement of 1802 whenever favorable opportunities arose, and he advised that the State government should seize the occasion to insist upon a cession from the Cherokees.[a] The assembly was, as usual, not unresponsive to such advice.

During its session in the following year the legislature addressed to the Central Government another remonstrance, dealing to some extent with the theoretical issue. "It has been the unfortunate lot of our State to be embroiled in the question of territorial right almost from the commencement of her existence," the protest ran. "The State of Georgia claims a right to the jurisdiction and soil of the territory within her limits. She admits, however, that the right is inchoate, remaining to be perfected by the United States in the extinction of the Indian title, the United States * * * acting as our agents."[b]

The Indian tribes were indisposed for further cessions; the Federal Administration declined to coerce the tribes; the State government grew more radical in its demands. George M. Troup succeeded John Clarke as governor, and introduced a new régime in Indian policy. He sent to the assembly in December, 1823, a message couched in no doubtful wording. He urged that the legislature should demand of the United States Government liberal appropriations and the proper steps for extinguishing the Indian title to all lands in Georgia. He said that the Central Government had been niggardly in its actions; that the state of things had been growing worse and worse. He referred to the occasion in 1814 when the United States required the Creeks to cede a large amount of land in the Alabama valley, but only a worthless district in Georgia. He emphasized, as a special grievance, that in 1814 the United

[a] Niles's Register, vol. 20, p. 181.

[b] Prince, Laws of Georgia to 1820, p. 531. U. S. Executive Papers, No. 57, 17th Cong., 2d sess., vol. 4.

States had guaranteed to the Creeks all the lands not ceded by them at Fort Jackson.[a]

On December 15 a committee of the State senate made a report in consonance with the governor's message, and in language as strong as the governor had used. This was quickly adopted in the senate with a unanimous vote, in the house without a division, and received the governor's signature on December 20. The memorial thus prepared, and presented to Congress April 5, 1824, had as its burden that Georgia hoped to see "her laws and her sovereignty coextensive with the limits within which she had consented to confine herself."[b]

On March 10, 1824, the Georgia delegation in Congress addressed a remonstrance to the President on the dilatory policy then being followed. The answer of Mr. Monroe appeared on March 30 in a message to Congress. Differing from the opinion of the Georgians, he stated that the United States Government had steadily been doing its duty in regard to the compact with Georgia; that the Creeks and Cherokees refused to cede more lands; that the Government was not bound to remove the Indians by force; and he intimated that Georgia would have to wait for her lands until the Indians should change their minds.

At this time matters had reached a new stage with the Creeks. They had been making successive cessions of land from 1814, and felt cramped for room. The territory which they had yielded, up to this point, was what had been formerly their hunting grounds; but when all the district east of the Flint River had been given up, and when the Georgians still demanded more, it became a question of abandoning their homes and migrating to a strange country. The nation had advanced considerably in the arts of civilization, and could afford to do without extensive hunting grounds; but when the lands as far as the Chattahoochee were demanded, the Creeks resolved to stand upon the guarantees of their territory in the treaty of Fort Jackson, and firmly refused to sell their homes. Meanwhile the Cherokees had reached the same conclusion, and went so far as to send a delegation to Wash-

[a] W. Harden, Life of G. M. Troup, p. 197.

[b] Acts of Georgia General Assembly 1823, p. 218. Harden's Troup, p. 200. Indian Affairs, vol. 2, p. 491.

ington to make positive statement that their nation would cede no more lands for any consideration.[a]

In this state of things it seemed that the United States authorities must simply let matters rest until the Indians could be induced to sell out. Such would probably have been the case had not George M. Troup been governor of Georgia; but this fact became an important one as further developments took place. Referring to Monroe's message, Troup wrote to J. C. Calhoun, then Secretary of War, "The absolute denial of our rights, as we understand them and have long understood them, at the moment when we believed that they would have been most respected, is a subject of mortification and regret."[b] His course of action from that time was toward the end of removing that cause of Georgia's mortification.

President Monroe, without expecting any substantial results, appointed as commissioners to treat with the Southern Indians James Meriwether and Duncan G. Campbell, two citizens of Georgia. These gentlemen proceeded to arrange a conference with the Creek chiefs at Broken Arrow December 7, 1824. Their request for a cession of lands was met by a reference to the guaranties contained in the treaties of 1790 and 1814, and a refusal to sell any territory. The commissioners, however, discovered that the chiefs of the Lower Creeks were in favor of moving beyond the Mississippi, while the Upper Creeks were opposed to the idea and were intimidating the treaty faction. Meriwether and Campbell at once adjourned the meeting to consult the Federal authorities regarding a change in their instructions.

They requested of the President powers to hold a convention with the Georgia Creeks alone, representing that the Upper Creeks were under the control of Big Warrior and opposed to a cession; that the Cherokees, and especially John Ross, were urging the Creeks against ceding; that the United States Indian agent refused to give them any aid, while the subagent perfidiously opposed them. Nevertheless, they stated, the Lower Creeks were willing to cede their lands, following the advice of their great chief, William McIntosh, who was the principal chief of the eastern half of the nation.

[a] Niles's Register, vol. 26, pp. 101 and 139. U. S. Senate Doc. No. 63, 18th Cong., 1st sess., vol. 4.

[b] Niles's Register, vol. 26, p. 276.

Upon the refusal of the President to grant the powers requested, the commissioners made an alternative request for power to negotiate a treaty with McIntosh for a cession of the lands of the Lower Creeks, the cession to be valid upon ratification by the whole Creek Nation. Mr. Monroe stated his approval of the second plan offered, reprimanded the agent, Colonel Crowell, for his indifference, and discharged the sub-agent, Walker, for his obstruction of the work of the commissioners. The Lower Creek chiefs memorialized the President on January 25, 1825, that the party opposed to the cession, called the "Red Sticks," were plotting for the destruction of the friendly chiefs and asked for protection by the United States from Big Warrior and his followers. At the same time they appointed McIntosh and seven other Creek chiefs to arrange for a cession of the Creek lands in Georgia.

Meriwether and Campbell assembled the Creeks anew at Indian Spring on February 10, 1825. In their report of the proceedings it is stated that nearly 400 chiefs and headmen were present, with only a few from Alabama, and that these latter withdrew after protesting that the partial assembly had no power of cession. A proposition was made the Lower Creeks to exchange all their lands in Georgia for an equal acreage west of the Mississippi, with a bonus of $5,000,000 from the United States. This was agreed to as the basis of the treaty, and on February 12 the instrument was signed by practically all the chiefs present.[a]

The treaty was at once hurried off to Washington with accompanying documents. On the next day Colonel Crowell, in a letter to the Secretary of War, gave his version of the negotiations, endeavoring to prevent the ratification of the treaty. He wrote that only eight towns of the fifty-six composing the nation were represented at Indian Spring, that the treaty was signed by McIntosh and his party alone, and that only two of the signers besides McIntosh himself were chiefs of high grade. The authorities at Washington had already been informed by the Georgia representatives that Crowell's opposition to a cession by the Creeks was due to his antagonism to Governor Troup in State politics.

The treaty of Indian Spring was approved by the Senate

a Indian Affairs, vol. 2, pp. 571 to 582.

and signed by the President on March 5, 1825. Governor Troup issued a proclamation on March 21 that the Creeks had ceded to the United States all their lands in Georgia, to pass into the possession of the State on or before September 1, 1826, and warned all persons against intruding upon the Indian lands for any purpose whatsoever. He soon began negotiations with McIntosh, however, to secure the privilege of having the lands surveyed before the date set, in order that they might be occupied as early as possible in the winter of 1826. McIntosh wrote on April 12, 1825, that he would consent to the survey if the United States Indian agent did not object. On April 25 he gave the desired consent on behalf of the friendly Creeks without attaching the condition of the agent's approval.

The Red Stick Creeks had for some time been vowing vengeance against McIntosh and his supporters. A party numbering more than a hundred warriors surrounded his house on the night of April 29, 1825, set fire to it, and shot McIntosh to death as soon as he showed himself. By this murder, followed by that of two other chiefs of their party, the whole body of the friendly Creeks were thrown into terror and fled for their lives to the white settlements.[a]

The friendly Creeks and the Georgians had for some time suspected Crowell and other white men of inciting the Red Sticks to violence. Governor Troup informed the United States Government of his suspicions and on June 16 appointed commissioners on behalf of the State to take evidence regarding Crowell's guilt or innocence. Upon the arrival of T. P. Andrews as a special agent of the United States, the governor demanded Crowell's suspension from office. Andrews accordingly suspended Crowell, but a few days later wrote him an open letter apologizing for having done so upon false charges. Troup wrote Andrews on June 28 that he had read his letter in the Milledgeville Patriot, and ordered him to suspend intercourse with the government of Georgia. General Gaines was also sent down from Washington to inquire into the true state of things. Upon his taking side with Crowell and Andrews an acrimonious correspondence ensued between the governor and himself. Finally Troup read an open letter from Gaines

a Indian Affairs, vol. 2, pp. 579 to 583, 618, 770, and 771.

to himself in the Georgia Journal, and wrote Gaines on August 6, "I have lost no time to direct you to forbear further intercourse with this government." On the next day the governor demanded of the President that Gaines be recalled, as a punishment for his intemperance of language and disrespect to the constituted authorities of a sovereign State and the great bulk of its people. Upon the publication of a second letter by Gaines in the same temper as the former one, Troup, in the name of the government of Georgia, demanded "his immediate recall, arrest, trial, and punishment under the articles of war." The Secretary of War replied to Troup on September 19, "The President has decided that he can not, consistently with his view of the subject, accede to your demand to have General Gaines arrested." [a] Andrews and Gaines continued to publish letters defending themselves and reflecting upon the Georgia government. Troup nursed his wrath in silence.

The duty for which Andrews and Gaines had been sent among the Creeks was to inquire into the manner in which the treaty of Indian Spring had been negotiated. Upon receiving preliminary reports against the justice of the treaty, President Adams began steps to have the survey of the lands postponed. Governor Troup informed him, however, that since the legislature had decided that the treaty had vested the jurisdiction and the right to the soil in Georgia, and had authorized the governor to have the lands surveyed for distribution, the survey would promptly be made.

The reply of the President was delayed until the receipt of a report from General Gaines that a very large majority of the Creek chiefs denounced the treaty for intrigue and treachery. Tne Secretary of War wrote to the governor of Georgia, July 21, 1825: "I am directed by the President to state distinctly to your excellency that, for the present, he will not permit such entry or survey to be made." [b] For the time being the governor had nothing further to say, so he waited for the meeting of the legislature. He seems to have yielded the question of immediate survey to fall back upon the more important position of defending the validity of the treaty itself.

---

a Indian Affairs, vol. 2, pp. 603, 804, 807, 813, 815, and 817. Niles's Register, vol. 28, p. 196, and vol. 29, p. 14.

b Indian Affairs, vol. 2, p. 809.

The legislature very early in its session showed its attitude by a unanimous resolution of both houses, expressing belief in the fairness of the treaty, and thanking Messrs. Campbell and Meriwether for their services in obtaining the cession. A further resolution was adopted and approved December 23, 1825, that full reliance ought to be placed in the treaty of Indian Spring, that the title to the territory acquired by it had become an absolute vested right, that nothing short of the whole territory acquired by it would be satisfactory, and that the right of entry upon the expiration of the time set in the treaty would be insisted upon.[a]

The Georgia delegation in Congress stated to the Secretary of War, on January 7, that the State refused to grant the invalidity of the treaty at Indian Spring upon any grounds yet advanced, and declared that the President knew, and had informed the Senate before sending the treaty for ratification, of all the objections to its validity which had subsequently been urged.

Notwithstanding these utterances on the part of the authorities of the State of Georgia, Mr. Adams instituted negotiations for a new treaty with the Creeks. At Washington on January 24, 1826, a treaty was signed by the Secretary of War and "the chiefs of the whole Creek Nation." By it the Creeks ceded all their lands in Georgia except a district lying west of the Chattahoochee, and the United States guaranteed to the Creeks such lands as were not ceded. The President, on January 31, submitted to the Senate the new treaty as abrogating and replacing the treaty of Indian Spring, which he said had been ratified under the belief that it had been concluded with a large majority of Creek chiefs, and would soon be acquiesced in by the remainder, whereas, in fact, the ratifying party had proved small and impotent, and, after the death of their two principal chiefs, were not able to put the treaty in force, though they still claimed all the moneys for themselves. He hinted at unworthy practices in negotiating the former treaty, but failed to mention the chicanery which took place in connection with the latter one.[b]

[a] Nov. 18, 1825: Ga. Senate Journal, 1825, p. 56. Ga. Senate Journal, 1825, p. 838. Indian Affairs, vol. 2, p. 741.

[b] Indian Affairs, vol. 2, pp. 612, 613, and 747. See Benton and McKenney on the corruption of the chiefs in the negotiations at Washington: T. H. Benton, Thirty Years' View, vol. 1, p. 164. Indian Affairs, vol. 2, p. 665.

During the summer of 1826 Governor Troup held little communication with Washington, but his few utterances and his actions show that he was not charitably disposed toward Mr. Adams. In June the Georgia government, with the consent of the President, began a survey of the boundary between Georgia and Alabama. On June 29, Troup wrote the Secretary of War that the Cherokees had stopped the surveying party with threats of force. The Secretary replied, August 6, that the President protested against any use of force to complete the survey. Troup retorted that he had said nothing about using force, and that if he had done so it would not have concerned the President, since "Georgia is sovereign on her own soil."[a]

The treaty of Indian Spring gave Georgia the right of entry and possession of the lands involved from September 1, 1826. Governor Troup not recognizing any abrogation as valid, ordered the State surveyors to begin their work on the day set, although by the treaty of Washington the Creek title was to continue until January 1, 1827. When the survey began, some of the Creeks protested to the President. On September 16, the Secretary of War protested in the name of the President against any survey before the end of the year. On October 6, Troup wrote the Secretary that the survey had been practically accomplished and no opposition had been encountered.[b]

Upon the assembling of the legislature the governor reviewed the progress of Indian affairs in his message of November 7, and exhibited the then existing status. "The new treaty," said he, "prescribed new boundaries for Georgia, and by its perpetual guarantee made them permanent." The executive could not allow such a violation of the constitution of Georgia. He declared that there was such a radical difference between the United States Government and the Georgia government as to the rights of sovereignty and jurisdiction which the State claimed under her charter over the territory within her limits that harmony could not continue if the Indians were to remain.[c]

The resolutions which the general assembly adopted on December 22 show that the situation was considered a very

[a] Indian Affairs, vol. 2, pp. 742 and 743.   [b] Ib., pp. 742 and 743.   [c] Ib., p. 786.

serious and distressing one. The preamble set forth that "the unfortunate misunderstanding between the General Government and the State of Georgia has been marked by features of a peculiar character, and plainly indicating a force and power in the former which should have formed the subject of concern, if not alarm, to our sister States; but we regret to say that the very reverse has been the fact, and a cold, if not reproachful, indifference has taken the place of a much more deserved regard." It then proceeded to set forth what Georgia considered the true state of the case. "It is not for forfeited privileges we supplicate, but we seek the redress of violated 'rights. * * * It is a sovereign, and not a subject, that sues; it is an equal, and not an inferior, that remonstrates." The resolutions which followed declared that Georgia owned exclusively the soil and jurisdiction within her existing chartered and conventional limits, and that the attempted abrogation of the treaty of Indian Spring in so far as it would divest Georgia of any rights acquired under the treaty was illegal and unconstitutional.[a]

Following the spirit of the legislature's resolutions, and ignoring the treaty of Washington, Troup directed his surveyors to cover the whole of the Creek lands in Georgia in their surveys; but when they entered the district not ceded in the last treaty they were menaced by Creek Indians. Troup wrote the Secretary of War of this on January 27, stating that there was reason to believe that the United States agent was the instigator of the Creeks, and demanding whether he was acting under orders. Before receiving this letter the Secretary of War wrote Governor Troup, January 29, that complaints of intrusions had reached Washington through the Indian agent; that the action of the surveyors was in direct violation of the treaty of Washington, which was among the supreme laws of the land, and that, "charged by the Constitution with the execution of the laws, the President will feel himself compelled to employ, if necessary, all the means under his control to maintain the faith of the nation by carrying the treaty into effect." On the next day the Secretary directed R. W. Habersham, United States attorney for

---

[a] Acts of Ga., 1826, p. 227; Indian Affairs, vol. 2, p. 733. For large collection of documents on Creek affairs to January, 1827, see U. S. House Executive Doc. No. 59, 19th Congress, 2d sess., vol. 4 (404 pp.).

the district of Georgia, to obtain the proper process to have the United States marshal arrest the intruding surveyors.[a]

Having taken these steps, Mr. Adams saw fit to ask Congress to share his responsibility. He therefore stated his view of the whole case in a message of February 5, 1827. Citing the United States statute of 1802, that any person attempting to settle or survey lands belonging to the Indians should be punished, he stated that he had begun civil process against the surveyors. In abstaining in the early stage of proceedings from the use of the military arm he said that he had been governed by the consideration that the surveyors were not to be considered in the light of solitary transgressors, but as the agents of a sovereign State. Intimations had been given, he continued, that should the surveyors be interrupted they would at all hazards be sustained by the military force of the State, whereupon a conflict must have been imminent. Fearing a collision between the State and Federal governments, the President begged to submit the matter to Congress for legislation.[b]

Without waiting for definite Congressional action, Mr. Adams dispatched Lieutenant Vinton to Milledgeville in the capacity of aide of the commanding general of the United States forces, with a communication to the effect that the governor must stop the survey at once or the United States would take strong measures to have it stopped.

The climax of the whole matter was now reached. Though Troup's course of action had excited some criticism within the State as well as a vast amount of it outside, the people of Georgia to a man were in strong support of the governor in this time of need. Mr. Habersham resigned his office as United States attorney, refusing to array himself against his native State, to which he owed higher duties than to the United States, while all his friends applauded his action. The whole State rang with the slogan of "Troup and the treaty."

George M. Troup was never known for half-heartedness in word or deed, but upon this occasion he fairly surpassed himself as a hotspur. He wrote on February 17 to the Secretary of War, in reply to the document received from the hand of

[a] Indian Affairs, vol. 2, p. 865. Harden's Troup, p. 482.
[b] Indian Affairs, vol. 2, p. 863.

Lieutenant Vinton: "You are sufficiently explicit as to the means by which you propose to carry your resolution into effect. Thus the military character of the menace is established and I am only at liberty to give it the defiance which it merits. You will distinctly understand, therefore, that I feel it my duty to resist to the utmost any military attack which the Government of the United States shall think proper to make upon the territory, the people, or the sovereignty of Georgia, and all the measures necessary to the performance of this duty, according to our limited means, are in progress. From the first decisive act of hostility you will be considered and treated as a public enemy, and with the less repugnance because you, to whom we might constitutionally have appealed for our own defense against invasion, are yourselves the invaders and, what is more, the unblushing allies of the savages whose cause you have adopted."[a]

On the very day of his letter of defiance to the President the governor took what he considered the proper measures to counteract the usurpations of the Federal authorities. First, in regard to the civil arm of the State, he ordered the attorney and solicitor general to take legal measures to liberate any surveyors who might be arrested by United States officers and to make indictments against all such officers. Then, clothing himself with his military prerogative, George M. Troup, commander in chief of the army and navy of the State of Georgia, issued the following order from headquarters at Milledgeville: "The major-generals commanding the Sixth and Seventh Divisions will immediately issue orders to hold in readiness the several regiments and battalions within their respective commands to repel any hostile invasion of the territory of this State. Depots of arms and ammunition, central to each division, will be established in due time."[b]

When the documents were published throughout the country, great interest was aroused in the very unusual state of things which they exhibited. Everyone was on the qui vive for further developments, but those were disappointed who looked for exciting occurrences. Certain events had already taken place which led to the relief of the strain. January 31 the Secretary of War wrote Colonel Crowell, who was still

a Harden's Troup, p. 485. Niles's Register, vol. 32, p. 16.
b Harden's Troup, p. 487. Niles's Register, vol. 32, p. 16.

the agent to the Creeks, that the Department of War had just received reliable information that the Creeks would not refuse to sell their remaining lands in Georgia, and ordered Crowell to negotiate to that end.[a]

Very soon after his orders of February 17 Governor Troup learned of the efforts which were making for the final cession, and took the news, as well he might, to mean that the President was retreating from his position and that Georgia was victorious in her contest.

Troup wrote to the Georgia Congressmen February 21, expressing his pleasure at learning that the President would try to obtain the remaining Creek lands for Georgia. This letter is both a pæan of victory and a disquisition on the Federal Constitution. "I consider all questions of mere sovereignty," he wrote, "as matter for negotiation between the States and the United States, until the proper tribunal shall be assigned by the Constitution itself for the adjustment of them. * * * The States can not consent to refer to the Supreme Court, as of right and obligation, questions of sovereignty between them and the United States, because that court, being of exclusive appointment by the Government of the United States, will make the United States the judge in their own cause. This reason is equally applicable to a State tribunal. * * * Of all the wrongs wantonly and cruelly inflicted, none have been borne with more patience than the charge of seeking a dissolution of the Union. My intentions have been to cement and perpetuate it by preserving, inviolate, the rights of the parties to the compact, without which the compact would be of no value; and to this end I have unceasingly labored."[b]

After the excitement had subsided reports were made in Congress by the committees to which the President's message of February 5 had been referred. Accompanying its report with an exceedingly voluminous collection of documents, the House committee advised, on March 3, that it would be expedient to purchase the Indian title to all lands in Georgia, and "that, until such a cession is procured, the law of the land, as set forth in the treaty of Washington, ought to be maintained

a U. S. House Executive Docs. No. 238 (p. 7), 20th Cong., 1st sess., vol. 6

b Harden's Troup, p. 490. Niles's Register, vol. 32, p. 20.

by all necessary and constitutional means." [a] The report of the Senate committee, presented by its chairman, Mr. Benton, on March 1, was a strongly reasoned document, well calculated to restore public tranquillity. Making a résumé of the trouble from the beginning, the report first set forth President Adams's motives for his actions and tacitly expressed approval for what he had done. Then, investigating the claims made by Georgia, it set them forth with the usual arguments in their support. It showed that the State founded her claim to jurisdiction over all her chartered territory not ceded in 1802 by virtue of the independence of the sovereign States at the time of the Declaration of Independence, and that she appealed to the decision in the case of Fletcher *v.* Peck that the Indian title was not inconsistent with the title in fee in the State to the lands occupied by the Indians. It set forth the contention that under the agreement of 1802 the United States had simply the function of negotiating and ratifying treaties with the Indians of Georgia and no other power in the premises; that if the United States agents had committed a fraud in connection with the treaty of Indian Spring, the Federal authorities could not interfere with the rights of Georgia, completely vested by the ratification of that treaty, but must find some other way to indemnify the Creeks. The report practically justified Georgia in all that she had done and urged that not the slightest preparation be made for military force to coerce a sister State. [b]

Negotiations were in progress during the summer of 1827 for a further cession by the Creeks, for which the treaty was concluded on November 15. [c] It was afterwards found that even this treaty left a small amount of Georgia territory in the possession of the Creeks, and a final treaty was made in January, 1826, which extinguished the Indian title to the last strip of Creek land in Georgia. [d]

[a] Harden's Troup, p. 488.
[b] Indian Affairs, vol. 2, pp. 869 to 872.
[c] U. S. House Exec. Docs. No. 238 (p. 16), 20th Cong., 1st sess., vol. 6.
[d] Athenian (pub. at Athens, Ga.), Jan. 25, 1828.

CHAPTER III.—THE EXPULSION OF THE CHEROKEES.

At the beginning of the American Revolution the hunting grounds of the Cherokees were conceded to extend from the eastern slopes of the Blue Ridge to the neighborhood of the Mississippi River, and from the Ohio River almost as far south as central Georgia. Most of their villages, however, were located in eastern Tennessee and northern Georgia. The settlement of the country by the whites, and the acquisitions of the Indian territory by them, was naturally along the lines of least resistance. That is to say, the Cherokees first ceded away their remote hunting grounds and held most tenaciously to the section in which their towns were situated.

At an early stage in the Revolution a body of militia from the Southern States made a successful attack upon the eastern villages of the Cherokees, who were in alliance with the British. The tribe was at once ready for peace, and signed a treaty with commissioners from Georgia and South Carolina at Dewits Corner, on May 20, 1777, acknowledging defeat at the hands of the Americans, establishing peace, and yielding their title to a section of their lands, lying chiefly in South Carolina.

The Cherokee families which had lived upon the lands conquered now moved westward, extending the settlements of the tribe farther along the course of the Tennessee River. At the same time five new villages were built by the most warlike part of the nation on Chickamauga Creek and in the neighboring district southeast of Lookout Mountain.[a] Before the end of the Revolution the Cherokees were again at war with the Americans, and Gen. Elijah Clarke led an expedition against this settlement on the Chickamauga. The sudden raid caused such terror in the Indian villages that the

[a] Public Lands, vol. 1, p. 59. Indian Affairs, vol. 1, p. 431. Stevens, vol. 2, p. 413.

inhabitants eagerly promised great cessions of land in order to be rid of the invaders. Clarke made what he called a treaty at Long Swamp, but the agreement was necessarily informal and extra-legal. The fact that it was not followed up by the proper authorities caused Clarke to think that the people had not benefited sufficiently by his exertions. The injury to his feelings in this connection was probably responsible in part for his attempted settlement on Indian lands in 1794.

At the close of the Revolution, as we have already noted, the Cherokees ceded to Georgia their claim to a district about the sources of the Oconee, which they held as hunting ground in joint possession with the Creeks. In the territory which the Cherokees retained, the districts near the Georgia settlements were less attractive than the Creek lands to the south. The upland region in the State was being rapidly settled, however, and new lands were in demand. The State made occasional attempts between 1785 and 1800 to obtain further cessions. Frequent conventions were held by commissioners of the United States and the Cherokee chieftains, at some of which representatives of Georgia were present. But the tribe held fast to its Georgia lands. By the treaty of Hopewell in 1785 the Cherokee Nation placed itself under the protection of the United States and agreed to specified boundaries for its territory, but it made no cession which concerned Georgia. The agreement of Hopewell was confirmed at a convention on the Holston River in 1791, and again at Philadelphia in 1793, but the boundaries on the southeast remained practically unchanged.[a]

The treaty of Philadelphia was rendered necessary by hostilities arising with the tribe in 1793; the Chickamauga towns, as usual, provoked the unpleasantness on the Indian side, while the settlers on the frontier of North Carolina and Tennessee were quite as much to blame on the side of the whites. Considerable excitement prevailed for several months, and raids were made by each party; but the fact that the Creek country intervened between Georgia and the chief settlements of the Cherokees directed the warlike energies of the tribe to the north and northeast.

[a] Indian Affairs, vol. 1, pp. 83, 124, and 543.

After 1795 no considerable portion of the Cherokee Nation was at any time seriously inclined to war. Those of its members who preferred the life of hunters moved away to the far West, while the bulk of the tribe remaining settled down to the pursuit of agriculture. The chief complaint which Georgia could make of them in later years was that they kept possession of the soil, while white men wanted to secure it for themselves.

The invention of the cotton gin in 1793 had the effect after a few years of increasing the preference of the Georgians for the warm and fertile Creek lands, over the Cherokee territory which was ill adapted to cotton with the then prevailing system of agriculture. For this reason it was not until all of the Creek lands had been secured for settlement that the State authorities began to make strenuous efforts for the expulsion of the Cherokees. In the intervening years certain moderate steps were taken, which must now engage our attention.

As early as 1803 Thomas Jefferson suggested the advisability of removing all of the southern Indians west of the Mississippi, and in 1809 a delegation of Cherokees, at the instance of the United States Indian agent, Return J. Meigs, made a visit to the Western lands. At that time a considerable part of the Cherokee Nation favored removal, but the matter was postponed. General Andrew Jackson reported, in 1816, that the whole nation would soon offer to move West. When negotiations were made for a treaty in the next year it was found that there was a division of opinion. The Lower Cherokees, who lived chiefly in Georgia, were disposed to emigrate, while the Upper or Tennessee division of the nation preferred to remain and to change from their wild life to the pursuit of agriculture. By the treaty signed at the Cherokee Agency, July 8, 1817, a tract of land was ceded in Georgia, and arrangement was made that such Indian families as so desired might take up new homes in the Far West.[a]

Within the next two years about one-third of the Cherokees moved into the Louisiana Territory; but it happened quite unexpectedly that each section of the nation had altered its disposition, so that a large part of the Upper Cherokees moved

[a] C. C. Royce, The Cherokee Nation, in Report of U. S. Bureau of Ethnology, 1883–84, pp. 203 and 215. Indian Affairs, vol. 2, pp. 125 and 129.

away from Tennessee, while most of the Lower Cherokees remained in Georgia. Thus, when a treaty came to be made in 1819, it was found that a large area had been vacated to the north and east, but only a small district could be obtained in Georgia. It further appeared that, owing to the influence of a powerful chief named Hicks, the westward movement had almost completely stopped.[a]

The treaties of 1817 and 1819 provided that the head of any Cherokee family living in the district ceded to the United States might at his option remain in possession of his home, together with 640 acres of land, which should descend to his heirs in fee simple. The Georgia legislature, of course, protested against this provision as violative of the rights of the State, while Congressional committees declared that in so far as the treaty provided for Indians to become citizens, it infringed upon the powers of Congress.[b] The agreement was accordingly modified and the Cherokee family holdings were gradually purchased during the next few years.

Georgia was at this period beginning to grow insistent upon obtaining possession of the Cherokee lands as well as those of the Creeks. In March of 1820, President Monroe requested appropriations from Congress to extinguish by treaty the Indian title to all lands in Georgia. When the Cherokees were officially approached upon the subject in 1823, the council of chiefs replied to the commissioners, Messrs. Campbell and Merriwether: "It is the fixed and unalterable determination of this nation never again to cede one foot more of our land." That part of the tribe which had emigrated had suffered severely from sickness, wars, and other calamities, and the remainder refused to follow them. To emphasize their decision a delegation proceeded to Washington, where they declared to the President that, "the Cherokees are not foreigners, but the original inhabitants of America, and that they now stand on the soil of their own territory, and they can not recognize the sovereignty of any State within the limits of their territory."[c]

[a] Indian Affairs, vol. 2, pp. 187, 188, 259, and 462. O. H. Prince, Laws of Georgia to 1820, p. 321.

[b] U. S. House Journal, 16th Cong., 1st sess., p. 336. Prince, Laws of Georgia to 1820, p. 531. U. S. Reports of Committees, No. 10, 17th Cong. 1st sess., vol. 1 (Jan. 7, 1822). U. S. Reports of Committees, No. 4, 17th Cong., 2d sess., vol. 2 (1823).

[c] U. S. House Journal, 16th Cong., 1st sess., p. 315 (Mar. 17, 1820). Indian Affairs, vol. 2, pp. 468 and 474.

It may easily be surmised that the chiefs who delivered this declaration were not full-blooded, wild Indians. As a matter of fact, the average member of the tribe, while not savage, was heavy and stupid; but the nation was under the complete control of its chiefs, who were usually half-breeds, or white men married into the nation. Many of these chiefs were intelligent and wealthy, but their followers continued to live from hand to mouth, with little ambition to better themselves Each family cultivated a small field, and perhaps received a pittance from the annual subsidy of the United States; but, as a rule, the payments for cessions of land never percolated deeper than the stratum of the lesser chiefs. The attitude of the United States had undergone a great change. Formerly the tribes near the frontiers had been held as terrible enemies, but they had now become objects of commiseration. The policy of the Government had once been to weaken these tribes, but that had given place to the effort to civilize them.[a]

It is remarkable that the United States Government was still inclined to regard the Indian tribes in the light of sovereign nations. The Cherokee delegation was received at Washington in 1824 with diplomatic courtesy, and its representations attended to as those of a foreign power. The Congressional Representatives of Georgia viewed the matter from the standpoint of their State. They accordingly remonstrated with the President, March 10, 1824, against the practice of showing diplomatic courtesy to the Cherokees. They said that too much time had been wasted, while the Indians were further than ever from removal. If a peaceable purchase of the Cherokee land could not be made, they demanded that the nation be peremptorily ordered to remove and suitably indemnified for their pains.

Mr. Monroe replied in a message to Congress on March 30 that the United States had done its best in the past to carry out the agreement of 1802, and that the Government was under no obligation to use other means than peaceable and reasonable ones. Governor Troup entered his protest against the message on April 24, urging that Georgia had the sole

---

[a] Message of Governor Gilmer, Dec. 6, 1830, Niles's Register, vol. 39, p. 339. Cf. Letter of Superintendent of Indian Affairs to Secretary of War, Mar. 1, 1826, Indian Affairs, vol. 2, p. 658.

right to the lands, and denying that the Indians were privileged to refuse when a cession was demanded. The Cherokees, for their part, held to their contention for national rights, appealing to the clause in the Declaration of Independence "that all men are created equal," and reiterating their determination to give up not an inch of their land.[a] As far as concerned results, the Cherokees had the best of the argument. The effort to drive them west was given up for the time.

The delegation returned home to lead their tribesmen still further in the ways of civilization. A Cherokee alphabet was devised by Sequoyah in 1825, a printing press was set up at the capital, New Echota, in the following year, and soon afterward steps were taken to formulate a written constitution for the nation. Meanwhile the Cherokee population was increasing with considerable rapidity. In 1818 an estimate had been made which placed the number east of the Mississippi at 10,000, and it was thought that 5,000 were living on the Western lands. A census was taken in 1825 of the Cherokee Nation in the East. Of native citizens there were numbered 13,563; of white men and women married in the nations, 147 and 73, respectively; of negro slaves, 1,277.

The Cherokee national constitution was adopted in a convention of representatives on July 26, 1827. It asserted that the Cherokee Indians constituted one of the sovereign and independent nations of the earth, having complete jurisdiction over its territory, to the exclusion of the authority of any other State, and it provided for a representative system of government, modeled upon that of the United States.[b]

Of course Georgia could not countenance such a procedure. Governor Troup had just worsted President Adams in the controversy over the Creek lands, and the State was prepared at least to hold its own against the Cherokees. The legislature, on December 27, adopted resolutions of no doubtful tenor. After praising Governor Troup for his able and patriotic conduct regarding the Creek lands, the preamble showed that since the agreement of 1802 the Indians had been removed entirely from Ohio, Kentucky, North and South

[a] Niles's Register, vol. 26, pp. 100, 103. Indian Affairs, vol. 3, pp. 476, 502, 736.

[b] Indian Affairs, vol. 2, pp. 651, 652. Royce, The Cherokee Nation, p. 241. For text of the Cherokee constitution see U. S. Executive Document No. 91, 23d Cong., 2d sess., vol. 3. Cherokee Phoenix, Feb. 28, 1828.

Carolina, Tennessee, and Missouri, from nearly all of Arkansas and Alabama, and that large cessions had been obtained in Mississippi, Illinois, Michigan, and Florida. The resolutions followed: "That the policy which has been pursued by the United States toward the Cherokee Indians has not been in good faith toward Georgia. * * * That all the lands, appropriated and unappropriated, which lie within the conventional limits of Georgia belong to her absolutely; that the title is in her; that the Indians are tenants at her will, * * * and that Georgia has the right to extend her authority and her laws over her whole territory and to coerce obedience to them from all descriptions of people, be they white, red, or black, who may reside within her limits." The document closed with the statement that violence would not be used to secure Georgia's rights until other means should have failed. [a]

When a year had passed with no developments in furtherance of the policy of the State, Governor Forsyth advised the passage of an act to extend the laws of Georgia over the Cherokee territory, but suggested that such law should not take effect until the President should have had time again to urge the Indians to emigrate. The legislature accordingly, by an act of December 20, 1828, carried out its threat of the previous year, enacting that all white persons in the Cherokee territory should be subject to the laws of Georgia, providing that after June 1, 1830, all Indians resident therein should be subject to such laws as might be prescribed for them by the State, and declaring that after that date all laws made by the Cherokee Nation should be null and void. [b]

Before any further legislative steps were taken, a new and unexpected development arose which tended to hasten some early solution of the complex problem. In July, 1829, deposits of gold were found in the northeastern corner of the State, and the news rapidly spread that the fields were as rich as those being worked in North Carolina. As soon as the news was known to be authentic there came a rush of adventurers into the gold lands. In the summer of 1830 there were probably 3,000 men from various States digging gold in Cherokee Georgia. The intrusion of these miners into the Chero-

---

[a] Acts of Georgia General Assembly, 1827, p. 249. For a defense of Georgia see Benton, Thirty Years' View, vol. 1, p. 163.

[b] Athenian, Nov. 18, 1828. Dawson, Compilation of Georgia Laws, p. 198. Prince, Digest of the Laws of Georgia to 1837, p. 278.

kee territory was unlawful under the enactments of three several governments, each claiming jurisdiction over the region. The United States laws prohibited anyone from settling or trading on Indian territory without a special license from the proper United States official; the State of Georgia had extended its laws over the Cherokee lands, applying them, after June 1, 1830, to Indians as well as white men; the Cherokee Nation had passed a law that no one should settle or trade on their lands without a permit from their officials.[a]

A conflict of authorities was imminent, and yet at that time no one of the three governments, nor, indeed, all of them combined, had sufficient police service in the section to check the great disorder which prevailed. The government of Georgia was the first of the three to make an efficient attempt to meet the emergency. Governor Gilmer wrote to the President October 29, 1830, stating that the Cherokee lands had been put under the laws of Georgia, and asking that the United States troops be withdrawn.

General Jackson,. whose view of the Indian controversy was radically opposed to that of Mr. Adams, did not hesitate to reverse the policy of the Government. He had already expressed his belief that Georgia had a rightful jurisdiction over her Indian lands, and he lost no time in complying with Mr. Gilmer's request to withdraw his troops. The general assembly of Georgia was called in special session in October for the purpose of making additional laws for the regulation of the gold region. By an act of December 22, 1830, a guard of 60 men was established to prevent intrusion and disorder at the gold mines. By the same act it was made unlawful for any Cherokee council or legislative body to meet, except for the purpose of ceding land, while the same penalty of four years' imprisonment was fixed to punish any Cherokee officials who should presume to hold a court. Not content with this, the legislature enacted by the same law that all white persons resident in the Cherokee territory on March 1, 1831, or after, without a license from the governor of Georgia or his agent, should be guilty of a high misdemeanor, with the penalty provided of not less than four years' confinement in the penitentiary. The governor was empowered to grant

[a] Athenian, August 4, 1829. Georgia Journal, September 4, 1830. G. White, Historical Collections of Georgia, p. 136.

licenses to those who should take an oath to support and defend the constitution and laws of Georgia, and uprightly to demean themselves as citizens of the State.[a]

The attitude of the judge of the Georgia superior court, who had most of the Cherokee territory in his circuit, had already been shown in a letter which he, Judge A. S. Clayton, wrote Governor Gilmer June 22, 1830, suggesting a request to the President for the withdrawal of the United States troops. Nine citizens of Hall County had just been brought before him by the Federal troops for trespassing on the Cherokee territory. He wrote: "When I saw the honest citizens of your State paraded through the streets of our town, in the center of a front and rear guard of regular troops, belonging, if not to a foreign, at least to another government, * * * for no other crime than that of going upon the soil of their own State, * * * I confess to you I never so distinctly felt, as strong as my feelings have been on that subject, the deep humiliation of our condition in relation to the exercise of power on the part of the General Government within the jurisdiction of Georgia."[b]

Three months later Judge Clayton, in a charge to the grand jury of Clarke County, expressed his belief in the constitutionality of the recent extension of Georgia's laws, and his intention to enforce it. He said that he would disregard any interference of the United States Supreme Court in cases which might arise before him from the act of Georgia. "I only require the aid of public opinion and the arm of the executive authority," he concluded, "and no court on earth besides our own shall ever be troubled with this question."[c]

It was with good reason that the State officials were determined if possible to keep the Cherokee questions out of the Federal courts. The policy of Chief Justice John Marshall was known to be that of consolidating the American nation by a broad interpretation of the Federal Constitution, and a consequent restriction of the sphere of the State governments.

The Cherokee chiefs had learned to their sorrow that Presi-

a Athenian, October 19 and 26, 1830. Niles's Register, vol. 39, p. 263. Acts of Georgia General Assembly, 1830, p. 114. Prince, Digest of Georgia Laws to 1837, p. 279. Georgia Journal, January 1, 1831.

b The original of this letter is among the archives in the State capitol, Atlanta, Ga. (MSS.).

c Niles's Register, vol. 38, p. 101.

dent Jackson readily conceded all that Mr. Adams had struggled to deny to Georgia. The hostile legislation of Georgia had paralyzed the working of the Cherokee constitution. The President admitted the right of the State to survey the Indian lands, to extend its laws over them, and to annul the laws of the Cherokees. He refused to recognize the Cherokee constitution and denied that the nation had any rights as opposed to Georgia. With such cold comfort from the Executive, the chiefs determined to resort to the judicial branch of the Federal Government in a final effort to save their homes from the rapacity of Georgia.

Mr. William Wirt was engaged as counsel by the Cherokees. On June 4, 1830, he wrote Governor Gilmer suggesting that the State and the Cherokee Nation make up a case before the United States Supreme Court to test the constitutionality of the attempt of Georgia to extend her laws over the territory in question.[a] In very curt terms the Governor declined the suggestion, stating that the court mentioned had, under the Constitution, no jurisdiction in the matter. Mr. Wirt continued in his championship of the Indian cause, and introduced a motion before the Supreme Court for an injunction to prevent the execution of the obnoxious Georgia laws.

Before the motion for injunction was argued a case arose which the Cherokees thought might test the matter. George Tassel, a Cherokee Indian, had been convicted of murder in the Hall County superior court and lay in jail under sentence of death. Upon a writ of error being carried to the United States Supreme Court, the State of Georgia was cited, through its governor, December 12, 1830, to appear and show cause why the writ should not be decided against the State. Governor Gilmer, in a message of December 22, submitted the citation to the legislature, stating in his own behalf, "So far as concerns the executive department, orders received from the Supreme Court in any manner interfering with the decisions of the courts of the State in the constitutional exercise of their jurisdiction will be disregarded, and any attempt to enforce such orders will be resisted with whatever force the laws have placed at my command." The response of the general assembly was a resolution requiring the governor to

[a] Niles's Register, vol. 38, pp. 69 and 71.

use all his legal power to repel every invasion upon the administration of the criminal laws of the State from whatever quarter. It "Resolved that the State of Georgia will never so far compromit her sovereignty as an independent State as to become a party to the case sought to be made before the Supreme Court of the United States by the writ in question." The governor was authorized to send an express to Hall County to have the sheriff execute the laws without fail in the case of Tassel.[a]

The test case of the Cherokee Nation *v.* Georgia was soon afterwards reached upon the docket of the Supreme Court.[b] The bill set forth the complainants to be "the Cherokee Nation of Indians, a foreign state, not owning allegiance to the United States, nor to any State of this Union, nor to any prince, potentate, or state other than their own." It alleged that, as evidenced by numerous treaties named, the United States had always shown an ardent desire to lead the Cherokees to a higher degree of civilization; that the Cherokee Nation had established a constitution and form of government, a code of civil and criminal laws, with courts to carry them out, schools, and churches; that the people had become agriculturists; and that under severe provocations they had faithfully observed all their treaties with the United States. The bill claimed for the Cherokees the benefit of the clauses in the Constitution that treaties are the supreme laws of the land, and judges are bound thereby, and that no State shall pass any law impairing the obligation of contracts. It stated that, in violation of the treaties, the Georgia legislature had, in December, 1828, passed an act to add the territory of the Cherokees to Carroll, Dekalb, and other counties, and to extend the laws of the State over the said territory; that in December, 1829, another act was passed to annul all laws of the Cherokees. It further set forth that application for protection and for the execution of treaties had been made to the President, who replied, "that the President of the United States had no power to protect them against the laws of Georgia." The complainant asked that the court declare null the two laws of Georgia of 1828 and 1829; that the Georgia officials be enjoined from interfering with Cherokee lands, mines,

a Niles's Register, vol. 39, pp. 338 and 339.
b For report of the case, see R. Peters, jr., U. S. Supreme Court Reports, vol. 5, p. 1.

and other property or with the persons of Cherokees on account of anything done by them within the Cherokee territory; that the pretended right of the State of Georgia to the possession, government, or control of the lands, mines, and other property of the Cherokee nation, within their territory, be declared by the court unfounded and void.

On the day appointed for the hearing the counsel for the complainant filed a supplementary bill, citing as further grievances of the Cherokees that, in accordance with a resolution of the Georgia legislature and in defiance of a writ of error allowed by the Chief Justice of the United States, the man called Corn Tassel, or George Tassel, had actually been hanged by a Georgia sheriff; that the Georgia legislature had passed additional laws of objectionable character, providing for a survey preparatory to the disposition of the Cherokee lands, forbidding the exercise of powers under the authority of the Cherokee Indians and their laws, and authorizing the governor to take possession of all gold mines in the Cherokee territory; and that the governor of Georgia had stationed an armed force of Georgians at the mines to enforce Georgia laws. The case was argued on the part of the complainant by Mr. Sergeant and Mr. Wirt. No counsel appeared for the State of Georgia.

The opinion of the court, as rendered by Chief Justice Marshall, granted that the counsel for the plaintiffs had established that the Cherokee Nation was a State and had been treated as a State since the settlement of the colonies; but the majority of the court decided that an Indian tribe or nation in the United States was not a foreign state in the sense of the Constitution and could not maintain an action in the courts of the United States. The decision concluded accordingly, "If it be true that the Cherokee Nation have rights, this is not the tribunal in which those rights are to be asserted. If it be true that wrongs have been inflicted and that still greater are to be apprehended, this is not the tribunal which can redress the past or prevent the future. The motion for an injunction is denied."

In a separate opinion Mr. Justice Johnson held that the name "State" should not be given to a people so low in grade of organized society as were the Indian tribes. He contended, with the treaty of Hopewell as an illustration, that the

United States allotted certain lands to the Cherokees, intending to give them no more rights over the territory than those needed by hunters, concluding that every advance of the Indians in civilization must tend to impair the right of preemption, which was of course a right of the State of Georgia.

Mr. Justice Thompson gave a dissenting opinion, in which Mr. Justice Story concurred, that the Cherokee Nation was competent to sue in the court and the desired injunction ought to be awarded.

It was clear that nowhere in the opinion of the court was it stated that the extension of the laws of Georgia over the Cherokee territory was valid and constitutional. This one case had been thrown out of court because no standing in court could be conceded to the plaintiffs. The decision was against the Cherokee Nation for the time being; but it did not necessarily follow that a subsequent decision would bear out the claims of the State of Georgia.

Messrs. Wirt and Sergeant had brought their action against the State of Georgia in the name of the Cherokee Nation only because no promising opportunity for making a personal case had arisen. One of the complaints in the bill for injunction was that the cases where the Georgia laws operated in the Cherokee territory were allowed to drag in the Georgia courts so as to prevent any one of the Cherokee defendants from carrying his case to the United States Supreme Court by writ of error. An attempt had been made to utilize the Tassel case, but the prompt execution of the criminal put an early end to the project. The first case which arose of a character suitable for the purpose of the attorneys was upon the conviction of Samuel A. Worcester for illegal residence in the Cherokee territory. The history of the case was as follows:

The act of the Georgia legislature approved December 22, 1830, which we have noticed, made it unlawful for white persons to reside in the Cherokee territory in Georgia without having taken an oath of allegiance to the State and without a license from the State authorities. This law was directed primarily against the intruding gold miners; but the message of the governor had stated the expediency of considering all white persons as intruders, without regard to the length of their residence or the permission of the Indians. The law was accordingly made one of sweeping application.

There were at the time resident among the Cherokees twelve or more Christian missionaries and assistants, some of them maintained by the American Board of Commissioners for Foreign Missions. These men were already suspected of interfering in political matters and would probably have been made to feel the weight of the law without inviting attention to themselves, but they did not passively await its action. They held a meeting at New Echota December 29, 1830, in which they passed resolutions protesting against the extension of the laws of Georgia over the Indians and asserting that they considered the removal of the Cherokees an event most earnestly to be deprecated.[a]

After sufficient time had elapsed for the intruders to have taken their departure, if so disposed, the Georgia guard for the Cherokee territory arrested such white men as were found unlawfully residing therein. Among the number arrested were two missionaries, Messrs. Worcester and Thompson. On writ of habeas corpus they were taken before the superior court of Gwinnett County, where their writ was passed upon by Judge Clayton. Their counsel pleaded for their release upon the ground of the unconstitutionality of the law of Georgia. The judge granted their release, but did so upon the ground that they were agents of the United States, since they were expending the United States fund for civilizing the Indians. Governor Gilmer then sent inquiries to Washington to learn whether the missionaries were recognized agents of the Government. The reply was received that as missionaries they were not governmental agents, but that Mr. Worcester was United States postmaster at New Echota. President Jackson, upon request from Georgia, removed Mr. Worcester from that office in order to render him amenable to the laws of the State. The Cherokee Phœnix, the newspaper and organ of the nation, expressed outraged feelings on the part of the Indians at the combination of the State and Federal executives against them.

The governor wrote Mr. Worcester, May 16, advising his removal from the State to avoid arrest. May 28 Col. J. W. A. Sandford, commander of the Georgia Guard, wrote each of the missionaries that at the end of ten days he would arrest

[a] Athenian, January 25, 1831. Gilmer, Georgians, p. 381. White, Historical Collections of Georgia, p. 139.

them if found upon Cherokee territory in Georgia. Notwithstanding their address to the governor in justification of their conduct, they were arrested by the guard, the Rev. Samuel A. Worcester, the Rev. Elizur Butler, and the Rev. James Trott, missionaries, and eight other white men, for illegal residence in the territory. Their trial came on in the September term of the Gwinnett County superior court. They were found guilty, and on September 15 were each sentenced to four years' confinement at hard labor in the State penitentiary. But a pardon and freedom were offered to each by the governor on condition of taking the oath of allegiance or promising to leave the Cherokee territory. Nine of the prisoners availed themselves of the executive clemency, but Worcester and Butler chose rather to go to the penitentiary, intending to test their case before the Supreme Court.[a]

On the occasion of their second arrest the missionaries had been taken into custody by a section of the Georgia Guard, commanded by a subordinate officer, Colonel Nelson. During the journey from the scene of the arrest to the place of temporary confinement the treatment of the prisoners was needlessly rough, extending in the cases of Messrs. Worcester and McLeod to positive harshness and violence. These two clergymen complained to the head of their missionary board of having been put in shackles, and of other indignities. The State government condemned the severity of the guard, and ordered an inquiry made into Nelson's conduct. That officer explained that his course of action had been rendered necessary by the unruly character of his prisoners. The controversy was practically closed by the retort of the Rev. Mr. McLeod that Colonel Nelson's statements were false and his conduct villainous.[b]

The cases of Worcester and Butler, who refused the governor's conditions for pardon, were appealed to the United States Supreme Court, from which a writ of error was issued on October 27, 1831.

Wilson Lumpkin, who had become governor of Georgia, submitted to the legislature on November 25, 1831, copies of the citations of the United States Supreme Court to the State

[a] White, Historical Collections of Georgia, p. 140. Niles's Register, vol. 40, p. 296, referring to Cherokee Phoenix, May 28, 1831. Niles's Register, vol. 40, p. 296. Georgia Journal, Sept. 29, 1831. Niles's Register, vol. 41, p. 176.

[b] Gilmer, Georgians, pp. 414, 536. Georgia Journal, Oct, 6, 1831, and Dec. 5, 1831

of Georgia to appear and show cause why the judgments which had been made against Worcester and Butler should not be set aside. With the documents went a message: "In exercising the duties of that department of the government which devolves upon me, I will disregard all unconstitutional requisitions, of whatever character or origin they may be, and, to the best of my abilities, will protect and defend the rights of of the State, and use the means afforded me to maintain its laws and constitution."

The legislature on December 26 adopted resolutions upholding the constitutionality and the soundness of policy in the recent enactments of the State, declaring that it had become a question of abandoning the attempt to remove the Indians or of excluding from residence among the nation the white persons whose efforts were known to be in opposition to the policy of the State. Regarding the citation received, the legislature resolved, "That the State of Georgia will not compromit her dignity as a sovereign State, or so far yield her rights as a member of the Confederacy as to appear in, answer to, or in any way become a party to any proceedings before the Supreme Court having for their object a revisal or interference with the decisions of the State courts in criminal matters." [a]

The hearing on the writ of error in Worcester's case came up before the Supreme Court during the course of the year 1832.[b] The case was argued for the plaintiff by Messrs. Sergeant, Wirt, and E. W. Chester, the State of Georgia, of course, not being represented. The Chief Justice, in delivering the opinion of the court, went into an extensive historical argument. He stated that the right acquired by the English discovery was the exclusive right to purchase, but the "absurd idea that the feeble settlements on the sea coasts * * * acquired legitimate power to * * * occupy the lands from sea to sea did not enter the mind of any man." The grants of the king, he said, were grants against European powers only, and not against the natives; the power of war was given for defense, not for conquest. He then discussed the treaties of the United States with the Cherokees, declaring that in the treaty of Hopewell the expressions, "the

[a] Niles's Register, vol. 41, p. 313. Acts of Georgia General Assembly, 1831, pp. 259, 268.
[b] For report of the case Worcester v. Georgia, see 6 Peters, p. 515 et seq.

Cherokees are under the protection of the United States," certain lands are "allotted" to the Cherokees for their "hunting grounds," "the United States shall have the sole right of managing all the affairs" of the Cherokees, did not mean that the Cherokees were not recognized as a nation capable of maintaining relations of peace and war. Taking up the later treaties and the laws of the United States, the opinion was further supported that the Cherokees had been and should be recognized as constituting a distinct national state.

The conclusion was reached that "the Cherokee Nation, then, is a distinct community, occupying its own territory, with boundaries accurately described, in which the laws of Georgia can have no force. * * * [The whole intercourse is vested in the United States Government.] The act of the State of Georgia, under which the plaintiff was prosecuted, is consequently void, and the judgment a nullity. It is the opinion of the court that the judgment of the Georgia county superior court ought to be reversed and annulled." The case of Butler v. Georgia, similar in all respects to that of Worcester, was in effect decided in the same manner by the opinion rendered in Worcester's case.

The judgment for which the Cherokees had so long been hoping was thus finally rendered; but they rejoiced too soon if they thought that by virtue of it their troubles were at an end. Governor Lumpkin declared to the legislature, November 6, 1832, that the decision of the court was an attempt to "prostrate the sovereignty of this State in the exercise of its constitutional criminal jurisdiction," an attempt at usurpation which the State executive would meet with the spirit of determined resistance. He congratulated himself that the people of Georgia were unanimous in "sustaining the sovereignty of their State." [a]

The unchanged attitude of Georgia boded ill for the hopes of the Cherokees. But the position of the Federal Executive rendered the situation desperate in the last degree for those Indians who were still determined not to give up their homes. President Jackson simply refused to enforce the judgment of the Supreme Court. He intimated that now that John Marshall had rendered his decision, he might enforce it. Of

course the chief justice had no authority beyond stating what
he thought right in the case. Worcester and Butler remained
at hard labor in the Georgia penitentiary, and the Cherokee
chiefs began at length to realize that no recourse was left
them against the tyranny of the State.

As far as the two missionaries were concerned, they felt
that their martyrdom had been sufficiently long, and adopted
the course of conciliating the State in order to secure their
liberation. They informed the attorney-general of Georgia
on January 8, 1833, that they had instructed their counsel to
prosecute their case no further in the Supreme Court.
Appreciating the change in their attitude, Governor Lumpkin pardoned both of them January 10 on the same conditions
that he had offered them some months before, and ordered
their release from prison.[a]

Most of the people of Georgia approved of the pardoning
of Worcester and Butler under the circumstances, but that
action of the governor found many critics among the ultra-
montanists. A meeting of citizens of Taliaferro County,
which lay in the center of the hot-head section, resolved, on
April 23, 1833, with only one dissenting vote, "That the
executive of Georgia, in the case of the missionaries, did,
by his conduct, sacrifice the dignity of the State and prove
himself incapable of sustaining her honor. * * * Resolved,
further, that there is no one so well qualified to repair the
tarnished honor of the State as our patriotic fellow-citizen,
George M. Troup."

The attacks upon Mr. Lumpkin grew so strong that in view
of his prospective candidacy for a second term as governor
his friends saw fit to publish the various documents and
considerations which had led to the release of the two missionaries [b]

In the course of the year 1834 a final tilt occurred between
the State of Georgia and the Cherokee Nation, supported by
the Supreme Court. The case was very similar to the former
one of George Tassel. A citation of the Supreme Court,
dated October 28, 1834, summoned the State of Georgia to
appear and show cause why the error shown in the writ of

[a] Southern Recorder, January 17, 1833. Date of pardon given as January 14 in Niles's
Register, vol. 43, p. 382.
[b] Niles's Register, vol. 44, pp. 202 and 359.

error in the case of James Graves, tried and convicted of murder, should not be corrected. On November 7 Mr. Lumpkin sent a copy of the citation to the legislature, stating that it constituted a third attempt to control the State in the exercise of its ordinary criminal jurisdiction. "Such attempts, if persevered in," he said, "will eventuate in the dismemberment and overthrow of our great confederacy. * * * I shall * * * to the utmost of my power, protect and defend the rights of the State." The legislature adopted resolutions which it considered appropriate to the occasion, referring to the "residuary mass of sovereignty which is inherent in each State * * * in the confederacy.[a] Graves was executed in due time, according to the sentence of the Georgia court.

The case of Graves was superfluous so far as it concerned the status of the Cherokee Nation. The fiasco of the decision in Worcester's case established the permanent triumph of Georgia's policy, and rendered it only a question of a very few years when the Indians would be driven from their territory within the limits of the State.

As far as regards the Federal Executive, the government of Georgia stood upon the vantage ground, after 1827, which it had won by its victory over Mr. Adams. General Jackson approved of the contention of the State, and from the time of his inauguration used his influence for the removal of the Indians. In a message of December 8, 1829, he stated, in reply to the Cherokee protest against the extension of Georgia laws over them, that the attempt by the Indians to establish an independent government in Georgia and Alabama would not be countenanced by the President. During 1829 and 1830 his agents were urging the Cherokee chiefs to make a cession and at the same time persuading individual tribesmen to move west. In the latter year he threw open the lands vacated by the piecemeal removal for disposition by Georgia, but ordered a stop to the removal of the Cherokees in small parties with the purpose of building up a strong cession party within the tribe east of the Mississippi.[b]

a Niles's Register, vol. 47, p. 190. Georgia Senate Journal, 1830, p. 139. Acts of Georgia General Assembly, 1834, p. 337.

b Athenian, December 22, 1829. message of Governor Gilmer, Niles's Register, vol. 39, p. 339. Royce, The Cherokee Nation, p. 261.

The State government was not unmindful of its advantageous position. In 1831 the legislature directed the governor to have all the unceded territory in the State surveyed, and to distribute the land among the citizens of the State by the land-lottery system. An act of December, 1834, authorized the immediate occupation of the lands thus allotted, though it gave the Indians two years in which to remove from their individual holdings.[a]

President Jackson persisted in his attempts to persuade the Cherokees to remove in a body. Early in 1834 it was discovered that a treaty party was developing in the nation. This party sent a delegation to Washington, which signed a preliminary treaty looking to a cession, but John Ross, the principal chief of the nation, protested, May 29, 1834, with such a show of support by the great bulk of the nation that the treaty failed of ratification.[b]

The division among the Cherokee leaders had at length opened a way for the final success of Georgia's efforts. In February, 1835, two rival Cherokee delegations appeared at Washington, with John Ross at the head of the orthodox party and John Ridge as the leader of the faction in favor of emigration. John Ridge, Major Ridge, Elias Boudinot, and other chiefs had finally come to see the futility of opposition to the inevitable, and were ready to lead their people westward.[c] The Ridge party signed a treaty of cession on March 14, which required the approval of the whole Cherokee Nation before becoming effective; but in a council of the Cherokees, held at Running Waters in June, Ross succeeded in having the treaty rejected.[d]

The maneuvering of the two factions in the following months engendered ill-feeling among the Cherokees and strengthened the position of Georgia. In December, 1835, a council was called by United States commissioners to meet at New Echota. The meeting was a small one, because of the opposition of the Ross party; but on December 29 a treaty

[a] Acts of Ga. Gen. Assem., 1831, p. 141. Acts of Ga. Gen. Assem., 1834, p 105. Prince, Digest of Ga. Laws to 1837, p. 262.

[b] Royce, The Cherokee Nation, p. 275.

[c] Cf. Their memorial to Congress, Nov. 27, 1834, U. S. Exec. Docs. No. 91, 23d. Cong., 2d. sess., vol. 3. Cf. Also defense of the Treaty Policy, in letters by Elias Boudinot, formerly editor of the Cherokee Phoenix, Southern Banner, Jan. 7, 1837, ff.

[d] White, Historical Collections of Ga., p. 143. Royce, The Cherokee Nation, p. 279. Southern Banner, Apr. 16 and June 18, 1835.

was signed with the chiefs attending which provided for the cession of all the remaining Cherokee lands east of the Mississippi River for $5,000,000 and lands in the West. The Ross party protested against the treaty, but were not able to prevent its ratification at Washington.[a]

The news of the definitive ratification served only to increase the discontent among the Indians. A confidential agent of the Secretary of War reported, September 25, 1837, that upon investigation be found that the whole Cherokee Nation was irreconcilable to the treaty and determined that it should not bind them.[b]

Public sentiment throughout the United States, especially among the opponents of the Administration, became deeply stirred with sympathy for the Indians. Within the halls of Congress Webster, Clay, and Calhoun were vigorous in their condemnation of the New Echota treaty.[c] President Van Buren was so influenced by this torrent of remonstrance and criticism as to suggest to the governors of Georgia, Alabama, Tennessee, and North Carolina, on May 23, 1838, that an extension of not more than two years be allowed in which the Cherokees might move away. Mr. Gilmer, who had again become governor of Georgia, replied, on May 28, that he could give the plan no sanction whatever. He feared that the suggestion was the beginning of another attack upon the sovereignty of the State, and declared his determination to take charge of the removal in person if the Federal Government should fail in its duty.[d]

There was, however, to be no further contest. General Scott had already arrived in the Cherokee country to direct the removal. He issued a proclamation, May 10, 1838, that every Cherokee man, woman, and child must be on their way west within a month. On May 18 John Ross made a last ineffectual offer to arrange a substitute treaty. The emigration was at once pushed forward, and on December 4 the last party of the Cherokees took up their westward march.

[a] Acts of Ga. Gen. Assem. 1835. p. 342. Niles's Register, vol. 49, p. 343. Benton, Thirty Years' View, vol. 1, p. 624. Royce, The Cherokee Nation, p. 282.

[b] Royce, The Cherokee Nation, p. 286.

[c] Benton, Thirty Years' View, vol. 1, p. 625. Royce, The Cherokee Nation, p. 290.

[d] Gilmer, Georgians, pp. 240 and 538.

CHAPTER IV.—THE TROUP AND CLARKE PARTIES.

In nearly all of the constitutional and political matters which we have treated in the preceding chapters the people of Georgia acted as a compact body. The ratification of the Federal Constitution was unanimous; the condemnation of the Yazoo sale was overwhelming; the demand for the Creek and Cherokee lands proceeded from the whole people, as well as from the officials. Thus, to the outside world, the State presented a united front. Yet internal contests were almost continuously waging. From the close of the Revolution to the time of the Civil War there were factions and political parties in Georgia which, though they underwent several changes of name and of policy, preserved a certain degree of continuity through the whole period.

This continuity of parties was due not only to tradition in families and localities, but very largely to inequalities in the economic condition of the population. The character of these inequalities and the consequent differentiation of the classes of the people will perhaps be best understood after an investigation of the process by which the territory of the State was settled.

The establishment of Oglethorpe's colony at Savannah and the settlement of the coast region are well known and need no discussion here. A fact to be remembered is that Savannah, Frederica, Darien, Ebenezer, St. Marys, and the adjacent districts in the low country were settled by colonists who had come directly from Europe, whether English, Scotch, or German. The source of settlement of the hill country in middle Georgia, however, was quite different. The early inhabitants were chiefly of English, Scotch, and Irish extraction, but they came into Georgia by way of Virginia and North Carolina instead of through Savannah.[a] They had

a G. R. Gilmer, Georgians, pp. 8 and 175.

become Americanized before reaching the boundaries of Georgia. As a rule they had been engaged in raising tobacco in their former homes. The system of tobacco culture was such as to exhaust the soil quickly and to require the periodical shifting of the farmer to new fields. When the best lands of the two early tobacco States had become exhausted, there began an exodus of a part of their population in search of fresh territory. Westward was the natural trend of migration; but when the Alleghenies barred progress in that direction, smiling valleys were seen to stretch to the southwest and were usually followed by the seekers for new homes. Thus the piedmont region of the Southern colonies was gradually settled, and at the close of the Revolution several thousand people were living in middle Georgia.

These settlers were hardly such typical frontiersmen as those who crossed the mountains and explored the Mississippi basin; yet they were very different from the dwellers upon the seaboard. Each family had moved slowly across the country with its loaded beasts of burden, its horned cattle, and an occasional slave, but without vehicles, for bridle paths were the only roads by which to travel.[a] Hogs, sheep, and poultry were not to be found about the earthen-floored and mud-plastered log cabins of the early settlers, for that kind of property was too troublesome to drive or to carry.[b] The very boldness of these pioneers in breaking their bondage to the river bank is evidence of the difference in their temperament from that of their lowland brethren, who considered themselves out of reach of the world when not within stone's throw of a creek or an inlet. This movement across the country began some thirty years after the founding of the colony; at the close of the Revolution it gathered strength and continued steadily to increase. The bulk of the population of Georgia to-day is composed of the descendants of the immigrants from the neighboring States to the East.

There were, then, two centers of immigration in the early history of the State, and each came to have its own frontier, the one to the south bordering the seaboard region and not far from navigable waterways, so depending upon the coast towns for market; the other on the edge of the Virginia and

[a] G. Andrews, Reminiscences of an Old Georgia Lawyer, p. 12.
[b] Gilmer, Georgians.

North Carolina settlement in middle Georgia, independent of watercourses in the immediate vicinity, but relying for necessary trading upon the villages at the head of navigation on the several large rivers in the State. The backwoods families of both frontiers were similarly placed in many respects— their contact with the Indians, their isolation from society, their necessity for self-reliance, and their general dearth of property in slaves. A peculiar result of the settlement of the State from these two nuclei was the development of what we may call a semi-frontier between them. This area lay just to the north of the rank of seaboard counties and extended from the neighborhood of the Savannah River to the edge of the Indian country, where it joined the true frontier. It had nearly all of the features of the Creek and Cherokee border, but differed in having a few members of the planter class scattered among its Cracker[a] citizenry and in never having alarms from the Indians. The region long remained thinly settled on account of its reputation for sterility, and its inhabitants yielded but very gradually to the elevating influences working both from the seaboard and from the hill country.

During the Revolution, Whigs and Tories were almost equal in number in Georgia. Partisans on either side carried on the local contest with such determination that the severity of the warfare in the extreme South was probably exceeded nowhere on the continent.[b] The proportion of Tories in the uplands was probably greater than on the seaboard, because the inland population was little concerned with taxation at the seaports levied upon articles which rarely found their way to homes where food and clothing were produced within the household and where luxuries were unknown. In fact, the whole revolutionary spirit among Georgians was due rather to sympathy with the northern colonies than to any sense of great oppression in their own cases. The active revolutionary movement in the colony originated with the settlers from

[a] An early account of the Georgia Crackers is given by Anthony Stokes, sometime chief justice of the colony of Georgia, writing just at the close of the American Revolution. Anthony Stokes, "A View of the Constitution of the British Colonies," London, 1783, pp. 140 and 141. Stokes designates as Crackers the great crowd of immigrants then pouring into the inland region of Georgia from western Virginia and North Carolina. The stories which reached him at Savannah of their method of life were distorted and fantastic and yet, with proper allowance for the author's cockney point of view, his account gives a valuable side light upon conditions in that period.

[b] H. M'Call, History of Georgia, vol. 2.

New England in St. John's parish, or Liberty County, and was caused largely by a feeling of indignation at the hardships of the people in Boston. The desire for independence was not rapid in spreading to the remote districts in Georgia; yet in the later years of the war the hill country patriots became more strenuous against the British and the loyalists than were their colleagues in the New England settlement or in Savannah.

After the achievement of independence, the whole remaining population of Georgia was anxious to enjoy and perpetuate its advantages. For that reason the people were practically unanimous in approving the Federal Constitution. The Constitution was regarded largely as a means to an end. The unanimity of the convention of January, 1788, in its favor need not indicate that the Federalist party would later control the State, for other influences, such as the need of the State for national protection against the Indians on the west and the Spanish in Florida, were more powerful than any party allegiance in causing the solid vote in favor of strong central government.

The Federalist and Republican parties began to develop soon after the establishment of the new frame of government. The former, which should have been called the Nationalist instead of the Federalist party, adopted the policy of a broad construction of the Constitution, with the principle as a basis that that instrument established an American nation in place of a confederation of States; the Republican party, on the other hand, favored a strict or narrow construction of the powers given by the Constitution to the General Government, which it held to be simply a central government in a federation of States, each of which had previously been sovereign, and each of which had retained for itself all rights and jurisdiction not expressly ceded in the literal wording of the Constitution. Chiefly on account of tne peculiar course of Indian affairs, and the suit of Chisolm against the State, the majority of the people in Georgia adopted the views of the Republican party.

During Washington's second administration, there may have arisen a good deal of local discussion over the correct interpretation of the Constitution; but the Yazoo controversy arising in 1793 and 1795 dwarfed all other issues then before the State. Some of the Federalist leaders were found to be prominently connected with the bribery in the Yazoo sale, and we may suppose that the strength of their party was diminished in consequence.

The vote recorded in the choice of electors to vote for a successor to President Washington gives us an opportunity to examine the local situation of the adherents of the two national parties of the period. This vote occurring in 1796, while the Yazoo affair was fresh in men's minds, was undoubtedly affected by the excitement over the fraud; but as it affords the only source of knowledge to be found for the relative strength of the Federalist and the Republicans, the county returns must be utilized for what they may be worth. The Federalists were badly beaten, carrying only 4 counties out of 21 and almost tying the vote in two others.[a] South Georgia, as far as can be learned, was uniformly Republican and with large majorities. The remoteness of the southern seaboard counties from the sanctum of the "Augusta Chronicle and Gazette of the State," to which we are indebted for our information, is probably responsible for the failure of returns from those counties. Middle Georgia, though also carried by the Republicans, was divided in opinion. From the returns which we have, the indication is plain that the two centers of population of the State were at some variance in their political views, and further that there was a tendency for the frontier of each to support the views of its respective mother settlement.

After 1796 the few facts which can be gleaned indicate that there was a dwindling in the number of voters who were professedly Federalists, while parodoxically the general attitude of the Federalist party came to be assumed in considerable degree by the government and people of the State. We have no record as to the character of the action taken by the legislature of Georgia in response to the Virginia and Kentucky resolutions of 1796. A message of Governor James Jackson is extant, dated January 6, 1799, in which he states to the Georgia legislature that according to the request of the governor of Kentucky, he transmits certain resolutions of the legislature of that State on the subject of the alien law of the

[a] Augusta Chronicle, Dec. 17, 1796.

United States.[a] The journals of the legislative houses of Georgia for 1799 do not now exist, the explanation being that they were probably among the papers destroyed by Sherman's army during the invasion of the State in 1864. But there is a manuscript index to the house journal which contains the item, "Alien and sedition laws, resolutions relating thereto, 430."[b] Thus we know that some action was taken, but what that action was no one can say.

We have already noticed the extremely modest and loyal tone of the address and remonstrance to Congress adopted by the Georgia legislature in 1800. It is clear that the hand which wrote the document and the official body which approved it were under very strong Federalist influence. For some twenty years succeeding the date of that address there was practically a cessation of the remonstrances from Georgia to the Central Government, which had been so common in the later years of the eighteenth century, and which after 1823 became a fixed habit of the legislature for each succeeding session.

Before the occurrence of the Presidential election of 1800 the choice of electors of the Federal Executive was again assumed by the general assembly.[c] The reason for its removal from the hands of the people was that the election of State officers coming in October and the choice of Presidential electors in November the voters of the Commonwealth were too frequently called to the polls in each fourth year. In 1800, as in 1796, the electoral vote of Georgia was cast for Mr. Jefferson against Mr. Adams, but we can not estimate the relative strength of the candidates in Georgia.

The Federalist party as such lived in Georgia for a decade or more after its defeat in 1796, but gradually lost strength and dwindled away. Its contentions were upheld by the Augusta Herald, but after 1804 that paper gave up its extreme partisan attitude, tacitly acknowledging the dissolution of the active party in the State. But, on the other hand, that a strong remnant of the Federalist faction was remaining in Georgia as late as 1810 is shown by the fact that President Meigs, of

[a] Minutes of the Georgia Executive Department MSS., volume for 1798–99, p. 357.

[b] I. e., page 430 of the MSS. Journal for 1798–99. See MSS. Index of Journals of the House of Representatives, 1781 to 1820, p. 9, under "November session."

[c] Augusta Herald, Nov. 5, 1800.

the University of Georgia, was in that year forced to resign his position chiefly on account of the friction of his Jeffersonian doctrines with the Federalist tenets of the influential citizens in the neighborhood of Athens.[a]

In the early years of the new century nearly all of the political thinkers in the State were agreed in the support of the Republican party, and the so-called era of good feeling, to arrive at a later time to the nation as a whole, was preceded by a similar condition of affairs in Georgia. But if the era of good feeling is a misnomer in national politics, it would be much more so if applied to affairs in Georgia for the period at which we now arrive. The recriminations and enmities of Yazoo times had not then died away, while Federalist and Republican disputants were still to be heard; but the prominence of those former disputes was dwarfed by a new contest, the origin and basis of which was in the purely personal antagonisms of men in a struggle for political glory and civic authority.

Although these personal enmities did not begin to attract general attention until about 1807, their origin dated from before the time of the Yazoo sale.[b] While the Yazoo question was not a party issue with the Federalists and Republicans, the great majority of the Republicans were apparently against the sale, and the Federalists were weakened by the charge that their party leaders had been among its supporters. The legislature which met in 1796 to rescind the sale of the lands was dominated by James Jackson, of Savannah, who resigned his seat in the United States Senate in order to return to Georgia and fight the Yazoo cabal. Though Jackson won his battle in the legislature and before the people, he did not convince everyone that the sale of the lands had been utterly vicious. It was only natural that those who were attacked by him should actively defend themselves. We accordingly find that for some years a part of the State was divided into Jackson and anti-Jackson factions.

[a] W. H. Meigs, Life of Josiah Meigs, p. 51.

[b] An anonymous pamphlet entitled "Cursory remarks on men and measures in Georgia," printed in 1784, states that in that year there were two factions in the State, the one made up of men eager for the extensive confiscation of loyalist property which they themselves might buy at a fraction of its value, the other composed of honest, conservative men who were, however, too passive to hold the radicals in check. This document enables us to trace at least as far back as the close of the Revolution the origin of the factions which became conspicuous at the time of the rescinding of the Yazoo sale.

From this beginning developed the system of personal politics in Georgia. The rescinding of the Yazoo sale was the work of the conservative class of Georgians and of this class James Jackson was distinctly the leader. A distinguished veteran of the Revolution, he was a strong type of the old school of Georgia gentlemen in politics. Of gentleness in the usual sense he had little, for he was bold to a degree, and intolerant of all opposition. His principles were high and his convictions strong. Like many men of his temperament, he could see only one side of a question. Thinking his opponents to be knaves, he was accustomed in important debates to overwhelm them with the volume of his voice and the strength of his condemnation backed by his custom of supporting his statements upon the field of honor when occasion arose. And yet withal Jackson was a most attractive man to those with whom he held friendly intercourse. He recognized as friends those only who were harmonious in all relations. A political opponent could not be upon cordial social terms with him. Jackson was a lover of learning, and was a founder of the University of Georgia. He was an aristocrat and a leader of the aristocrats of his State. And above all he was a Georgian with his whole heart. His traits of character are important because from conscious imitation or from the similar influence of the same environment the same traits were possessed in large degree by the successive leaders in Georgia for decades after his death.

General Jackson remained in Georgia for several years after the passage of the Yazoo rescinding act, serving as governor of the State from 1798 to 1801. In 1801 he was again sent to the United States Senate. He died at Washington before the expiration of his senatorial term.

It was Jackson's policy to attract to his circle of friendship the promising young men of the several sections of Georgia.[a] Prominent among those whose attachment he cultivated was William Harris Crawford, a young up-country lawyer, who had already won sufficient distinction to be chosen by the legislature as one of the editors of the first accepted compilation of Georgia laws. Upon Jackson's withdrawal from Georgia politics, Crawford became the acknowledged leader of a strong

[a] Letter of Jackson to John Milledge, Charlton's Life of Jackson, p. 184.

faction in the State, consisting of his own friends and the friends of Jackson. Opposed to this were the enemies of both, led by John Clarke and his brother, Elijah Clarke the younger. With the advent of Crawford as a prominent character in politics, the inland section of Georgia came to be of greater consequence in political matters. As years passed this development continued, until the seaboard counties became comparatively unimportant in State politics. The great bulk of the population came to be in the interior, and a broad expanse of pine barrens hindered intercourse between the seaboard and the political center of the State.

William H. Crawford has left little record of his work as a statesmen and politician which will enable the student to form a well-defined conception of his true place in history. From the dearth of other material, the average American historian has followed the views of John Quincy Adams, who has written most fully of Crawford, but who was his most bitter and prejudiced adversary. In this way injustice has been done the man. Crawford, however, belongs to the history of the United States rather than to that of Georgia, and even if the necessary evidence were at hand this would not be the proper place to rehabilitate him. We are here concerned only with his influence upon local developments, and we need only notice his personality in so far as it shows what kind of man the people of that time were most ready to follow. He was a fine specimen of physical manhood, very tall, and so dignified that his critics called him haughty. Yet his manner was frank and unconventional, and his speech blunt and to the point. To his very numerous personal friends he was cordial and gracious, especially so over his glass of toddy, of which, like the typical Georgian of his day, he was very fond. Crawford's judgment was strong, and he had the courage of his convictions when any question of personal honor was in any way involved. But his service as a statesman, if at any time he rose to that distinction, was greatly hindered by his persistent ambition. His greatest power lay in his faculty for organizing men in personal alignments in support of himself as their leader.

There were no questions of large policy at issue between the Georgia factions. The situation was one which demanded

an able politician and not a statesman. For the leadership of
a faction in such a condition of things Crawford as a young
man was eminently fitted. A native of Virginia, his capacity
for leadership placed him at the head of the Virginia element
in the population of Georgia. The importance of this element in the politics of the State was largely the result of the
fact that the early immigrants from Virginia settled in one
neighborhood about Broad River, chiefly in Elbert County.
This Virginia settlement came to have a strong self-consciousness, and it developed a feeling which was handed down
through generations, that men of Virginian lineage should
stand together. The Virginia spirit was heightened by the
fact that a strong settlement from North Carolina was planted
a short distance to the south of Broad River, chiefly in Wilkes
County.[a] The rivalry which sprang up came to find its chief
expression in politics. Largely through the friendship of
Jackson and Crawford, an alliance was formed between the
Virginia faction in the uplands and the aristocratic element
on the seaboard.

As years passed and as prosperity came to the cotton belt,
a new development set in for the differentiation between the
well-to-do folk and the people without any considerable
means. Planters became distinct from farmers in the uplands
as well as in the lowlands. The whole white population was
embraced within these two agricultural classes, for townsmen,
as such, were so few as to be a negligible quantity. The
Virginians had from the first considered themselves the aristocratic element, and their opponents could not deny their
claim. The Virginians tended to attract to their faction all
unconnected planters, while on the other hand the farmers
who did not succeed in accumulating wealth, i. e., lands and
slaves, drifted to the alignment of the North Carolinians.
The tendency, then, was for the differentiation of parties
upon an economic basis.

The alliance between Jackson and Crawford constituted a
power which for a period of years was able to carry any contest which it resolved to win in State politics. After the death
of Jackson the mantle of the south Georgia leadership fell upon
George Michael Troup, whom Jackson had attached to himself
as one of the promising young men of the State. Though

[a] W. H. Sparks, Memories of Fifty Years, p. 28. G. R. Gilmer, Georgians, passim.

Troup had been born among the Indians in the Alabama valley, he was distinctly an aristocrat. He had attended school at Savannah and at Flatbush, Long Island, and had finished with a course at Princeton College.[a] He achieved distinction in Georgia politics by his service as a member from Chatham County in the legislature. He was acquiring some substance as a planter when he was elected a member of Congress in 1807. We may learn of his character and temperament from the account of his deeds which forms an integral part of the history of the struggle for State rights.

Crawford and Troup, then, were at the head of the Jackson-Crawford-Troup combination in Georgia. Supported by the same adherents, Crawford was sent to the United States Senate in the same year that Troup was elected to the lower house of Congress. A few years later, Crawford's occupation with national affairs removed him from intimate contact with Georgia politics, while Troup became more and more the moving spirit of the local faction.

In the North Carolina settlement in Georgia, the Clarke family had been prominent from the first.[b] We have already noticed the independent, headstrong, care-naught qualities of General Elijah Clarke of Revolutionary fame. John Clarke was the worthy son of such a father. Educated as much on the Indian warpath as in the log-cabin school, with more to fear from arrows and bullets than from the schoolmaster's rod, and perfectly fearless of either, he developed into an adroit Indian fighter, carried his rough and ready principles into politics, and so became a politician of the extreme Andrew Jackson type. He was not a very able man. Wilson Lumpkin, his strongest political colleague, has written that he supported Clarke more from sympathy than from any appreciation of his ability. Clarke's liking for personal broils of any kind was illustrated in his quarrel with Crawford in which bloodshed on the duelling ground was a mere incident. As the leader of the Carolinians in Georgia, it was John Clarke's agreeable duty to oppose the Virginians to the full extent of his power. In the Kentucky mountains such a state of things would have brought on a series of hereditary feuds. But in Georgia the hostile spirit found its outlet in the formation of hereditary political factions.

[a] Harden, Life of Troup, p. 11.   [b] Gilmer, Georgians, p. 198.

In the first decade of the century, the Crawford or Troup clique was stronger than the Clarke organization, but the two factions did not embrace the whole population of the State. Neither group of leaders followed an invariable practice of nominating a full ticket for all of the offices to be filled at each general election, and neither gave much attention to town and county offices. It was not until some years after the close of the war of 1812 that the factions spread over the whole State and took on more distinctly the characteristics of true political parties.

It is very difficult to obtain a trustworthy table of the relative strength of the two parties in the various parts of the State before 1826, because the governor (until 1825) and the Presidential electors (1800 to 1826, inclusive) were chosen by secret ballot of the general assembly, and it is impossible even to trace the votes of individual legislators to their respective counties and districts. Members of Congress were always elected upon a general ticket, and not according to the district system. Each voter wrote on his ballot the prescribed number of the names of the candidates whom he considered worthiest. The whole population of the State wanted to see Georgia represented in the national assembly by as strong a delegation as possible, and a man of recognized ability when a candidate for Congress usually had no effective opposition from the other faction.

The steps in the growth of the Clarke party are almost completely hidden from our view until six years after the time when it succeeded in placing its leader in the office of governor of the State. We are able only to catch rare glimpses of it before 1825 from a few Congressional elections and from contests in the State legislature. On the general ticket for Congress in 1806, the names of Elijah Clarke and George M. Troup are to be found with those of eight other candidates, while four of the ten were to be elected. Clarke was defeated, receiving a higher vote than Troup in six counties, an equal vote in two, and a smaller vote in fourteen.[a] In 1806 Judge Murry Dooly, a follower of Clarke, ran for Congress, but carried only four counties over Troup.[b] In 1810 Elijah Clarke again entered the contest, but defeated Troup in not a single county.[c] These contests were of course

[a] Augusta Chronicle, Oct. 11, 1806, ff.   [b] Ib., Oct. 6, 1808, ff.   [c] Ib., Oct. 13, 1810, ff.

not directly between any two of the candidates, yet the votes given show approximately the number of adherents of each of them. It seems that during these years the Clarke party was losing strength. Then, and for several years afterwards, John Clarke on account of his interest in military affairs, was not conspicuous in politics.

From 1810 to 1816 extended a period of comparative quiet in State politics. It was a period of mutterings of war, and of actual conflict between the United States and foreign powers. As was natural in such a case, petty disputes were at least nominally dropped for the time, to give way to an undivided support of the policy of the General Government.

The whole of the South was eager for measures of retaliation for the indignities which England heaped upon America. Georgia was strongly in support of the non-intercouse act and the embargo, and later became anxious for the declaration of war. The governor expressed great enthusiasm in the American cause, in 1812 and 1813,[a] and without being gainsaid in the State, anathematized as traitors all who opposed the war.[b] The quota of troops assigned to the State was quickly supplied by volunteers.[c] This enthusiasm, moreover, was not of the inexpensive variety. Though Georgia anticipated little experience of actual warfare with the British, she expected trouble with the Spanish in Florida and with the Indian tribes. Then, too, the stopping of the exportation of products was a decided hardship upon the people.[d] The editor of a prominent newspaper advised the people during the war that, since little prospect existed that the price of cotton would ever again pay the cost of cultivation, some other product, such as wheat, must be resorted to as an export commodity.[e] It was considered patriotic in that period to discourage all import of English or French goods. Upon a public occasion on February 22, 1809, each student of the University of Georgia, agreeably to a resolution of the student organization, appeared in a complete suit of homespun cloth.[f] Domestic manufactures of various kinds were urged upon the people,[g] but the

a Niles's Register, vol. 3, p. 193.　　b Ib., vol. 5, p. 209.　　c Ga. Journal, Jan. 8, 1812.
d Ib., Jan. 6, 1812.　　e Ib., Mar. 11, 1812.　　f Georgia Express (Athens), Apr. 1, 1809.
g A motion prevailed in the Ga. House of Reps., Nov. 5, 1814, to authorize commissioners to establish a lottery to raise $7,000 to enable Henry Heald and others to erect a woolen factory in the upper part of the State: Ga. House Journal, 1814, p. 50.

making of coarse cloth could alone be advanced to any satisfactory point. At the end of the war the dearth of cotton in Europe made the price of that article so high that all energies in the cotton section were directed to the cultivation of the staple,[a] and with plenty of ready money the planters fell again into the habit of buying their manufactures from Europe, though from that time forward the products of the Northern States began to enter the South in increasing quantities.

The Troup-Clarke antagonism did not become of engrossing interest in Georgia until after the year 1818. The period immediately following the treaty of peace with Great Britain was too prosperous to admit of much dissension of any kind. It is probably not accidental that the gradual decline in the price of cotton from the close of 1818[b] coincided in time with the rise of political parties which tended to be made up, the one of the prosperous class of citizens, the other of the less prosperous class. In the hard times during the war of 1812 all classes had stood together against the foreign enemy and against the disaffection in New England. The peace which followed brought prosperity and contentment. When the price of cotton was 30 cents a pound no man was disposed to find fault with his neighbor. But when economic conditions again reached the normal, the political differences which were characteristic of the time and place again became important.

Early in 1819 it became generally known that John Clarke would be a candidate for election as governor of Georgia. The opposing faction took this news as a challenge to combat, and replied by announcing that Troup would resign his seat in the United States Senate to oppose Clarke in the gubernatorial contest.[c] In the summer of 1819 the period of quiet in local politics was fully at an end. The State rang with discussion.

Though the stump speaker did not at that time exist as an

[a] Ga. Journal, July 19, 1815.

[b] *Average price of cotton, 1815–1821.*

	Cents.			Cents.
1815	21		1819	24
1816	29		1820	17
1817	26		1821	14
1818	34			

[c] Ga. Journal, Sept. 29, 1816.

institution, the partisan editor was very well developed. Not only did editors themselves write in support of their candidates, but the columns of their papers were filled with the partisan writings of numerous contributors, always, of course, on the side with the editors of the respective journals. Farmers adjourned from the cotton fields to the crossroad stores, where opinions were exchanged and extensive arguments delivered upon the engrossing topic of Troup and Clarke. A correspondent wrote in the columns of the Georgia Journal that electioneering was running higher in the State than he had ever witnessed in any preceding year, and proceeded to deprecate the evils of the times.[a] The excitement culminated in the election of governor by the legislature in November, which resulted in the triumph of Clarke over Troup with thirteen votes majority.[b]

After the crisis had passed, politics were quiet for nearly two years. The Congressional election of 1820, like others of the time, tells us nothing. It happened that there was no strong Clarke candidate in the contest of that year. The opponents of the successful Troup candidates were of such little weight that it is even difficult to determine which faction gave them their support. But, as the time approached for the next gubernatorial contest, the State again became excited.[c] The two candidates, who were the same as before, were praised or criticised in the newspapers by "Veritas," "Homo," "A Georgian," "A Planter," "An Up-Country Man," and numerous other anonymous scribblers. Clarke was accused of having shot at an effigy of General Washington and of having been a Federalist. Troup's father was said to have been a Tory. A Clarke adherent railed at "that class of electors who had become so slavishly accustomed to the triumph of the candidates put forward annually or biennially by Crawford and his friends at Athens."[d] Another wrote that the Crawford party was determined to defeat Clarke because a show of strength in Georgia was essential to Crawford's election to the Presidency. As November approached it became evident that the race would be exceedingly close. The unheard of practice was instituted of voting for candidates for the legislature according to their

[a] Ga. Journal, Sept. 28, 1819.   [b] Harden, Life of Troup, p. 168.
[c] Ga. Journal, Mar. 26, Apr, 17, June 26, July 27, 1821.   [d] Ib., Sept. 18, 1821.

known preference for one or the other of the gubernatorial candidates.[a]

Election day finally arrived. The united general assembly met in the hall of the lower house and the ballot for governor was taken. The gallery was crowded with spectators, and many who could not gain entrance waited for news on the steps and on the grounds of the statehouse. The pervading anxiety was as great as if the freedom of the country were in suspense instead of the election of one hot-head or another as governor of Georgia, with no appreciable question of policy at stake. The result of the ballot was the election of Clarke, with only two votes majority.

The defeat served only to increase the determination of the Troup party. The Clarke men were no less resolute upon winning the next contest.

The campaigning for the next two years was quiet, but steady and earnest. Troup again stood for the coveted office of governor. Clarke did not try for a third election, but his party put forward Matthew Talbot as its champion. The two houses of the legislature met in joint session on November 6, 1823, to cast their ballots, and the contest was as doubtful as before. The same evidences of suspense were visible as in 1821, both in Miliedgeville and in the State at large. Within the hall of assembly the partisans had wrought themselves into a state of acute tension. It so happened that when 162 ballots had been counted the tally stood 81 and 81, with 4 votes still in the hat. These proved to be all for Troup, and the house went wild.[b] A picturesque figure was that of Jesse Mercer, who staggered out overcome with joy, loudly praising heaven that he had lived to see the day.

This old man was for many years a prominent clergyman of the Baptist Church in Georgia. He mixed politics with his gospel to such an extent that he never failed to carry his county overwhelmingly for Crawford or Troup or the candidates of their party. Governor Lumpkin lays at his door many of the votes that were cast against him in his numerous campaigns, saying that although the Baptist Church was not

[a] Ga. Journal, Sept. 11, 1821.
[b] Sparks, Memories of Fifty Years, p. 128. Cf. Harden, Life of Troup, p. 170.

a unit in politics, yet Mercer always carried the bulk of its members for the Troup candidates.[a]

Troup had at last won the governor's chair, but neither success nor defeat could put an end to the local strife. Before the next election occurred the Clarke party, as it claimed, had succeeded in having the choice of the chief magistrate given into the hands of the people,[b] and the election of governor in 1825 was the first popular one in the history of the State. For that struggle John Clarke again authorized the use of his name as a candidate, opposing his old adversary, George Troup. The fact that the election was to be in the hands of the people was not calculated to make the contest the less spirited. The candidature of both men was announced early in April of 1825,[c] though the voting was not to occur until October 3.

This was one of the hardest fought battles ever waged in State politics upon a personal question. Every doubtful voter was besieged, cozened, and probably bribed where possible, by zealous partisans. Troup's administration had been a strong one, but Clarke had also given very general satisfaction in his four years' tenure of the office. Criticisms were made upon the past official acts of both candidates, and more upon Troup's than upon Clarke's, but Troup had dealt with the more difficult questions, and his management of them found enthusiastic praise as well as strong condemnation. Election day arrived and passed and the struggle was ended, but weary days and weeks dragged past before anyone could know who had been elected.[d] At length the returns from the counties on the farthest frontier reached Milledgeville, and it was known that Troup had been elected with a majority of 683 votes. It is of interest to note that the majority in the State assembly elected on the same day was of the Clarke faction, which means that Troup would probably have been defeated if his election had depended upon the old system.[e]

At this point we have a direct vote of the Troup and Clarke parties. By making a map showing the vote in each county, several interesting phenomena are brought into view which

---

[a] Wilson Lumpkin, incidents connected with the life of W. Lumpkin, vol. 1, circ., p. 670. (MSS.)

[b] Ga. Journal, Feb. 3, 1824.   [c] Hardin, Life of Troup, p. 334.

[d] Ib., p. 396.   [e] Ga. Journal, Dec. 27, 1825.

would otherwise be obscure if not entirely hidden.   It is to be remembered that in 1796 the Federalists were chiefly in the up-country and that the Republicans tended to have their heaviest majorities near tide water.   The map before us now bears little resemblance to that of the former period, but it shows the connection or lack of connection between the two parties in the State at the two epochs.   Governor Wilson Lumpkin, whose manuscript autobiography the writer has had the privilege of reading in part, states that in the second decade of the century there were a greater number of men in the State holding Federalist views than was generally suspected, and that most of them had joined the ranks of the Clarke party.[a]   From such individual cases as can be traced this seems to be borne out.   Yet the Federalists gradually abandoned their party alignment and again there were great numbers in the Clarke party who had never advocated Federalist doctrines, and the connection can not be depended upon as being at all vital.

The map of the vote of 1825 shows that parties had become divided territorially upon a basis entirely different from that of the former period.   It shows that Troup's stronghold coincided with the two centers of immigration, while on the whole frontier Clarke's majority was uniformly heavy; that the older and more advanced parts of the State supported Troup, and all of the backwoods region was against him.   There are two exceptions to be observed in this broad statement of the county vote, and only two.   One of these occurred in the case of three of the easternmost counties of middle Georgia, which were among the very first to be settled in that region, and which contained many of the most progressive citizens of the State.   Yet these three counties were carried for Clarke against the general tendency.   The reason for this exception is readily discovered.   Lincoln County was the home of Judge Dooly, one of the foremost leaders of the Clarke constituency, and probably the ablest politician of all Troup's opponents. Richmond County was carried for Clarke by the efforts of a small band of its citizens bound to him by personal ties, conspicuous among whom was W. J. Hobby, a brother-in-law of Clarke and the owner of the Augusta Chronicle.[b]   The outspoken hostility of his paper toward Troup was probably

---

[a] Lumpkin, Incidents (MSS.), vol. 1, circ., p. 30.   [b] Ga. Journal, Sept. 6, 1826.

responsible for the Clarke majorities in both Richmond and Columbia. These two and Lincoln were adjoining counties, and were very sympathetic. It was a period of personal politics, and it is not surprising that the personal advocacy of intimate friends of the two candidates was extremely influential in deciding the local vote. Furthermore, these counties had been settled largely by North Carolinians, who were clannishly disposed to rally round any one of their fellows who needed their support. The other exception was in the case of a line of counties along the Oconee and Altamaha rivers, viz, Laurens, Montgomery, and Tattnall. They were situated at the junction of the semi-frontier, previously characterized, with the Indian border counties, and we should expect the vote in them to be in favor of Clarke; but the fact that the counties went against him is fully explained by the statement that they lay in Troup's home section, an argument more weighty then than now.[a]

The contrast between the old settlements and the frontier was only an evidence of the more fundamental contrast in the economic conditions of the classes of the people in the State. When the map of the election of 1825 is compared with a map drawn to illustrate the returns of the State census of 1824, a very close relation is seen to exist between the two. With the exceptions of Lincoln, Columbia and Richmond, and Laurens, Montgomery and Tattnall counties, already explained, the counties giving Troup majorities were almost identical with those having more negroes than whites in their population. This striking similarity of the maps is highly significant, for the reason that the presence in a county of a large proportion of negroes, 99 per cent of whom were slaves, is conclusive evidence, in view of the system prevailing, that a large proportion of the white people of that county were of the well-to-do class. With this line of reasoning and illustration we reach a conclusion which strongly supports our former statement that the slave owners, who constituted the well-to-do class in Georgia, were as a rule members of the Troup party, and that the poorer whites, who tended to be the more numerous on the edges of settlement, were as a rule members of the Clarke party.

In the eighteenth century the economic geography of

[a] Harden, Life of Troup, p. 399.

Georgia was such as to cause a strong contrast between the seaboard and the uplands. But the invention of the cotton gin and of other textile machinery, and the extensive introduction of cotton culture into the red hill section of the State, brought a fundamental change in the relationship of the sections. Cotton culture made slave labor distinctly profitable, and accordingly the plantation system came to thrive in the uplands as on the seaboard. After the industrial systems of the two areas had grown similar, their political and social views did not long remain in contrast. In 1825 the economic, and therefore the political and social, distinction was between the old settlements and the frontier.

It was largely accidental that the first strong settlement in the uplands was made in the later cotton growing section; but it was quite natural that the older counties in the cotton belt should be the first in that belt to become prosperous and to develop aristocratic feeling. At a later time, when the soil of the eastern counties had become partly exhausted, there was a migration of planters westward; but before 1825 the tendency was for those who were gaining wealth and increasing their number of slaves and acres to remain in their homesteads and buy up the lands of their less prosperous neighbors, who would then remove to the frontier or to the districts to the north or the south of the cotton belt, which were ill adapted to the plantation system.

It is essential to remember that, although the fact was not frequently stated at the time, the Troup and Clarke parties were based upon a fundamental difference in the economic conditions of the people. As we follow the developments in the succeeding decades, we shall see that these parties changed their names more than once, and attempted to change their character, but that the division of parties according to economic and social conditions and dependent upon economic geography was more powerful for continuity than were the influence of leaders or the dictates of policy when they tended toward a disorganization of the alignment.

Industrial and social conditions were of course nothing more than the general basis for the division of the people into political factions. There was nothing like an invariable custom that a man who had slaves should vote for Troup and a man who had no slaves should vote for Clarke, nor that the possession of five slaves or more should support one candidate while the owner of four negroes or less should rally to the other. The line of separation between the classes was itself vague and varying. The great bulk of the slaveholders were slaveholders in a very small way. It was the ambition of most of these to increase the number of their servants and their acres, and it was the hope of most of the poor whites that at some day they themselves might become slave owners. Thrift and improvidence caused elevation and retrogression in the scale of wealth in many individual cases. The existence of professional men and merchants as a part of the population tended to prevent the exclusive ranking of citizens by their holdings of slaves and lands.

The contrast between the extremes of wealth and poverty in the South has been exaggerated. A score of slaves was considered a large number for one family to own in the cotton belt in this period. This meant only a moderate degree of comfort for the family, and that only when the plantation was well managed and the price of cotton satisfactory. It is manifestly absurd to speak of the planters as manorial lords. On the other hand the condition of the poor whites was far from the extreme of human misery. The land lottery system adopted by the State government for the distribution of the public domain either gave to each family a homestead outright, or rendered it very easy for settlers to buy land in the frontier districts at very low prices. As a rule each farmer owned his land and his live stock. His farm produced the necessities of life, in abundance dependent upon the degree of his industry. He had such small luxuries as fruit and melons of his own raising, game of his own killing, and often liquors of his own or his neighbor's distilling. The sale of his market crop enabled him to purchase in limited amount such commodities as he did not produce. The hardship of his remoteness from markets was not peculiar to his own lot as contrasted with that of the planter.

The social system was by no means rigid in the cotton belt. Such wealth as the planters had gained was of too recent acquisition to permit of their being supercilious about manual labor. The average slaveholder encouraged his negroes in the fields by following his own plow or by leading the cotton choppers with his hoe in his hand, and not by watching them from a stump in the shade or by driving them by the flourish of a whip. The hard-working poor man had the recognition and respect of the planters. It was only the slovenly and shiftless "poor white trash" who had the contempt of self-respecting white men and self-respecting negroes.

The political situation, far from being absolutely fixed by industrial relations, was strongly influenced by personal friendships or antipathies, and by inherited affiliations. But on the whole it is correct to say that as a very general rule the poorer class of citizens, who were chiefly on the edges of settlement, were the chief supporters of Clarke, while the slaveholders were usually members of the Troup party.

During the existence of the Troup and Clarke parties there was no antagonism between them upon the ground of any policy followed by the State or the Central Government. The only occasion upon which the local factions took different sides on any political matter outside of the State was that of the Presidential contest of 1824; while that contest was one of a personal character, not involving any platform or policy. The candidates for the office were John Quincy Adams, Andrew Jackson, William H. Crawford, and Henry Clay. The Troup party in Georgia was of course very enthusiastic in support-ing Mr. Crawford, who had for years been at its head. The leaders of the Clarke party persuaded many of their followers to rally around Jackson's banner in opposition. Mr. Craw-ford's chances for election were excellent, until a short time before the date of balloting he was stricken with paralysis, too severely in the opinion of many people to discharge the duties of the Presidency. His friends in Georgia, however, refused to forsake his cause, and the legislature chose Craw-ford electors with a vote of about two to one. The electoral college failing to make a choice in this instance, the United States House of Representatives elected Mr. Adams, who was probably less acceptable to Georgians than any other one of the candidates.

There was the appearance of some difference of principles in 1825, when Governor Troup had some unpleasantness with the Indian agent, Colonel Crowell, causing that official to bestir himself in an effort to prevent Troup's reelection.[a]

[a] Savannah Republican, June 15, 1825. Harden, Life of Troup, p. 336. cf. also, Indian Affairs, vol. 2, p. 580.

Thus the few who were opposed to the expulsion of the Indians from the State took sides with Clarke and seemed to be in unison with his party. But the fact that the treaty which Troup succeeded in having made with the Creeks was approved by the Georgia house of representatives with a unanimous vote,[a] shows the real agreement of the local parties upon the Indian question.[b]

We have already noted that the legislature elected in 1825 had a majority of Clarke members.[c] This assembly passed a law dividing the State into Congressional districts, providing that only one Congressman could be elected from each district, but permitting each voter to vote for one candidate in each district.[d] Some gerrymandering appears upon mapping the districts according to the act, but as the governor was known to be opposed to the majority in the assembly, the act had to be framed so as not to incur his veto. The object of the act was to give the Clarke party more chance of representation in Congress. All of the best-known men in the State lived in the eastern counties and were of the Troup party; but after the passage of the act a certain number of candidates from the west were guaranteed election, while these men were most likely to be of the Clarke party. This movement then is seen to have been merely for party advantage, and is no evidence of a division upon true policy.

For several years after 1825 there was comparative quiet in the State, no considerable questions of policy arising to cause disagreement. The parties maintained their organization, and seem to have come into better understanding of their own respective composition and circumstances. In 1827 a correspondent of Clarke leanings wrote in the Augusta Chronicle, then the most influential of the Clarke journals, explaining to persons outside the State the real points of difference between the two local factions.[e] His statements substantiate the distinctions above set forth in regard to social and economic classes, and show that some differences of policy were springing into existence. But he goes further to claim democratic principles in the past as against the Troup aristocrats, which a more impartial critic will hardly

a Savannah Republican, Nov. 22, 1825.　　b Ib.. July 2, 1825.
c Georgia Journal, Dec. 27, 1835.　　d Ib., Dec., 1825, and Jan., 1826.
e Augusta Chronicle, Jan. 24, 1827.

grant in full. He claims that the Clarke party had put the election of governor and of Presidential electors into the hands of the people against Troup opposition. This is not fully corroborated in other material, which shows the voters on the questions to have been very generally divided between sections and parties. It was true in general that the Troup party was the more aristocratic and the Clarke party the more plebeian, but on account of the personal equation there was so much intermixture of classes in each party that any partisan statement beyond this must be accepted only with allowance for the point of view.

Troup's second term expired in the fall of 1827, and both sides prepared for the coming fray, but the Clarke party was greatly dismayed by the death of their candidate, Mathew Talbot, only a few days before the election, and John Forsyth obtained the chair without opposition.[a] At the same time as the gubernatorial election of 1827 occurred a contest for a vacant seat in Congress, which is of some interest, although no heavy vote was cast. George R. Gilmer and Thos. U. P. Charlton, both Troup men, offered themselves as candidates.[b] Some of the Clarke leaders decided to put Charlton under obligations by supporting him in the race; but the Troup party, resolving not to permit their adversaries to have the balance of power, concentrated upon Gilmer. Thereupon the Clarke party, seeing that it could not gain its enterprise, broke ranks and let its adherents vote as they chose. Gilmer was victorious, with a heavy majority.

It was generally recognized that nearly all the lawyers in Georgia were in the Troup ranks, and that the men of the bar were leaders in politics. We may reasonably suppose that the men were from the ranks of the budding Clarke party who in 1810 presented to the legislature a petition begging the abolition of "the most useless pest that ever disgraced civil society—the lawyers."[c] Since most of the lawyers were "Troupers," the Clarke party occasionally lacked a leader. This was the case in 1829 when two Troup men became contestants for the executive chair. The Clarke party really possessed the balance of power in this election, and it was

a Augusta Chronicle and Ga. Journal, October, 1827.
b Ga. Journal, Savannah Republican, and Augusta Chronicle, Sept., 18ʳ
c Augusta Constitutionalist, Oct. 21, 1831.

owing to its support that Gilmer obtained a tremendous victory over his competitor, Joel Crawford.[a] But the schemers were finally balked in their plans, for Gilmer declined to consider himself under obligations to return any favors which an opposing faction had shown him while seeking its own interests.[b] Naturally this attitude on the part of the new governor was not pleasing to his quondam supporters, who accordingly resolved to defeat him at all costs should he try for reelection.[c]

After the close of the great gubernatorial contest in 1825 an increasing dissatisfaction was evident in the State regarding the personal character of the political factions into which the people were divided. There were continual complaints of this from intelligent voters, and demands were made that there be a change "from men to measures" as a basis for political difference. The comparatively quiet period from 1825 to 1832 was a suitable time for such a change to be brought about, but for some years no question of policy could be found upon which the parties could disagree. Upon Indian affairs, upon the tariff, upon internal improvements, upon slavery, and in less degree upon the United States Bank, the leaders of each party had ideas, sometimes of decided character, but in each case these ideas happened to be practically the same.

A germ of party disagreement, however, was developing from the course of Indian affairs. The history of the friction over the Creek lands has shown us that in this period Georgia assumed a very pronounced position in the contention for State rights. It was natural that the slaveholders, courageous and masterful in their disposition, should take the lead in such a movement and should carry it forward with heightened zeal when the Federal authorities threatened to make trouble.

The aggressive and belligerent policy of Governor Troup at the head of the hotspurs brought severe criticism from without the State. After a time this had the effect within the State of showing the leaders of the Clarke party that although Troup had gained the material part of his contention against Adams, such radical action was not admissible as a general

a Athenian (Athens, Ga.), Oct. 7, 1829.

b Augusta Chronicle and Ga. Journal, October, 1827.

c Gilmer, Georgians, p. 459.

rule. This disapproval of Troup's policy by his local adversaries seemed to open a way for the substitution of measures for men as the chief consideration in the party alignment. Meanwhile John Clarke had withdrawn from Georgia politics by removing to Florida. The plan was suggested by some one that the Clarke party change its name to that of the Union party. The plan was informally approved by the rank and file of Clarke's former colleagues, and the name of the old champion gradually lost its usage as a shibboleth.

The Troup leaders were nothing loth to answer the challenge. They replied by avowing State rights as their principle and using it as their slogan. Their followers assented to the change. After the lapse of a few years, in which both sets of titles were in use by the people, the names State Rights and Union came to designate the local organizations. The process of name changing was begun in 1829 and was completed in 1832, though for some years afterwards the parties continued to be spoken of occasionally by their personal titles.

We shall see in a later chapter how well or how ill the policies suggested by their new names were maintained by the two parties respectively.

CHAPTER V.—THE STATE RIGHTS AND UNION PARTIES.

The preceding chapter has prepared us to follow the history of parties and politics in Georgia after 1830; but it is well, before proceeding, to make another and final review of the previous decade, dealing with such matters as internal improvements and the protective tariff, which, in addition to Indian affairs, were instrumental in bringing about the existing complexion of things and made possible the course which history pursued for the following thirty years.

We have already seen that from about 1798 to about 1823 there stretched a period of comparative reaction in Georgia against advanced theories of State sovereignty, or at least a period of quiescence on the subject. It may be observed that as late as December 12, 1821, there was introduced into the State senate, apropos of the controversy which had lately been waging elsewhere over the constitutionality of the United States Bank, a resolution which well expressed the attitude of the people during the quiescent period:

"In the conflict between the Federal and State authorities the State of Georgia will not enlist herself on either side. She regards the Federal union of the States as the best safeguard against intestinal discord, and the injuries of foreign powers. She is disposed to concede to the Federal and State governments, respectively, those powers which are intrusted to the former and reserved to the latter in the Federal Constitution." [a]

The policy of a protective tariff to industries, which later aroused so much hostility in Georgia, was adopted by the American Government as a result of certain developments during the war of 1812. At the beginning of that struggle America imported nearly all of her manufactured articles

---

[a] Niles' Register, vol. 21, pp. 296.

H. Doc. 702, pt. 2——8   113

from abroad. But when the British warships swept the Yankee trading and fishing vessels off the seas, the attention of the New England people was turned to manufactures as a substitute occupation. At the end of the war the industries which had recently been flourishing in the enjoyment of a monopoly of the home market were sadly hurt by the revived stream of imports from Europe. The Eastern States clamored for help from Congress, and in consequence the beginning of the protective system was made.

During the course of the war of 1812 the people of Georgia had strongly approved of domestic manufacture as a patriotic enterprise, especially when carried on in Georgia. But, when peace had arrived, the plan for a high tariff did not find approval in the State. An editorial in the Georgia Journal in 1820 declared against protective duties and condemned domestic manufactures.[a] The question, however, did not arouse much general interest until some years later, when the advocates of high tariff became more successful in their cause.

Many of the leading citizens of Georgia were strongly in favor of increasing the advantages of its people by a system of internal improvements in the shape of good roads, canals, etc. The first plan was to make these improvements at the expense of the State; but when the idea arose of national expenditures in these lines, the State mildly approved, and desired to have some of the improvements so placed that Georgia would derive advantage from them. The State rights advocates did not realize that internal improvements savored of paternalism until it became clear that that policy had become closely associated with the plan of protective duties.

Governor Troup very strongly desired a complete system of canals or horse-power railroads throughout the State.[b] He urged the State legislature to appropriate money, and on June 29, 1824, he wrote to the President of the United States that, since Congress had seen fit to pass an act authorizing the President to procure surveys and estimates for roads and canals, he felt it his duty to urge Georgia's claims for a share of the benefit, and to suggest a canal to connect the waters of

[a] Georgia Journal, Feb. 1, 1820   [b] Harden, Life of Troup, p. 181.

the Savannah with those of the Tennessee, and one to connect the St. Marys with the Suwanee River in Florida.[a]

Aside from the matter of the Creek lands, the subject of the African Colonization Society was the first to bring forth emphatic declarations from the Georgia legislature on the sovereignty of the States. At the time of its establishment the society had had the support of very many Southern people, but when it adopted emancipation propaganda the Georgia leaders turned squarely against it. The legislature on December 27, 1827, adopted resolutions which began with gravely and firmly protesting against the right of Congress to appropriate money to aid the society, and from this starting point ranged into an elaborate exposition of the constitutional limitations of the General Government. They declared that it was only when the governor of Georgia, to oppose the threat of armed coercion by the President, "threw himself upon the ramparts of the Constitution, there to sacrifice himself in its defense, it was only then that the people of the South were roused from their fatal lethargy. It is only now that the people of the South begin deeply to feel that the preservation of their happiness and prosperity depend upon the preservation of that Constitution, as it came from the hands of its makers—and feelingly to know that this can only be effected by union among themselves, and by a firm determination and manly resistance to any attempts to merge these free and sovereign States into one grand, unlimited, consolidated government. The Federal compact was a compact made between independent sovereignties for the general benefit and welfare of the whole, by which each, to effect that object, relinquished portions and like portions of its sovereign power, reserving to itself the residue, and by which all became mutual guarantees of each of the absolute and exclusive enjoyment of that residue. All the powers which could be exercised by each in a way sufficiently beneficial and without clashing or interfering with the exercise of the same powers by the others were intended to be retained and were retained by the States in their separate capacities. It irresistibly follows that Congress can not, by implication, derive from that compact power to do any act which can interfere with the just and full exercise by the

States of powers which each can within itself exercise in a way sufficiently beneficial to itself. Such are the powers of each State to make roads and canals and regulate its slave population." Congress therefore has no power to appropriate money for internal improvements or to aid the colonization society.[a]

A year later, on the subject of a controversy on slavery between South Carolina and Ohio, resolutions of the Georgia legislature declared that the States had an unquestionable right, in case of a breach of the general compact, to complain, remonstrate, and even to refuse obedience to any measure of the General Government manifestly violative of the Constitution.[b] The work of the Northern abolition societies was already beginning to add still another reason why Georgia should battle strongly in the particularist cause.[c]

The colonization society soon lost its prominent position; the project of Federal aid to better avenues of internal communication was slowly killed by the development of railroads for steam locomotion by private capital, frequently aided by the State governments; the Creek tribes of Indians disappeared from the public view; but there remained, in addition to the general question of slavery and the controversy over the Cherokee lands, the subject of the protective tariff, which from 1824 steadily grew more important as influencing the cotton States to place stronger emphasis upon the particularistic theory until the crisis of nullification times was reached in 1833.

The tariff of 1816 had been the first one possessing noteworthy protective features; those of 1820 and 1824 were successive advances along the line of protection, while in 1827 Congress was considering a still higher rate of tariff. The report of a committee was adopted by the Georgia legislature in December, 1827, setting forth in a lengthy preamble an historical argument on the powers of the General Government and of the States. It declared in rather mild opposition to protection that "Any law regulating commerce for its sole advantage, or for the purposes of revenue, which shall incidentally promote the interest of manufactures * * * [is

a Acts of Ga. Gen. Assem., 1827, p. 194. U. S. House Exec. Doc. No. 126, 20th Cong., 1st sess., vol. 3.

b Dec. 20, 1828; acts of Ga. Gen. Assem., 1828, p. 174.

c Cf. resolution of Ga. Leg., Dec. 19, 1829, acts of Ga. Gen. Assem., 1829, p. 235.

constitutional], but the moment it loses sight of either of these objects [it becomes unconstitutional]. An increase of tariff duties will and ought to be resisted by all legal and constitutional means so as to avert the crying injustice of such an unconstitutional measure." It concluded by directing the report to be laid before Congress and before the legislatures of the other Southern States.[a]

The Congressional Representatives of Georgia were not backward in voicing the opinions of their constituents. But Mr. Gilmer, then a Congressman, complained that he found a sad apathy and stupidity in the lower House when the matter arose of interpreting the Constitution.[b]

The sections interested in protection, disregarding the opposition of the South, pushed on their policy, and in May, 1828, enacted a new tariff law increasing the duties upon wool, hemp, and manufactures. There at once arose a great agitation in the cotton States to secure the repeal of the measure, which was felt to be very burdensome to the South and beneficial only to a rival section. South Carolina had already in 1827 protested vigorously against protection, and had received some support from Georgia. From the spring of 1828 the people of Georgia took a more vivid interest in the cause. A great number of mass meetings were held throughout the State condemning the tariff;[c] county grand juries made presentments against it;[d] the students of the University of Georgia resolved to wear Georgia homespun at the commencement in 1828, to show their hostility to the tariff,[e] and the trustees of the institution commended their resolution.[f] A great meeting was held in the University chapel at Athens August 7, at which nearly all of the leading politicians of the State were present. Strong resolutions against the consitutionality of the tariff were adopted without opposition.[g] Almost the only note of dissent to the general attitude of the State was an editorial in the Savannah Mercury protesting that since the tariff had not had such awful results as were

[a] Dec. 24, 1827; acts of Ga. Gen. Assem., 1827, p. 203. cf. also Athenian (Athens, Ga.), Jan. 24, 1828.
[b] Speech in Congress, Mar. 7, 1828; Athenian, June 3, 1828.
[c] E. g. Niles's Register, vol. 35, p. 64.
[d] E. g. Niles's Register, vol. 35, p. 63.
[e] Georgia Journal, August, 1828.
[f] Minutes of the Univ. of Ga. trustees, Aug. 7, 1828, MSS.
[g] Niles's Register, vol. 35, p. 14.

predicted, all the excitement in the South had very little justification.[a]

Georgia was never so radical in its opposition to the tariff as was South Carolina. The message of Governor Forsyth on November 4, 1828, stated that the tariff act of 1828 had filled the whole Southern country with resentment and dismay. He noted the possibility of neutralizing the law by State action, but considered that it would be hardly wise or constitutional, at least until the usual method of seeking repeal had proved ineffectual.[b] The legislature adopted a memorial to be sent to the States opposing the tariff, urging them to work for the repeal of the unconstitutional act, and exhorting each of these States, as a policy of self-preservation, to ward off its effects by living as far as possible upon its own products.[c] Many Georgians agreed with Mr. McDuffie, of South Carolina, that if driven to it by the tariff, the South could manufacture its own articles of consumption. In the line of carrying this theory into practice, the first cotton factory in Georgia was built at Athens in 1829 with local capital.[d] Another larger factory was built at Athens in 1883,[e] which remained in operation for many years. The smaller mill was burned in 1835, but was later rebuilt.[f]

After 1828 the agitation against the tariff died down for a few years, in Georgia. The legislature of 1829 was satisfied with directing the Georgia Congressmen to use their best efforts to obtain the repeal of the act.[g] In 1830 the general assembly paid little attention to the tariff, but requested the Congressmen to vote against internal improvements as a system.[h] It is clear that there was a period of comparative quiet in the State as regards the particularist struggle, from 1829 to the beginning of 1832.[i] This was largely due to the confidence of the people in Andrew Jackson, whom they expected to be a champion of the cause.

The influence of Andrew Jackson upon Georgia politics is

[a] Niles's Register, vol. 35, p. 136.

[b] Athenian, Nov. 18, 1828.

[c] Acts of Ga. Gen. Assem. 1828, p. 173.

[d] Ga. Journal, Apr. 3 and Apr. 10, 1830; Athenian, Feb. 2, 1830.

[e] Augusta Constitutionalist, May 17, 1833; Ga. Journal, Nov. 19, 1832.

[f] Augusta Constitutionalist, Mar. 31, 1835.

[g] Acts of Ga. Gen. Assem., 1829, p. 241.

[h] Dec. 29, 1830; U. S. House Exec. Docs. No. 60, 20th Cong., 1st sess., vol. 3. cf. also U. S. Exec. Docs., No. 91, 22d Cong., 2d sess., vol. 2.

[i] Cf. editorial in Macon Messenger, June, 1830, quoted in Niles's Register, vol. 38, p. 337.

worthy of attentive study. In the Presidential contest of 1820 Jackson and Crawford were the only candidates who had any following in Georgia. The local campaign, in so far as it involved any other than personal issues, was not unlike the campaign in the country at large. It was a question of the continuance of the "Virginia dynasty" in the Government or the election of the popular hero who had arisen from the masses. The Troup party, aside from its personal attachment to Crawford, was, from its aristocratic composition, inclined to support such a man as he, who stood for the "Cabinet succession" to the Presidency. The local support of Jackson was not different from that in the other States in which the effort to gain control was made by the lower classes.

Both Jackson and Crawford were defeated in the Presidential contest. Crawford soon disappeared from the national arena. Henry Clay cast his lot with the Administration of Adams, and Adams became so distasteful to the Georgia politicians that they were prepared to give the most loyal and undivided support to the opposition candidate for the election of 1828. In the popular conception Jackson filled all possible requirements for the candidacy. As early as December, 1826, a resolution was adopted by the Georgia legislature and signed by Governor Troup, stating that the people of Georgia looked with confidence to the election of Andrew Jackson to the Presidency. On December 21, 1827, 68 members of the State senate, out of a total of 69 voting, declared their preference for Jackson, and only one member could be found in favor of Adams.[a] During the next year each local party tried to outshine the other in its support of Jackson. Independent tickets of electors were put into the field by each party, but every candidate upon each ticket was pledged to vote for Jackson and Calhoun, as President and Vice-President.

The principal issue which caused the unanimity was that of the Indian lands. Upon this issue we have seen in a former chapter that Jackson as President faithfully carried out the expectations of the Georgians. So long as that issue was a vital one, both of the local parties remained steadfast in his support, notwithstanding the occurrence of disconcerting developments in other matters. The anti-Masonic movement

[a] Savannah Republican, Jan. 19, 1828.

at the North in 1829 was regarded in Georgia as merely an
electioneering scheme in Clay's favor, and was given no
approval.[a] The tariff and internal improvements were of
secondary consideration for the time being. The unpleasantness between Jackson and Calhoun and the withdrawal of
Berrien from the Cabinet on account of the Eaton affair,
caused not a waver in the steady devotion of the great majority of Georgians to their champion. The State senate resolved
unanimously in November, 1831, that it favored the reelection
of Jackson, and opposed the election of Calhoun as President
or as Vice-President.[b]

The election of 1832 took place in a period of tension in
the Cherokee controversy. Jackson was sturdily upholding
the contentions of Georgia. It is not surprising that the
nomination of two independent tickets pledged to his support
was again a feature of the local campaign, and that hardly a
voice within the State was heard to praise the candidacy of
Mr. Clay.

But influences were at work which were to break this accord
as soon as the Cherokee question should subside. Jackson
and the Georgia leaders were too autocratic in temperament
to remain in perpetual harmony without complete identity of
interests and points of view. The local parties were inclined
to disagree wherever possible; and the disturbing developments of the time were already furnishing much ground for
discussion. The outcome was to be the merging, in the following period, of the local parties respectively with the two
national parties which were then beginning to differentiate.

Since 1828 the Southern representatives in Congress had
struggled for lower duties on imports, but had fought against
overpowering numbers. General Jackson had been looked to
as a leading opponent of the protective tariff; but his message
of 1830 approved of the principle and suggested the expendi-
ture of the surplus revenue in internal improvements. The
tariff act of July 14, 1832, gave no relief to the South, but
established protection as a fixed policy of the Government.
The people of Georgia felt very much injured by the act;
but his loyalty to the cause of their State in the Cherokee
dispute prevented their losing faith in the President.

Early in 1831 the doctrine of nullification in its then uncrys-

[a] Athenian, Sept. 1, 1829.　　　[b] Niles's Register, vol. 41, p. 272.

tallized form had begun to enter the view of the Georgia politicians; but the doctrine probably did not obtain serious consideration by any great number of the citizens before the beginning of the next year.[a] From that time forth it was the subject of much thought and discussion in the State. Except by a few extremists, nullification was considered to be too radical. But the popular discontent aroused by the tariff act of July 1832, and the evident determination of South Carolina to test her power against the tariff, in the capacity of a sovereign State, led to a very thorough consideration of the existing status.

The leaders of political thought in Georgia, after studying nullification in its relations to the several constitutional theories already before the country, reached in most cases a substantial agreement, and in the end, as will appear below, carried a large majority of the people with them.

The doctrine of State rights had no set formula for all time; but being a method of interpreting conditions and relations, it was subject to varying exposition by different philosophers and in different epochs.

The men of Georgia were not given to formulating intricate theories unless they were to serve concrete and immediate ends. In the matter of the Creek lands the chief question was of the right and power of the State to require the Central Government to carry out the terms of the bargain which it had made with the State government. In the Cherokee controversy the chief issue was upon the jurisdiction over the disputed territory. On the part of the Georgians there was a distinct wish to restrict the discussion in these cases to the immediate issue, and not to go far afield in generalizations. The sovereign rights of the State were frequently referred to, but were not expounded at length, for the reason that they were hardly in question. Even John Quincy Adams spoke as a matter of course of the authority and dignity of the sovereign States of the Union.

The principle of close construction of the Constitution was held by practically all Georgians at all times from the adoption of the instrument. This meant simply that the Constitution limited the Central Government and reserved to the several States all powers not expressly delegated. When

[a] cf. Augusta Constitutionalist, Oct. 21, 1831.

exigencies arose in which more radical theories would be useful there was no difficulty in formulating them and securing their local adoption. Conservative particularism was universal in Georgia. The advance to radical particularism was a matter of expediency and not of principle.

As long as the South could make any effective opposition in Congress to the protective tariff the ballot box was trusted to secure the observance of the fundamental law. But as soon as the majority showed its determination to override the Southern opposition and disregard Southern interests, the cry of unconstitutionality was raised. The wording of the Constitution made it necessary for the argument showing the unconstitutionality of protective duties to be of such extreme nicety that to sustain the contention the party of protest was driven from conservative ground. The condition of expediency having arisen, none of the local politicians and few of the rank and file balked at the advance from moderate to radical particularism—from the advocacy of State rights to that of State sovereignty.

Whereas the doctrine of State rights emphasized the powers reserved to the States in the terms of the Federal Constitution as the fundamental law, the theory of State sovereignty laid heaviest stress upon the independence and the sovereign character of the original States before they formed the Union or adopted the Constitution, and upon their continued sovereignty as members of the Union or Federation. The pivotal question was no longer as to what interpretation the Constitution was to receive, but as to where lay the proper authority to give to the instrument its official and final construction. From the premise of the sovereignty of the States meeting in convention in 1787 and establishing a Federal Government in 1789, it was argued that the States created the Central Government as their agent for the performance of certain specified functions and with certain delegated powers; that the agent, being subordinate to the sovereignties which created it, had no power to enlarge its own authority, and in the event of an attempt to assert such power it might be checked by the sovereign States or any of them.

A conservative wing of the State sovereignty theorists conceded to the Central Government the rights of sovereignty in its own sphere, which should not interfere with the soveignty of the States in their own spheres. In the event of a conflict of authority, the power of deciding as to the limitation of the spheres did not lie either in the State governments or in the Central Government; but unless the difficulty could be settled by mutual concession, recourse must be had to constitutional amendment. This doctrine did not of necessity rest upon a theory of divided sovereignty. The argument was, of course, that the people of the States were sovereign, and the people alone; that the people had delegated certain powers of sovereignty to the Central Government, and had continued the State governments in the exercise of other powers of sovereignty which were the residue of those powers with which these governments had been intrusted at a former time.

The latter or moderate State sovereignty doctrine was somewhat the more popular one in Georgia where the tariff issue had led the people to abandon distinctly conservative ground. But the difference between the moderate and the advanced doctrines of State sovereignty was so slight that all but the most acute and consistent thinkers were likely to shift from one to the other unconsciously.

Nullification was simply the radical doctrine of State sovereignty plus a formula for its specific application. The nullifiers had set to work to find an efficient means of overthrowing the protective tariff. They reasoned out the sovereignty of the States and the subordinate character of the Central Government. With this preparation for the concrete question at hand, they declared, as did all State sovereignty adherents, that Congress had exceeded its powers, and that the United States Supreme Court, being a part of the Central Government, which was itself nothing more than an agent, had no authority whatever to judge of the powers of the agent, but that the only authority for such judgment lay in the sovereign States. The nullifiers then proceeded to show how this authority could be exercised.

The machinery as described by Calhoun was not complex. A State by virtue of its sovereignty could declare the nullity of an unconstitutional act of Congress and prohibit its execution within the limits of that State. This prohibition was of absolute finalty as against any further power of the Central government acting in isolation. But Congress had one last recourse. It might submit to the States a constitutional amendment expressly justifying its own view of its powers.   If the amendment should fail of adoption, Congress must concede that its interpretation of its authority was not according to the will of the sovereign and must repeal the act in question. In the event of the ratification of the amendment by three-fourths of the States and its incorporation into the Constitution itself, the protesting State would be overruled and would have to submit or withdraw from the Union[a]

South Carolina adopted and applied the expedient of nullification.   Concerning the measures taken by the South Carolina convention and legislature, most of the Georgia leaders thought their underlying principle to be sound, but considered the interposition of the sovereignty of the State to be inexpedient without further remonstrance and without joint action by all of the aggrieved States.

To study the internal history of nullification in Georgia and its effect upon local politics, we must return to the beginning of the year 1831, when the doctrine first began to be taken seriously in the State.   Before that time the idea of a State veto had been entirely theoretical, and nullification had been a hazy conception without any distinguished champion.

It was in March, 1831, that the editor of the Georgia Journal discovered that Mr. Calhoun was at the head of the nullification movement, which was in the line of his own views as a Troup or State Rights partisan.   The discovery bade fair to disarrange existing alignments.   Crawford and others opposed to Calhoun, it was thought, must change to the Clarke or Union alignment.   This would bring on an extensive reorganization.   The conclusion of the editor was: "We reckon we had better wipe all out and begin afresh."[b]

The anticipations of the editor were not fully realized. Crawford had lost his position of consequence in the State. Andrew Jackson was in complete control of Georgia politics. The new doctrine was not to obtain speedy acceptance, nor at once to disconcert parties very seriously.

The gubernatorial contest of 1831 was of distinct interest as regards practical workings and as regards political theories. The earliest candidates to be announced were George R. Gilmer and Thomas Haynes, both of whom were members of the

[a] Collection of documents on nullification in Calhoun's Works, vol. 6.
[b] Ga. Journal, Mar. 17, 1831.

State Rights party. This promised the Clarke or Union leaders a chance to profit by the division of support.

The opponents of Troup and his successors had for some years been without a prominent leader, and without efficient organization. In 1830 an opportunity was given them to develop a party machine. The University of Georgia was in need of funds with which to rebuild a burned dormitory and to erect additional buildings. The board of trustees was filled with conspicuous Troup men, and could obtain no appropriations from the Clarke majority in the legislature. The problem was solved by doubling the number of the trustees by the addition of a group of Clarke leaders. The legislature was at once amenable and made adequate appropriations to the University.

The trustees of the university had formerly acted as the executive committee of the Troup party. After 1830 it comprised the executive committee of each party. At the time of each meeting of the board, there would be held in Athens two caucuses, made up of the partisans on the board together with other visiting members of the respective cliques. The first caucus of the Union party was held at Athens in May, 1831. The result of its deliberations was the announcement of Wilson Lumpkin as a candidate for the governor's chair.[a]

The principles and attitude of Mr. Lumpkin, who was thus put forward by the Union party to oppose Gilmer and Haynes in 1831, illustrate the unsettled and transitional condition of politics in the State. Lumpkin in his own memoirs gives evidence of his having been at the time of his candidacy a State rights man, and yet an advocate of moderate Union principles; an opponent of nullification (though not at that time pronounced, as contemporary material shows) and yet a friend and in other matters a political ally of Calhoun. When Lumpkin first entered politics in 1812 he received support from the Clarke party, and always thereafter kept faith with his colleagues in that organization. He was while in Congress a member of the opposition to Crawford at the time of the attempt to nominate him over Monroe in 1816; and as a member of the State legislature in 1824, he influenced most of the Clarke representatives to vote for Jackson as opposed to Crawford in the Presidential contest. But for the five years

a Augusta Constitutionalist, June 24, 1831.

126

preceding 1831 Lumpkin had been in Congress upholding the contentions of Georgia, in a way satisfactory to all his constituents, while State politics had been so temperate that the Troup party, forgetting his past opposition and knowing his State rights inclinations,[a] claimed him as an adherent.

Lumpkin's candidacy was at first a puzzle to the partisan editors. The State Rights papers thought him a third candidate of their own party and deplored the threatening disruption of the organization.[b] After a time it was made clear that he would be supported by the former adherents of Clarke. Then the uncertainty of his attitude toward nullification formed a topic for discussion, but the general opinion was that that doctrine had not grown to be of fundamental importance.

In August, 1831, it became evident that the Union party was solid for Lumpkin and that the State Rights party was divided between Gilmer and Haynes. At the University commencement in that month the State Rights caucus tried to bring down either Gilmer or Haynes from the candidacy.[c] Persuaded by the party press, Haynes withdrew in September,[d] and the contest lay between Gilmer and Lumpkin, the rival champions.

The supporters of Gilmer were anxious to have it believed that their candidate was more certain than any other one to defend the rights of the State. At a Fourth of July dinner held by them at Milledgeville, Troup and Gilmer and Andrew Jackson were toasted, and Clay and the tariff condemned. Governor Gilmer responded in a spirited toast to the rights of the States and declared his own devotion to the cause.[e]

The friends of Lumpkin asserted that their candidate was as loyal as anyone to the legitimate rights of the State. They sought to damage Gilmer's popularity by a reference to his opposition to distributing the lands in the gold-mining district among the citizens of the State by the land lottery, thence arguing that he had not the interests of the common people at

a Savannah Republican, Jan. 10, 1828; see for public letter of Lumpkin stating his conservative support of State rights.

b Ibid., May 31, 1831; Athenian, June 14, 1831.

c Augusta Constitutionalist, Aug. 12, 1831.

d Ibid., Sept. 13, 1831.

e Savannah Republican, July 12, 1831.

heart.[a] The outcome of the contest was the election of Lumpkin as governor, but in the legislature elected at the same time the State Rights party secured the greater number of seats.

The location of majorities in 1831, as shown by a map made according to the returns of the gubernatorial election, was strikingly like that in 1825. No conspicuous change occurred anywhere. As for the newly settled area, most of it went for Lumpkin, as might have been expected; but where the land was particularly fertile or the population decidedly high toned, Gilmer carried the county.[b] Corroboration of this lies in the comparatively large number of slaves in the Gilmer counties of the west, and in contemporary agricultural criticisms.[c] This similarity, we may almost say identity, of local situation demonstrates that the lines of cleavage continued to depend upon economic and social conditions, and had little connection with questions of public policy. In fact, the party leaders, immediately after the contest, underestimating the importance of nullification and its developments, prophesied that the only points of difference between the local parties for the next few years would be regarding the choice of the next Vice-President and of a successor to President Jackson at the expiration of his second term, a contingency then five years in the future.[d]

The editor of Niles's Register, in noting political events in Georgia from 1819 as far as 1833, hardly ever failed to protest at the conclusion of each article that it was impossible to understand Georgia politics and he could make no pretense of doing so. The editor was wise in his resolution to refrain from the attempt at exposition, for hardly anyone but a member of one of the Georgia cliques could have explained the anomalous conditions in the State.

The parties in Georgia had a certain intangibility resulting from the obscurity in their manipulations. Each was controlled by a ring which transacted business in caucuses and kept no minutes. The responsibility for any single measure could rarely be traced to any single originator or champion.

a Augusta Constitutionalist, Sept. 27, 1831.
b cf. ibid., Sept. 12, 1835.
c Ibid., Feb. 3, 1835. cf. also Chappell's Miscellanies of Georgia, vol. 2, p. 22. See also map herewith showing products of counties.
d Augusta Chronicle, Feb. 1, 1832.

The party newspapers as a rule did not adopt any one line of argument for a campaign and consistently hammer away at it, but they supplemented their meager editorials by opening their columns to their political friends who would contribute articles over pseudonyms. If attacks were made in these articles upon the policy or political reputation of an opposing candidate, it was not customary for the candidate to make personal reply, but he or his friends would write anonymous articles in defense or in counter attack and publish them in the organs of their own party. Thus the personal element in the situation is largely concealed from the historical student, while the evidence remains that personal influence was a very essential factor in the progress of events.

The local parties themselves were not fully conscious of their complete dependence upon economic, social, and personal affinities and differences. The adoption of the names State Rights and Union was a manifestation of their desire to establish points of difference of a distinctly political character. It was not until after much argument and important developments that genuine opposing policies of any kind were adopted by the parties as units.

The unanimity of the people upon external questions before them in 1831 was indicated by the unanimous adoption by the State senate in November of resolutions expressing its wish for General Jackson's reelection. The resolutions admitted that "recent events [e. g., those in Tassel's case] have been hailed in some of our sister States as a proof of the triumph here of J. C. Calhoun and his principles over the President, his friends, and his principles," but declared, "the great body of the people of this State have no feeling in common with the pretentions or with many of the principles of Mr. Calhoun, and especially those contained in his late address to the people of the United States on the subject of nullification."[a]

Within the next year the unanimity disappeared. The heated debate in Congress upon the revision of the tariff brought on an agitation in Georgia which failed of being superheated at an early stage only because everyone at first thought very nearly alike and no local dispute could be aroused. The Georgia Congressmen fought with might and main against the tariff. When they were overpowered by the final vote in July

[a] Niles's Register, vol. 41, p. 272.

one or two of them accepted the finality of the result with only a mild protest. The others did not give up the battle, but shifted the scene of their activity to the popular forum.

The people welcomed their returning representatives at the close of the session as heroes who had made a good fight in a worthy cause. The politicians in attendance upon the University of Georgia commencement, in August, arranged a public meeting for the consideration of the tariff and the grievances which it brought. The result was the adoption by the meeting of recommendations to the several counties of the State for the election of delegates to a convention to be held at Milledgeville in November. The purpose of the convention was to decide upon the course which Georgia should follow to secure the preservation of her rights. Mr. John M. Berrien and Judge A. S. Clayton were the leading spirits in the meeting and were appointed as the leading members of a standing committee of correspondence for the furtherance of the anti-tariff cause.[a]

Within the same month a great public dinner was arranged by the citizens of Oglethorpe County in honor of the State Rights congressmen from Georgia. In the political speech-making which followed the dinner, Mr. Berrien pleaded for the organization of the people against the tariff. He made a ringing appeal for the defense of the sovereign and inalienable rights of the States, and for the observance of the pledge contained in the protest of the Georgia legislature of 1828. Judge Clayton had recently distinguished himself as a nullifier in Congress. He now declared that the last hope of mitigation from the oppressors of the South was extinguished; that self-redress was the only recourse remaining; that the time was come to strike for liberty.[b]

The listeners gave their heartiest applause to the most radical sentiments. They unanimously declared that they would not submit to the tariff, and that they would help to defend any State against coercion by the central government. And yet a resolution was adopted, with only a few dissenting voices, which averred unshaken confidence in the patriotism of Andrew Jackson. The meeting appointed a committee of

[a] S. F. Miller, Bench and Bar of Georgia, vol. 2, p. 29.
[b] Niles's Register, vol. 43, p. 9.

correspondence, and seconded the call of the Athens meeting for the convention at Milledgeville.

Meetings were held in nearly every county to consider the problems before the country. A very poor cotton and corn crop increased the sense of hardship. The meetings were largely controlled by the radical element. Most of them chose delegates for the convention at Milledgeville, and instructed them of the wish of the county for radical action or for conservatism, as the case might be.

The convention met in the capitol on November 13, 1832. Of the eighty counties in the State, sixty-one were represented by a hundred and thirty-four delegates. Ex-Governor Gilmer was made president of the convention. At an early stage in the sessions Ex-Governor Forsyth moved the appointment of a committee on credentials. An acrimonious debate ensued, in which Messrs. Berrien and Clayton opposed Mr. Forsyth, who was the leader of the conservatives. Upon the rejection of his motion, Mr. Forsyth led a secession of fifty-three conservatives from the hall, and presented a protest denying the legitimacy of the convention. After the withdrawal of the dissentients the convention adopted a long series of resolutions, the doctrinal points in which approached very near to nullification. It declared the determined opposition of the people of Georgia to the protective tariff, and stated their resolution to resist the principle by the exercise of all their rights as one of the sovereign States of the confederacy and by concert with such other States as had kindred interests. The convention resolved that definite resistance should be postponed in order that Congress and the manufacturing States might have time to reconsider their oppressive policy, and it made arrangements for calling a convention of the Southern States, provided the action of the convention should be approved by the ballots of the people of Georgia.[a] The convention adjourned on November 17.

That all of the proceedings of the convention did not find undivided approval in the State was quickly shown by the action of the legislature. On November 20 a set of resolutions was introduced into the house of representatives as a conservative measure to counteract the radical propaganda of the convention. It expressed discontent with the tariff

[a] Georgia Journal, Nov. and Dec., 1832. Niles's Register, vol. 43, pp. 220 and 230.

law, but disapproved of the resolutions adopted by the late convention, which it said was composed of delegates of a minority of the people, and stated it to be the duty of the legislature to tranquilize the public mind. It embodied a scheme for calling a Southern convention, in the event of the approval of the plan by a majority of the citizens of the State at the time of the election of county officers in January.[a] These resolutions were adopted in the house by a vote of 97 to 57 and in the senate by 48 to 28. An additional resolution was adopted with a similar majority, which expressly repudiated the doctrine of nullification as being neither a peaceful nor a constitutional remedy, and warned the people of Georgia against adopting South Carolina's mischievous policy.[b]

The legislature seems to have had an afterthought that its resolutions were too pacific and submissive. On December 24 it resolved "That this general assembly does expressly declare that the Government of the United States does not possess the power under the Constitution to carry on a system of internal improvement within the several States or to appropriate money to be expended upon such improvement."[c] By the tenor of this resolution the legislature did not pretend to be a court with final authority of interpretation, but it merely saw fit to express its positive opinion as a body which had as much right as any other existing one to interpret the Constitution. This was in accordance with the moderate doctrine of State sovereignty, which was the doctrine at this time accepted by the majority of the people of Georgia.

The moderate State sovereignty doctrine necessarily depended upon a federal constitutional convention as the final resort in embarrassing circumstances. The Georgia legislature accordingly, in December, 1832, applied to Congress for the call of a federal convention to amend the Constitution in numerous details: To define more distinctly the powers of the General Government and those reserved to the States; to define the power in the General Government of coercion over the States, and in the States to resist an unconstitutional act; to settle the principle of the protective tariff; to establish a system of taxation which would bear equally upon all sections; to define the jurisdiction of the Supreme Court; to establish

---

[a] Niles's Register, vol. 43, p. 279.
[b] Dec. 14, 1832; Acts of Ga. Gen. Assem., 1832, p. 245. Niles's Register, vol. 43, p. 280.
[c] Dec. 24, 1832; Acts of Ga. Gen. Assem., 1832, p. 251.

a tribunal of last resort in disputes between the States and the General Government; to decide upon the constitutionality of the United States Bank and of internal improvements; to direct the disposition of the surplus revenue and of the public lands; to secure the election of President and Vice-President in all cases to the people and to limit their tenure of office to one term; and to settle the question of the rights of the Indians.[a] Such a convention was never called, and the desired amendments were never made. Having applied for the calling of a convention, the majority of the people of Georgia considered that they had done all that was required by the circumstances; and the legislature passed few more resolutions upon federal relations before 1850. The compromise tariff of 1833 closed the contest over the single issue of protection, but the threat of Jackson to coerce South Carolina roused antagonism in the South, and was more powerful than Calhoun's arguments in fostering nullification in Georgia: several years more were required for the dispute to die away.

The result of the agitation in the fall of 1832 and of the conflicting action of the convention and the legislature in November and December was a complication in local politics. A segment of the State Rights party adopted nullification, and was joined by bolters from the Union party.[b] Another section of the State Rights party, numbering about 5,000 of the 30,000 voters in the party at the last election, deserted their confrères to join the Union party. The names of Troup and Clarke were revived to distinguish between the two divisions of the new Union party. The remainder of the State Rights party, all of the nullifiers, and a few bolters from the Union party united for practical purposes under the banner of State Rights.[c] For the next four or five years Nullification, State Rights, Troup Union, and Clarke Union factions constituted the political alignment, the two former and the two latter groups voting respectively in combination, but struggling to obtain the nominations in their respective parties for men of their own coterie.[d]

Nullification, first conspicuous in 1831, possessed considerable strength in Georgia at the end of 1832, and continued to

a Dec. 22, 1832; acts of Ga. Gen. Assem., 1832, p. 249. U. S. House Ex. Doc. No. 92, 22d Cong., 2d sess., vol. 2.

b Augusta Chronicle, Aug. 25, 1832.

c Georgia Journal, Aug. 21, 1833.

d Ibid., Sept. 17, 1834.

gain supporters until 1834, after which it rapidly declined. Apparently it could at no time muster a majority of the State Rights party, which itself during these years was outnumbered by the Union party; so the nullifiers were never able to count a fourth of the voting population of Georgia. The doctrine had numerous supporters of a violent type, making more noise than comported with their number. Their efforts were strenuous but unavailing to bring the mass of the people or the most trusted leaders to approve the practice according to Calhoun's formula.

Judge A. S. Clayton was the only Georgian of decided prominence who was an outright nullifier. Judge Clayton did not differ from the typical Georgia hotspur except in the radical degree to which he carried his doctrines. He was thoroughly convinced of the righteousness of extreme particularism, and showed his consistency and his devotion to the cause by his defiance of the federal Supreme Court in Worcester's case[a] and by his bold attacks upon the bank and the tariff in Congress, as well as by his energy as a popular agitator for nullification. He was the chief owner in 1832 of the only cotton factory in Georgia; but he declared in Congress that, so far from leading him to favor protection, the knowledge of his own surprising profits from manufacturing served to clear his vision to the enormity of the tariff's oppression upon the planters.[b]

Mr. Berrien was an advocate of the advanced doctrine of State sovereignty, but he did not openly declare for nullification. As expressing the will of his State, he had delivered in the United States Senate in 1829 a strikingly eloquent defense of State sovereignty in his attack upon the constitutionality of the tariff.[c] As a member of Jackson's Cabinet from 1829 to 1831 he had been in harmony with the Administration, and was content to await developments. But the tariff act of 1832, following his resignation from the Cabinet in 1831, caused him to take up the cudgels again for extreme State sovereignty. The name of nullification had an unpleasant sound to many of the common people who did not study constitutional theories. His knowledge of the unpopularity

---

[a] Infra, p. 80.
[b] June 14, 1832; Niles's Register, vol. 42, p. 325. Register of Debates, 1831–32, p. 3850.
[c] Register of Debates in Congress, 1828–29, p. 22.

of this term was probably responsible for Mr. Berrien's failure to champion Calhoun's plan of a State veto. We shall have occasion in another chapter to observe that in the following decade Mr. Berrien, as a member of the Whig party, veered in his policy so far as to advocate a moderate protective tariff. His very great ability as a constitutional lawyer and his force as an orator made him a powerful champion of any cause which he adopted.

Mr. Gilmer was an advocate of State sovereignty, but was not a nullifier. In the anti-tariff convention he had moved the omission of one of the resolutions which contained a statement of doctrine very similar to nullification.[a] Upon the failure of his amendment, he gave his approval to the whole set of resolutions adopted by the convention, of which he was president. The strength of his State sovereignty convictions may be gathered from his executive policy toward the Cherokees, as set forth in the preceding chapter.

Mr. Forsyth was strongly opposed to any agitation on the ground of State sovereignty. He was in close touch with the President, and believed that matters would right themselves if time were given. Mr. Forsyth had been a leader of the Troup party in former years, but his distinct Union sentiments caused his separation from his former colleagues after 1832. His engrossing concern with international affairs led to his alienation from local politics. As Secretary of State from 1834 to his death in 1841, he remained in steady support of Jackson and Van Buren, while the State Rights party in Georgia drifted into the Whig party at large.

Mr. W. H. Crawford was habitually opposed to anything which Mr. Calhoun favored. He advised the calling of a constitutional convention as preferable to nullification or secession, either of which he thought would bring on war. If separation must be the final resort, he said, it would be well to learn how strong a Southern confederacy could be formed. On the whole it would be better to submit to the tariff than to form a dependent connection with any foreign state.[b]

Mr. Troup, upon being questioned, expounded State sovereignty as being above and having nothing to do with the Constitution. The United States Government being a mere agent,

a Niles's Register, vol. 43, p. 222.

b Letter of Crawford, Sept. 13, 1832, Niles's Register, vol. 43, p. 185.

he held that South Carolina had a right to do what she had done. Yet he blamed that State for not acting in concert with the other Southern States, and expressed his belief that if she had done so, "a certain and complete triumph of the Constitution [i. e., as limiting the Central Government] would have been the result."[a]

Governor Lumpkin's position was not different from that of Mr. Troup. Referring to the tariff in his annual message of 1832, he said: "Intolerable assumptions and usurpations * * * must be checked by some means; and the power to accomplish this end must unquestionably lie in the respective sovereignties." Yet he went on to say that it would have been at least the part of courtesy for South Carolina to have waited for joint action by the aggrieved States, and expressed his opinion that by conservative measures the existing unpleasant status might have been avoided.[b] Within the next year, Lumpkin expressed an increasing disrelish of nullification; but he did not hint at forsaking the doctrine of the sovereignty of the States.

The substantial agreement of Troup and Gilmer with Lumpkin upon doctrinal points shows that there was no adequate justification for the use of the names State Rights and Union by the respective parties. The Clarke or Union majority in the legislature of 1830 had stood squarely with Governor Gilmer when he refused to submit to the interference of the United States Supreme Court in Tassel's case. In the cases of Worcester and Butler and Graves, Governor Lumpkin continued Mr. Gilmer's policy without any noticeable modification. The State Rights party in 1832 did not allow the nullifiers to control it, and though its leaders, of course, approved the principle of the right of secession by a sovereign State, they did not advocate secession as a remedy for their existing wrongs. On the other hand, the Union party angrily resented the sobriquet of "submissionists" which their opponents sought to attach to them. Finally, it was the Unionist Lumpkin who, with the approval of both local parties, but in contravention of all precedent and in defiance of the dictum of the Supreme Court, declared the unceded Cherokee lands to be open for settlement.

[a] Letter of Troup, Sept. 25, 1834, Harden's Life of Troup, p. 522, and letter of Troup Feb. 10, 1833; ibid., appendix p. 1.
[b] Niles's Register, vol. 43, p. 207.

During 1833 an effort was made with some success to bring
the Union party to adopt a distinctly union policy. The
meeting of a State constitutional convention in May afforded
the occasion for a conference of Union party men from all
sections. The conference adopted resolutions approving the
Virginia resolutions of 1799 as defining the powers of the
Government, condemning the doctrine of nullification, protesting against protective duties, and approving the administration of Andrew Jackson.[a]

Two days later the members of the State Rights party in
the convention held a meeting. They adopted no formal
resolutions, but nominated Joel Crawford to oppose Wilson
Lumpkin in the gubernatorial contest.[b] Lumpkin was then an
avowed enemy of nullification, while Crawford refused to
commit himself.[c]

The presence of the nullifiers within the State Rights party
tended rather to weaken that party than to strengthen it. A
large number of voters in the old Troup party feared the influence of the radical doctrine to such an extent that they left
their usual alignment simply to oppose what they thought to
be political heresy.[d] Lumpkin obtained a decisive victory in
the large majority, as then considered, of above 2,000 votes.[e]

The returns for the northwestern part of the State in 1833
are interesting in that they show for several of the newly
organized and partially settled counties a Troup or State
Rights majority. This affords strong evidence that the men
of the oldest sections of the State were no less eager than the
frontiersmen to obtain the Cherokee lands. The lands in the
eastern part of Georgia were largely worn out by the exhaust-
ing system of cultivation in practice at the time. Cotton and
corn were the only commodities produced in large quantities,
while both of these were "clean" crops, exposing the soil to the
weather and diminishing its fertility. Commercial fertilizers
were unknown, and the planter's only recourse was to abandon his fields, at least temporarily, after some years of cultivation.[f] For these reasons several of the older counties in
middle Georgia lost nearly half their population through the

a Niles's Register, vol. 44, p. 258.

b Ibid., vol. 44, p. 224.

c Augusta Chronicle, July 13, 1833.

d Ga. Journal, Aug. 21, 1833.

e Augusta Constitutionalist, Oct. 18, 1833.

f M. B. Hammond, The Cotton Industry, p. 81.

removals to Cherokee Georgia.[a] A short period of residence in the northwestern district, however, led the immigrants from middle Georgia to realize that their new lands were as a rule unsuited to the system of cultivation by slave labor, and brought many of them to shift their party allegiance so as to oppose the aristocratic planters with whom they had formerly been in concert.

Several other features in the vote of 1833 deserve attention. The Clarke stronghold in Lincoln and Wilkes counties was carried by the enemy for the time being, on account of the popularity of the State Rights doctrine in that locality. Richmond County gave a majority of Union votes, though in 1831 it had been carried by Gilmer. This State Rights loss may be accounted for somewhat paradoxically by observing the existence in the county of the strongest nullification paper in the State. The Augusta Chronicle, formerly the Clarke organ, but at this time noisily in favor of nullification, insisted that the whole State Rights party believed in the most radical doctrine though it would not acknowledge its belief.[b] Such argument caused many State Rights men to vote the Union ticket in order to be certain that they were not upholding nullification.[c] The counties near Savannah changed from Troup to Union, partly upon principle and partly because of jealousy which arose between the eastern and the southern sections of the State seaboard.

Reflection by the State Rights party leaders upon the principles of the "force bill" and upon Jackson's proclamation against South Carolina led, after some months, to the adoption of a distinct platform for their party. This was done at an important State Rights meeting, held in Milledgeville on November 13, 1833, at which nearly all of the prominent men of the party were present. The meeting adopted a preamble stating the need of forming an association for counteracting the designs of those persons in Georgia and in the country at

[a] Macon Telegraph, Aug. 10, 1833. An institution of importance in making all the people wish to drive away the Indians was the land lottery. By the provisions of the lottery law a person was not required to go and dwell upon the homestead, but was given the privilege of selling his section of land. The governmental distribution of the lottery tickets to every family in the State gave to every Georgian a contingent interest in the lands, and made the classes vie with each other in the effort to have the lands thrown open for distribution and settlement. cf. Southern Recorder, May 1, 1835.

[b] Augusta Chronicle, Apr. 17, 1832.

[c] Ga. Journal, Aug. 21, 1833.

large who were inculcating the doctrine of consolidation and nationalism, and especially for systematically opposing the President's proclamation and the force bill, which had aimed a deadly blow at State rights. The preamble was followed by resolutions providing for the organization of a formal association to be known as the "State Rights party of Georgia," the creed of which was to be the Virginia and Kentucky resolutions as triumphantly acted upon by Georgia in her dealings with the Indians. They declared that laws infracting the rights of the States were null and void and would be resisted by the State Rights party. The resolutions repeated the condemnation of the force bill, and requested the Georgia Senators and Congressmen to demand its immediate repeal.[a]

From these resolutions, unanimously adopted by the meeting, it is clear that a rift had begun to appear between Andrew Jackson and the State Rights party of Georgia. The Union party in Georgia approved the force bill as one of the measures taken by the infallible Jackson. The State Rights leaders condemned the force bill, and necessarily criticised the President. It was not long before they were in outright opposition to Jackson and all that was Jacksonian.

Henry Clay had ingratiated himself with a large number of Southerners by proposing the compromise tariff of 1833. The common opposition of Clay and Calhoun and Berrien and Troup and Gilmer to Andrew Jackson, led in time to a coalition of all of them against Jackson and his friends. The breach of the State Rights party with Jackson had become complete in July, 1834, when Mr. Troup in a semi-public letter denounced the Administration as vicious and corrupt.[b] A further lapse of time was necessary, however, before the force of common enmity to a common foe could completely reconcile and combine the extreme anti-tariff men of the South with the champions of the "American system" elsewhere.

As the autumn of 1836 approached, the question of a successor to President Jackson became of engrossing interest. The Union party in Georgia had become an integral part of the "Jacksonian Democracy," and of course approved the candidacy of Van Buren. The State Rights leaders still claimed that their organization was a part of the true Demo-

---

aS. F. Miller, Bench and Bar of Georgia, vol. 1, p. 27.
eNiles's Register, vol. 46, p. 417.

cratic party, but they were thoroughly at loggerheads with Jackson and Van Buren. They followed a partly independent course in the campaign by supporting Hugh L. White, of Tennessee. The result of the contest in Georgia was a majority of some three thousand votes for Judge White over Mr. Van Buren.

Within the next year the Union party made a rally to retrieve its defeat in the Presidential campaign, but when the choice of governor was made in 1837 Gilmer, as the champion of State Rights, proved too strong for Schley,[a] who tried to obtain reelection. The election was very quiet, however, and the majority not a large one.

The years 1837 and 1838 were almost devoid of political interest, but were distinguished as a period of great financial depression. The chief matter of interest in the beginning of 1839 was the assembling of a State convention to reduce the excessive number of representatives in the legislature.[b] A similar convention had been held in 1833, but its recommendations had been rejected by the popular vote. The Union party had a majority in the convention of 1839, and used its power to some extent in arranging representation in a way to serve its own interests.[c] During the same year occurred a great agitation for temperance,[d] in the lead of which was Joseph Henry Lumpkin, who was made chief justice of the State upon the establishment of the supreme court some years later. In the gubernatorial election of 1839 the Union party was victorious, gaining for McDonald a victory over Dougherty.[e]

From 1837 to 1840 there was dragging a controversy between the State governments of Georgia and Maine. The governor of Georgia, according to resolutions of the legislature, demanded of the governor of Maine that two men at that time in the latter State should be given up to the authorities of Georgia to stand trial upon the charge of stealing slaves in Savannah. Maine refused the demand, and when Georgia's

---

[a] Augusta Chronicle, Nov. 9, 1837. In the election of 1835 William Schley, the Union candidate, had defeated Charles Dougherty by 2,571 majority; Savannah Georgian, Oct 30, 1835.

[b] Southern Banner (Athens), May 31, 1839.

[c] Ibid., June 7, 1839.

[d] Ibid., Aug. 16, 1839.

[e] Ibid., Oct. 19, 1839.

Congressmen decided that it would not be wise to push the matter at Washington the whole matter was dropped. [a]

In the Presidential campaign of 1840 the local parties in Georgia, following the indications which had been apparent for several years, became identified with the two national parties, and were known no more by the names of State Rights and Union.

To summarize the decade from 1830 to 1840, we have observed first a change working in response to the call "not men but measures," a change which culminated about 1833, but which at no time brought about a serious question of downright principle between the parties as actually constituted; then a retrograde tendency toward the former stage of personal politics, and finally a movement for the consolidation of the local with the national political parties, respectively. We noticed the strong power of economic and social differentiation and of personal habit and prejudice in keeping up the party organization on either side. At only one time was there any considerable bolting; a reorganization occurred in 1832–33, but the new parties retained, with slight changes, the constituencies of the parties which they had replaced. The county majorities in 1840 were by no means identical with those of 1825, but on the whole the relative situation of parties throughout the State in 1840 was very similar to that of fifteen years earlier.

The eastern section of the State continued its allegiance to the Troup party after it claimed the name State Rights, and indeed after it became part and parcel of the national Whig organization; while the whole of the mountainous north, much of the backwoods west, and most of the barren south maintained in the Union party the political opposition to the planter class. Large sections of western and southwestern Georgia were found to be fertile, and soon had a considerable proportion of aristocrats and State Rights voters in their population; but counties which contained lands not held in high esteem proved slow in yielding to the tendency to adopt State Rights principles. Slavery, as may be seen from any State or Federal census of the period, had spread to the westward, and also tended to increase in the southwest, but avoided the middle south.

[a] Southern Banner, Apr. 24, 1840.

The old semi-frontier still strikes the attention in the later maps. A description of the section, written by a traveler through it in 1831,[a] reminds one strongly of Irving's Sleepy Hollow. The people were poor, unenterprising, and unenlightened, but contented in their lowly circumstances. The pine woods stretched for scores of miles unbroken save by an occasional corn or cotton patch. The wire-grass beneath the pines, and here and there a few wild oats, furnished sustenance for ill-kept cattle. Few wagon roads existed, but bridle paths led from cabin to cabin. The State of North Carolina was dubbed the Rip Van Winkle of the South, but Emanuel and Tattnall counties and their neighborhood in Georgia could easily surpass any other section in sleeping ability. The people did not struggle against the enervating influence of their climate and surroundings. Without ambition or stimulus of any kind the life history of each generation was a repetition of that of the preceding one. Emanuel and Bullock counties of course continued to vote as of old, while Tattnall and Montgomery could not forget that Troup had honored them with his residence.

During the period from 1825 to 1840 there was unusual progress in Georgia in economic lines, chiefly regarding transportation. The great spur to enterprise was the need of better means of carrying cotton to market. In 1819 a steamboat began to ply from Milledgeville to Darien. Two years earlier the first ocean steamer to cross the Atlantic had sailed from the port of Savannah under the ownership of Savannah citizens.

There was much agitation concerning a system of canals for the State; but the first one of the proposed systems, dug to connect the Altamaha and Ogeechee rivers, proved a failure and damped the popular ardor for that kind of communication. Attention was then turned to railways as a better means of transportation. Wilson Lumpkin in 1826 surveyed a route from Milledgeville to Chattanooga for a railroad to be operated with mule power.[b] Steam locomotion on railways was accepted as feasible a few years later, and in 1836 and 1837 the work of building the "Central of Georgia" and the "Georgia" railroads was actually begun. The one was built northwestward from Savannah, the other westward from

[a] Augusta Constitutionalist, Oct. 18, 1831.
[b] W. Lumpkin, Incidents (MSS.).

Augusta, the main object of both being to connect the uplands of Georgia with the seaports.[a] In 1843 these two roads with their branches aggregated a total length of 400 miles, which was probably a greater mileage than was possessed by any other State at the time.[b]

Aside from the acquisition of new lands and the connection of her productive fields with the market, Georgia showed far too little enterprise in the period. Her railroads were not utilized in fostering any other industry than agriculture, and her resources did not increase as rapidly as did those of the Northern States. The belief was firm that cotton was king, that slavery was essential to its cultivation, and that it was not feasible to improve existing conditions. On the whole, the State was too much like its sleepy hollow; it preferred to go in well-worn ruts and to blaze no new paths. The attempt to introduce manufactures was only half-hearted, while in matters of statecraft the voting population was too willing not to worry itself with really important issues and to drop back into personal politics, with an occasional malediction upon the abolitionists, the protectionists, and the consolidationists in the North. Yet Georgia was quite as progressive as any of her neighbors, and no criticism can be laid upon her which must not be applied to the whole group of the Southern States.

[a] When completed, these roads reached a common terminus at the point from which the State of Georgia had already begun to build the Western and Atlantic Railroad to Chattanooga. At the point of junction a village was founded, which rapidly grew into the city of Atlanta. To this system was added a road leading through La Grange to Montgomery and the southwest. These radiating roads made Atlanta the strategic center of the whole South at the time of the civil war.

[b] Niles's Register, vol. 65, p. 272.

CHAPTER VI.—THE WHIGS AND THE DEMOCRATS: SLAVERY.

The Whig party, as a national organization, originated in a coalition of several smaller parties which in the beginning were not sympathetic with each other except in their antagonism to Andrew Jackson as President. The nucleus of the party existed as a faction hostile to Jackson in the all-comprehending Republican or Democratic-Republican party before 1832. During his second term of office Jackson's dictatorial proceedings alienated a number of his supporters, who in several groups joined the opposition. The most general reason for the defection was that the President was striving to exaggerate his prerogative beyond its natural and constitutional limits at the expense of the legislative branch of the Central Government. The one act of the President which excited most of the hostility against him was the destruction of the Bank of the United States by his executive edict.

But the State Rights party in Georgia was led to reverse its friendly attitude to Jackson through its resentment of his threat to coerce South Carolina in 1832–33. Although Mr. Clay was at the head of the combined anti-Jackson factions, it was Calhoun who was chiefly responsible for the course of action of the Georgia contingent. The crisis of the nullification struggle was reached early in 1833. In that year the attempt in Georgia to adopt political principles as differentiating the parties reached its nearest approach to success. The nullifiers approved of all of Calhoun's doctrines; the moderate State Rights faction sympathized with the nullifiers in their martyrdom to Federal tyranny. These two factions comprised the State Rights party of Georgia, which as a whole repudiated Jackson, and thereafter sought to defeat him and his followers. The assistance which the President had rendered Georgia in ridding her of the Indians was seen to have been rather from hostility to the red men than from

143

friendship to the rights of the State. The toast which he uttered in contrast to a sentiment on the rights of the States, "The Federal Union, it must be preserved," proved distasteful to State rights advocates, who, when they thought on the subject at all, took it as a matter of course that any State might secede from the Union at its pleasure.

Preparations were begun in Georgia as early as 1834 to defeat the wishes of Jackson in the choice of his successor in office. The arbitrary treatment of the bank in 1835 and 1836 added another count upon which its Georgia critics censured the Administration. But the breach had already been made; it could only be widened by this and later developments.

Martin Van Buren had never been held in very high esteem by the people of Georgia. The recent antagonism to the "American system" disqualified its champion, Henry Clay, as a candidate in the local field. But Hugh L. White was a very popular man in the State. The progress of opinion, then, brought it about that the State Rights party in Georgia should join the anti-Jackson or Whig party at large for the contest of 1836, and that Judge White, as its candidate, should receive the electoral vote of the State instead of Mr. Van Buren.

The fact that the local party acted with the Whigs at large in 1836 did not necessitate a permanent amalgamation with them, though it naturally had a tendency in that direction. The Whigs in 1836 stood upon no platform but that of opposition to Jackson, and did not even concentrate upon a candidate.[a] That there was no sympathy between the different divisions of the Whig party at the time of its birth, beyond that of opposition to a common adversary, is shown by the union within its ranks of the extreme high-tariff advocates in the East with the nullifiers, who were the extremists in the opposite direction, in the South.

The years of Van Buren's Administration were at the beginning of a period of reaction from political excitement in Georgia. The issues which had formerly been considered as crucial gradually lost their position of vital importance. The governor's message of 1839 stated that the Indian controversy was settled, that the high tariff and the exercise of doubtful powers had been abandoned by the Central Government, and that the spirit of fanaticism about slavery was being

[a] cf. Stanwood, History of Presidential Elections, p. 114.

overcome by reason.[a] But the peace and quiet did not strengthen the President. The financial stringency of 1837, which crippled all of the local banks, was laid at the door of Jackson and his right-hand man, Van Buren. The perversion of the executive patronage found many critics. The hard times not only continued for several years, but grew worse after a temporary improvement. Van Buren's strength in Georgia steadily grew less as the time approached for the election of 1840.

Throughout the interval from 1836 to 1840 the opposition at large was busy organizing its forces and consolidating its various factions into the Whig party, gradually approaching the adoption of positive political doctrines. The doctrines which its greater division favored were not entirely in accord with those of the State Rights party in Georgia, and that party was for the time placed in a position of indecision. The cardinal Whig plank was declared to be the checking of executive tyranny by strengthening Congress. With this the State Rights party agreed, though it held that a better check upon the President or upon Congress lay in the strict observance of the rights of the States.[b] Other items in the Whig creed were not so agreeable. It advocated the United States Bank, internal improvements, and a protective tariff. The issue of internal improvements, however, was deprived of importance by the development of railroads; the popular hostility to the bank had been greatly lessened by a counter hostility to Jackson's method of opposing it; while regarding the tariff, there was only a choice of evils—the Whigs were in favor of protection, and the Democrats had failed to live up to their promise against it. It was evident, too, that the Whig party stood in such need of assistance in the South that none of its doctrines would be pushed so far as to alienate the section. Both parties assumed practically the same position, for the time being, in regard to the slavery question in its various phases.

Other considerations than party platforms had weight in bringing the State Rights leaders to their decision. The Whigs nearly everywhere were the aristocrats, and so were congenial to the State Rights party in Georgia; the Union

a Niles's Register, vol. 57, p. 215.
b cf. Governor Gilmer's message of 1837, Niles's Register, vol. 53, p. 181.

party had already chosen the Democratic alignment, and it
was beyond the reasonable that their local opponents should
admit their superior wisdom in the choice of sides upon
national issues. The weight of the argument appearing to
rest with the Whigs, the majority of the State Rights party
decided to cast its lot with that organization. The strongest
statesmen of the nation were at that time in the Whig ranks,
viz, Webster, Clay, and, temporarily, Calhoun; and in
Georgia, Toombs, Stephens, Berrien, and Jenkins were the
equals or superiors of any others in the new generation of
political leaders in the State.

As was to be expected, there was some disagreement in
each of the local parties when they made their choice of alignment with the national parties. Early in 1840 it became
apparent that a good deal of confusion existed in State Rights
and Union ranks.[a] The leaders of the State Rights party
failed to agree upon supporting Harrison, and there were
three Congressmen in particular—Messrs. Black, Colquitt, and
Cooper—who openly supported Van Buren and entered the
Democratic ranks with a considerable number of State Rights
voters. These men were of course gladly received by their
new associates; they were at once returned to Congress, and
were later supported for other high offices by the Democratic
party.[b]

Ex-Governor Troup published a letter in June, 1840, approving of Van Buren's sub-treasury plan and showing that
some of the State Rights leaders would have preferred to
remain neutral in the Presidential contest.[c] Many members
of their party, whose sentiments were voiced by Alexander H.
Stephens, wished Troup himself to allow the use of his name
as a candidate;[d] but almost the whole party finally agreed
upon Harrison.

While Troup had become the prophet and honored adviser
of the State Rights party, Wilson Lumpkin held a similar
place among the Union voters. Lumpkin wrote several open
letters to the Union rank and file, declaring that Southern
people should not join the Whig party, whose Northern wing
was for abolition, and urging the candidacy of Van Buren as

a Southern Banner, June 26, 1840.
b Ibid., July 10 and 17, 1840, Jan. 21, 1841, and Oct. 28, 1842.
c Ibid., June 12, 1840.
d R. M. Johnston and W. H. Browne, Life of Alexander H. Stephens, p. 140.

against that of Harrison.[a] There was no bolting among the prominent Union leaders, but many voters for the time broke their connection with the party. Large districts of the back-woods were carried for Harrison in the "log cabin and hard cider" campaign, which usually voted with the Union party, and the Whigs carried the State with the very large majority of 8,340 votes. The strenuous labor of the Whig leaders in the State was partly responsible for the victory, but the dis-like for Van Buren and the popularity of "Tippecanoe and Tyler too" must account for its usual size.

The short period of the Whig party's strength, shown in Harrison's triumph of 1840, came to an end before the autumn of 1841, when McDonald of the Democrats defeated Dawson of the Whigs in the gubernatorial race with about 4,000 ma-jority. There was a good deal of excitement during the year over the proposed "relief laws," according to which the State was to borrow large sums of money, which were then to be loaned to such of the farmers as were in straitened circum-stances from the low price of cotton and the failure of crops. Owing mainly to the demonstration by Robert Toombs that the proposed laws were based upon faulty principles of finance they were defeated in the legislature, though most of the Democrats advocated their passage.[b] The project was a pop-ular one with the voters, and its defeat by the Whig leaders tended to hurt their party. The ascendancy of the Democrats continued through 1842, when their nominees for Congress were elected over the Whig candidates with an average ma-jority of 2,000 votes. That election was the last one in which Congressmen were chosen upon the system of the general ticket, for that system was superseded within the next two years by the method of election by districts, as now in use.

When George W. Crawford, a Whig, was elected over Mark A. Cooper in the gubernatorial contest of 1843 with a majority of above 3,000 votes, it was evident that the Demo-crats had in turn lost strength. The loss was explained, prob-ably with reason, by the statement that when the party had received into its ranks that section of the State Rights party which had refused to join the Whigs, the newcomers were so eagerly welcomed that nothing was considered too great for

[a] Southern Banner, May 22 and Sept. 11, 1840.
[b] P. H. Stovall, Life of Robert Toombs, pp. 34 to 37.

their reward; but when so many of the "State Rights Democrats" had so often been given support for office by the Union or "old line Democrats," the latter had grown lukewarm and the party had become weakened. The fact was pointed out that the candidate of the Democrats who had just been heavily defeated was himself one of the three Congressmen who had entered the party in 1840, and had constantly since then received that support which should in equity have been given to the older and more legitimate leaders of the party.[a] The policy of showering all their gifts upon the newcomers was then discarded by the Democrats, and its abandonment was probably one cause of their success in the next year.

During Tyler's Administration, from 1840 to 1844, the Whigs lost much of their strength in the South[b] because of the President's unusual deportment, and because the nationalist policy and the anti-slavery inclinations of the Northern wing of the party became more manifest. It became quite apparent that in joining the Whigs the State Rights party had in large measure abandoned its struggle for the particularist cause.

The preparations for the Presidential campaign of 1844 were begun almost as soon as the contest of 1840 had ended. The section of the State Rights party which had gone over to the Democrats in 1840 soon found itself again in harmony with Calhoun, and indeed urged his nomination for the Presidential contest of 1844;[c] for Calhoun had left the Whig ranks upon being convinced that he could not succeed in inducing the party to look upon the Federal Constitution from the point of view of State sovereignty. Many State Rights men who remained with the Whigs only decided to do so after much hesitation. The Whigs seemed almost declared enemies, and the Democrats were thought to have proved treacherous friends. The decision was finally made by such men as Stephens and Toombs to go with the Whigs, with the half-conceived intention of dominating the party and forcing it to act in a way suitable to the Southern interest. By this division of the South between the two national parties the section, which was in a decided minority, still controlled the legislation of the country for twenty years longer. It was a

[a] Southern Banner, Oct. 12, 1843.
[b] Lumpkin to Calhoun, Nov. 15, 1841, Calhoun's Letters, p. 832
[c] Southern Banner, May 12 and June 16, 1843.

wise course of action for the time being, but not so in view of the irrepressible character of the conflict then lowering.

The Whig leaders in Gergia were politicians of much adroitness. They realized the difficulty of their position and made the best they could of it. Their problem was, on the one hand, to keep the whole Whig party united, and, on the other, as far as possible to make the party recognize and uphold the principal claims of the South. To gain the confidence and full alliance of the Northern Whigs it was necessary to make ostensible concessions. To this end the Georgia Whig leaders made a show of supporting the plan of a protective tariff. We accordingly find Mr. Berrien addressing the United States Senate upon the subject on April 9, 1844. He said that he objected to the agitation in favor of lower duties. The United States should be industrially independent. The American workman should be protected from the competition of the pauper labor of Europe. The tariff of 1842, a revenue tariff with protective features, he considered not hurtful to any section. On the contrary, the whole country had been improved by the system of moderate protection, and that system ought to be continued. On the next day Mr. Colquitt, a Democratic Senator from Georgia, replied to Mr. Berrien. He showed the contrast between Berrien's position in 1831 and his position in 1844, and went on to answer his recent arguments before the Senate by advancing the doctrine and arguments of the State Rights party in 1831. Protection to industries, he thought, was now no less odious and unconstitutional than formerly, and the tariff of 1842, the work of the Whigs, was in his opinion the worst yet enacted. He concluded by censuring the Whigs for keeping the tariff in the background in the presidential campaign. On May 7 Mr. Stephens expressed sentiments in the House quite similar to those voiced by Mr. Berrien in the Senate.[a]

It is to be noted that these Georgia Whigs did not advocate an outright protective tariff. A very high tariff in which the revenue feature was distinctly secondary would not have been supported anywhere in the South. Such a tariff was not in contemplation in the Whig period. Berrien and Stephens and

[a] Speech of Berrien, Congressional Globe, Appendix, 1st sess. 28th Cong., pp. 492 ff. Speech of Colquitt, ibid., pp. 498 f. Speech of Stephens, ibid., p. 582.

Toombs[a] did not sacrifice a principle which was at that time important. Their policy was that of conciliation and ingratiation, and their concession upon the tariff was simply a means to an end in practical politics.

The Whig convention of 1844 nominated Henry Clay for the Presidency. Mr. Clay had many ardent admirers among influential Georgians, but he had destroyed his prospects of carrying any considerable portion of the South by committing himself against the annexation of Texas. The Southern Democrats were able to secure the nomination in their party for James K. Polk, who was known to be strongly in favor of annexing Texas.[b] Most of the local Whig leaders, however, stood firm in their loyalty to Clay. The strong organization of the Whig party and the personal popularity of its candidate, notwithstanding the Texas question, were exhibited by the comparatively small majority of 2,000 votes which Polk obtained in Georgia.

The composition and the development of the Whig party had not been quite rational from the beginning, and the elements composing the Democratic organization were but little more congruous. About 1845, the dissatisfaction of the populace of Georgia with the trend of national politics became quite manifest. The Whigs were successful in the State for the next four or five years, chiefly because of the strength and magnetism of their leaders and the popularity of the candidates put forward by them. The local leaders had tact enough to avoid national issues and to emphasize the personal reasons for supporting the candidates of their party.[c] Taylor and Fillmore carried Georgia in 1848, because many of the Democrats feared that Cass was not sufficiently proslavery.[d]

It was a matter of general note that the Southern wings of both parties had grown out of sympathy with the Northern divisions, especially in the case of the Whigs. It is remarkable that most of the Whig leaders in Georgia did not follow the lead of Calhoun in going over to the Democrats; but in truth the parties were not antagonistic upon the important

a For the position of Toombs in regard to the tariff, see Stovall's Toombs, p. 31.

b For anxiety of the Southern Democrats on the subject, see Southern Banner, May 23, 1844.

c Southern Banner. Sept. 4, 1845.

d Federal Union (Milledgeville, Ga.), Dec. 26, 1848.

issue of the epoch, i. e., slavery, and as a rule they stood as units only upon minor questions.[a]

The Southern wing of each party tried long and strenuously to control the actions and policy of its respective party as a whole, but toward 1850 the representatives from the North in Congress grew very restless under the domination, and issues at Washington assumed an alarming appearance. Disruption of the Union seemed imminent, but the disaster was still postponed for a decade by the last of Clay's great compromises.

The fundamental question of the perpetuity of slavery in America, which had for so many years been persistently held in the background by Southern statesmen, finally asserted itself during Polk's administration, as a crucial issue which could not thereafter be made to down until the arbitrament of civil war brought about its absolute settlement.

It is here advisable to make an investigation of the status of slavery in Georgia with its hardships and its mitigations, to study the sentiment of the people regarding the institution, and to notice the progress of opinion in other parts of the country.

The colony of Georgia was established by Oglethorpe on a plan which was truly Utopian. It was to be a refuge for honest people suffering from oppression, a land where every man should earn his bread by the sweat of his brow and live contented in honorable poverty, where there should be no envy, no harshness, and no riotous living. But the plans laid out for the colony were no more applicable than were the fundamental constitutions which John Locke formulated for Carolina. They disregarded human nature, the spirit of the times, and the climate and soil of the country to be settled. The cultivation of silk and grapes proved impracticable; the deprivation of alcoholic liquors would not be borne by the colonists; the subjugation of the rich swamp land near the coast was declared impossible except by slaves from Africa, who would not be affected by the miasma. The colony of Georgia remained a flat failure until the restrictions differentiating it from the typical English colony were removed. From that time the success and prosperity of Georgia were assured. The tradition of the hard times when slaves were forbidden tended to make later generations in Georgia the more doubtful of the

[a] Federal Union, Oct. 6, 1850.

possibility of prospering without the benefits of the peculiar institution.

As regards the lot of the negro slave, it was neither better nor worse than in the average American colony or slave State. The police regulations, as they appeared upon the statute books, were very harsh in several respects, but their rigor was considerably diminished as the years passed and as masters and slaves came the better to understand each the nature and disposition of the other. The first enactment regulating the status of slaves in Georgia was approved by the Crown, March 7, 1755, to be in force for three years. It was reenacted in 1759 to extend to 1764. It was continued with some modifications by a law of 1765 and was further changed in some details in 1770. Upon the achievement of independence the somewhat lightened system of slave law was continued by State authority.[a]

The following regulations were in force during the whole or a part of the period in which slavery existed in colonial Georgia. All negroes, mulattoes, mestizoes, and other persons of color, except Indians in amity with the colony, were presumed to be slaves unless the contrary could be established. A slave must not be absent from the town or plantation where he belonged without a ticket from his master or overseer. When found violating this law a slave might be punished by any white person. In case the slave should strike the white person, he might lawfully be killed. Patrols were organized throughout the province, with the duty of riding at least one night in each fortnight to visit the several plantations in each district, and to whip every slave found abroad without a ticket. Slaves might not buy or sell provisions or similar articles without a ticket.[b]

The following offenses were capital crimes when committed by a slave: Burning stacks of rice or stores of tar, or destroying similar valuable commodities; insurrection, or the attempt to excite it; enticing away slaves, or the attempt; poisoning, or the attempt; rape, or the attempt on a white female; assault on a white person with a dangerous weapon; maiming a white person; burglary; arson; murder of a slave or free

---

[a] Colonial acts of Georgia (Wormsloe Print), pp. 73 to 99, and p. 164. Marbury and Crawford, Compilation of the Laws of Georgia, pp. 419 and 424. Watkins's Compilation of Georgia Laws, p. 163. Lamar's Digest of the Laws of Georgia, p. 804.

[b] For patrol laws in a later period, see Acts of Ga. Gen. Assem., 1853–54, p. 101.

negro. A slave might be tried for a capital offense by two justices of the peace and three freeholders, or for an offense not capital by one justice and two freeholders. Free negroes were included under most of the slave regulations.

The earliest law was positively barbarous in some of its provisions, such as the offer of rewards for the scalps of slaves escaped beyond the Florida boundary, and the fixing of the limit of the legal working day for slaves at sixteen hours. The harshest provisions of the first laws were not continued longer than 1765.

In order to prevent the attempt of owners to conceal the crimes of their slaves, there was for a long time a provision of the law that slaves legally executed should be appraised and their value paid to the master by the province or State.[a]

There was perpetual fear of slave insurrection, though in the early decades of the nineteenth century there was less uneasiness than in the preceding or the succeeding period. The law required a white man to live constantly on each plantation, and it prohibited more than seven negro men from traveling on a road together without a white man in their company.[b] The institution of domestic servitude was considered to require that the slave remain without literary education. The acts of 1755 and 1770 forbade anyone to teach a slave to write.[c] In 1829 it was enacted that any negro or white person teaching a negro to read or write should be whipped, fined, or imprisoned.[d] A law of the same year prohibited, under a small fine, the employment of any negro in the setting of type in any printing office.[e] A frontiersman, more fearful than persons who lived in the black belt, urged that negroes should not be allowed to assemble to themselves because they were known to study their hymn books and so evade the law against negro education.[f]

Many of these laws stood unenforced, except on very rare occasions. In most cases the master rendered informal justice on his own plantation, except in very serious matters. The

---

[a] Law of 1755 (limit of £50); Colonial Acts of Georgia, p. 73. Law of 1770 (limit of £40); Watkin's Compilation of the Laws of Georgia, p. 163. Marbury and Crawford, p. 424. Repealed in 1793; Watkins, p. 530. Marbury and Crawford, p. 440.

[b] Law of 1755, supra. Law of 1770, supra.

[c] The penalty was fixed at a fine of £10 in 1770. Watkin's Compilation, p. 163.

[d] Dawson, Compilation of the Laws of Georgia, p. 413.

[e] Acts of Georgia General Assembly, 1829, p. 175.

[f] Article signed "Frontier," Georgia Journal, Dec. 12, 1831.

protection as well as the punishment of the slave was largely in the master's hands. But the law provided that in case of murder or malicious killing of a slave the trial and punishment should be the same as if the victim had been a white person.[a] A like regulation was made in regard to beating a slave without just cause.[b]

Slavery was distinctly a patriarchal institution. Except in the seacoast swamps and a few other malarial regions, the master lived throughout the year in the "big house" on his plantation, with the negro cabins grouped in "quarters" only a few yards away. The field hands were usually under their owner's personal supervision, while the house servants were directed by their mistress. The slaves were governed by harsh overseers only in very rare cases. Great numbers of slaveholders owned a very small number of slaves, and labored with them in the fields. The cabins of the negroes were frequently as good as those of the poorer whites. The fact that they were not always clean was due to the habits of their occupants.

It was, of course, to the interest of the master that his slaves should remain in the best possible condition. The Southern gentleman was widely known for his generosity and his innate kindness. The children of the two races were brought up as playmates, the mother of the pickaninnies frequently being the "mammy" of the master's children; and friendships enduring through life were contracted in early youth between the master and his hereditary servants. To illustrate the consideration which owners frequently felt for their slaves, we may cite an advertisement stating that several negroes were to be sold "for no fault, but merely on account of their unwillingness to leave the country with their master."[c]

The law did not recognize family relations among slaves, but public opinion condemned the separation of husband and wife or parent and child. Where such separation occurred through the division of estates or otherwise it was not unusual for one of the owners to buy the members of the family which he did not already possess.[d]

These considerations which indicate the existence of a softer

a Law of 1799; Marbury and Crawford, p. 443.

b Law of 1805; Clayton, Compilation, p. 269.

c Augusta Herald, Dec. 25, 1799.

d e. g. Sale by A. H. Stephens of a family of slaves to Mr. Scott, who owned the father, 1848; W. J. Scott, Seventy-one Years in Georgia, p. 30.

side to the slave system than that which such prejudiced observers as Olmsted and Frances Kemble have described, are not here cited to justify the perpetuation of slavery, but to show why the Southern people, who were intimately acquainted with negro character and with the mild nature of his servitude, were less prone to condemn the system than were those who stood afar off and ostentatiously washed their hands of the whole foul business.

Free persons of color were not generally held in high repute by the people of the South. In Georgia they usually numbered somewhat less than one per cent of the colored population. As a class they were considered lazy, trifling, and thievish, and were suspected of corrupting the slaves. There were a few brilliant exceptions in the State,[a] but by no means enough to affect the general sentiment.

All free negroes who were not industrious loved town life and avoided the country. A law passed in 1807 provided that " Whereas the citizens of Savannah and Augusta and their vicinities have heretofore and do now experience great injury and inconvenience from the numbers of free negroes, mulattoes, and mestizoes of vicious and loose habits who have settled and are daily settling therein," free negroes in Savannah, Augusta, Milledgeville, and Louisville were to be subject to the same police regulations as slaves. A penalty was set upon the hiring of any house to a free negro without permission of the city council or commissioners.[b]

Since the principles of sound policy were considered to require that the number of free negroes in the State should not be increased, an act, of 1818, forbade the entrance into Georgia of all free persons of color, with a few specified exceptions, fixing a penalty of a fine or sale into slavery. The provision for sale into slavery was repealed in 1824, but the law was reenacted in 1859, with only seamen excepted, and with the unvarying penalty of sale into life servitude. Another law of 1859 directed that vagrant free negroes be sold as slaves for a definite period for the first offense, and for life for a second offense.[c]

[a] E. g. Austin Dabney, in Gilmer, Georgians, p. 212. E. g. Wilkes Flagg, in Federal Union, June 11 and July 23, 1861.

[b] Clayton, Compilation of the Laws of Georgia, p. 369.

[c] Lamar, Compilation, p. 611. Acts of Ga. Gen. Assem., 1859, pp. 68 and 69. The reactionary legislation of 1859 was the result, of course, of the attempt of John Brown to arouse an insurrection.

Every free person of color in Georgia was required to have a guardian who was responsible for his good behavior, and whose permission must be obtained before the negro could have liberty to do certain things. Moreover, all free negroes must register annually with the county officials and be able to give a good account of themselves. No such persons were allowed to own or to carry firearms of any description.[a]

The ill esteem in which free negroes were generally held led to the policy of discouraging manumission. In 1801 all deeds of emancipation were made illegal except by act of the legislature. This was so far repealed in 1815 as to permit an owner to free his slave by will and testament. An act of 1818 rendered void all subsequent manumission by testament. This was later repealed, and was reenacted in 1859.[b] A prominent Georgia editor wrote, in 1829, that slavery was bad enough, but manumission in a slave State, without exporting the negroes, was dreadful. "Experience proves," he wrote, "that there is no condition of humanity which begets more wretchedness, more vice, more premature disease and mortality than that of emancipated negroes who remain without political rights in the midst of a free white population."[c] It was well known by those who took pains to inform themselves that, as compared with the free blacks in New England, the slaves in Georgia were frequently the better clothed, better fed, better taught, and better treated by their superiors.[d]

Although manumission was discouraged by law, it was by no means completely stopped as a custom. Special acts were passed nearly every year to give freedom to specified slaves whose masters wished to manumit them, usually on the ground of good service. In at least one case the legislature appropriated money to purchase a negro in order to set him free in reward for a praiseworthy deed.[e]

During the period before the abolition agitation, the leading thinkers in Georgia, and probably the bulk of the people,

[a] Prince, Digest of 1837, p. 808. Lamar, Digest, p. 811 (partially repealed in 1819). Prince, Digest of 1837, p. 808.

[b] Clayton, Compilation, p. 27. Lamar, Compilation, pp. 801 and 811. Acts of Ga. Gen. Assem., 1859, p. 68.

[c] Athenian, Aug. 25, 1829, referring to an article in the Baltimore American.

[d] Athenian, Feb. 9, 1830, referring to an article of the same tenor in the Genius of Universal Emancipation.

[e] Negro named Sam set free at cost to the State of $1,600, as a reward for extinguishing fire on the State House. Message of Governor Lumpkin, 1834; Ga. Senate Journal, 1834, p. 25.

considered slavery an evil. While no way of abandoning the system was seen to be practicable at the time, it was hoped that some feasible means would in the future be found to accomplish that object. Meanwhile the introduction of great numbers of slaves was considered undesirable.

We have seen in a former chapter that the delegates from Georgia in the Federal convention of 1787 insisted on legalizing the slave trade. But that the State authorities did not long hold the position of its delegates in 1787 is shown by the act of the legislature in 1798, which prohibited the importation of Africans from abroad after July 1 of that year.[a]

In the same year, 1798, a law was enacted against the interstate slave trade. This law was reenacted in 1817, repealed in 1824, reenacted in 1829, modified in 1836, repealed in 1842, and reenacted with alterations in 1851.[b] The general tenor of the law throughout the period was that a citizen of Georgia might introduce slaves into the State for his own service, or an immigrant might bring his slave property when settling in Georgia; but no one could bring in slaves for the speculative purposes of selling or hiring them. We have noticed that these statutes were not always in force. It is further true that they were openly violated with extreme frequency. The grand jury of Putman County presented as a grievance in 1817, that 20,000 slaves had been illegally brought into Georgia within the past year.[c]

The laws against the foreign slave trade were also sometimes violated. There were several conspicuous instances of this between 1815 and 1825.[d] The violations, however, were usually punished by the State authorities.[e] Gen. D. B. Mitchell, who had resigned the office of governor of Georgia to become United States agent to the Creeks, was concerned in the illegal introduction of Africans in 1819. General Clarke, then governor of the State, charged Mitchell with the offense and caused the President to dismiss him from the agency.[f]

a Dawson, Compilation, p. 673.

b Augusta Chr nicle, Sept. 26, 1817. Dawson, Compilation, pp. 411 and 673. Acts of Ga. Gen. Assem., 1829, p. 169. Acts of Ga. Gen. Assem., 1836, p. 254. Acts of Ga. Gen. Assem., 1842. Acts of Ga. Gen. Assem., 1851, p. 865.

c Augusta Chronicle, October 11, 1817.

d Special message of Governor Rabun, Nov. 11, 1818, Niles's Register, vol. 15, p. 359. Petition of R. H. Wilde, 1827, Niles's Register, vol. 32, p. 349.

e Lamar, compilation, p. 808. Georgia Journal, Aug. 16, 1818. Niles's Register, vol. 17, p. 221.

f Niles's Register, vol 18, p. 118, and vol. 20, p. 116.

The better enforcement of the law was secured in general by the offer of a reward by the State to persons seizing slaves illegally introduced.[a]

The invention of the cotton gin is usually said to have been very influential in prolonging the existence of slavery in America. This is quite true; but, on the other hand, negro labor was never considered absolutely essential in the cultivation of the short-staple cotton,[b] while in the district which produced rice and sugar and sea-island cotton it was almost fatal for white men to do agricultural labor. There was apparently a steady advance of sentiment in Georgia against the justice of slavery from the time of the adoption of the Federal Constitution until Garrison began his raging; no reaction is discernible as resulting from the extension of cotton production.

Gradual emancipation was thought to be the only practicable method of ridding the country of slavery; but the idea could not be borne of having the land filled with free negroes. The plan of colonizing the blacks in Africa was welcomed as a solution of the problem. The first colonization society in the United States was established in 1817.[c] The society soon became national. Numerous branches of it were established in Georgia, and considerable sums of money were subscribed for the furtherance of its objects. A number of Africans who had been illegally introduced were, by a legislative act, directed to be turned over to the colonization society[d] instead of being sold to the highest bidder, as was usually the custom.

The influence of the colonization society brought about a small wave of humanitarian feeling which was quite noticeable in Georgia.[e] One of the representatives of the State declared in Congress that he was desirous of seeing the negroes set free, though he condemned the plan of clothing them with American citizenship.[f] An editorial in the Georgia Journal, probably at that time the strongest newspaper in the State,

[a] Ga. Journal, Dec. 22, 1818.

[b] Cf. Niles's Register, vol. 18, p. 47 (Mar. 18, 1820).

[c] For the history of the colonization society, see J. H. T. McPherson, History of Liberia, in Johns Hopkins University Studies in Historical and Political Science.

[d] Act of 1817; Lamar, compilation, p. 808. For establishment of a branch of the colonization society at Milledgeville and subscription of money to carry back the negroes illegally imported, see Georgia Journal, May 11, 1819.

[e] Cf. Niles's Register, vol. 18, p. 25.

[f] A. H. Stephens, War between the States, vol. 2, p. 143. Annals of Congress, 16th Cong., 1st sess., p. 1025.

published as its conviction, "There is not a single editor in these States who dares advocate slavery as a principle." [a]

But the Southern people were not thoroughgoing in their desire to be rid of slavery. The movement in the North soon progressed further than the bulk of the Southerners were inclined to go. At once the South became sensitive and resentful of intermeddling with its institutions. Apropos of a resolution offered in Congress by Mr. King of New York that the proceeds of the sale of the public lands be applied to the purchase of the freedom of the slaves, and in anger at certain reputed remarks of the United States Attorney-General criticising slavery, Governor Troup sent a fiery message to the Georgia legislature in 1825. "Temporize no longer," said he. "Make known your resolution that this subject shall not be touched by them but at their peril. * * * I entreat you most earnestly, now that it is not too late, to step forward, and having exhausted the argument, to stand by your arms." [b] The leading organ of the Troup party applauded the governor's message, but the legislature was not disposed to adopt his extreme position at that time, though in 1828 it adopted resolutions which were as strong as Troup could have desired on the subject. [c]

As soon as the difference of opinion became apparent between the North and the South as to the feasibility of rapid emancipation, the colonization society was seen to be inefficient for the contingency. The South thought it too radical, the North considered it as a half-hearted project at best. The Georgia legislature roundly condemned the society in 1827, declaring in most positive terms that the General Government had no constitutional right to appropriate money for its assistance. [d]

The South always became extremely sensitive when any criticism on the moral rectitude of slavery was made by Northern writers. A Southern editor might obtain the attentive and even the approving notice of his readers when he demonstrated the evil of slavery and advocated its gradual abolition, but the same readers would feel outraged by attacks

a Georgia Journal, Jan. 9, 1821.
b May 23, 1825. Niles's Register, vol. 28, p. 238.
c Acts of Ga. Gen. Assem., 1828, p. 174.
d Acts of Ga. Gen. Assem. 1827, p. 109.

upon the institution which came from the North; and the very same editor would cry out to the South that its liberties and its constitutional rights were threatened with dreadful invasion from the determined enemies of the section.[a] The circulation of seditious pamphlets among the slaves was especially feared, and the penalty of death was set for anyone convicted of distributing them.[b] The better to prevent the success of such literature, the laws against negro education were made more sweeping.

The publication of violent abolition propaganda began to be noticed and resented by Georgia about 1828. Special attention was paid William Lloyd Garrison in 1831. An editor explained his actions on the ground of insanity, but urged the State executive to demand his rendition by the governor of Massachusetts, as an offender against the laws of Georgia.[c] The legislature adopted a different plan; it offered a reward of $5,000 for the apprehension and conviction in the Georgia courts of any of the editors or printers of the Liberator.[d] Of course this was not expected to lead to the capture and trial of Garrison, but was simply a manifesto showing the attitude of the State government toward the abolitionists.

The Southern leaders knew that the abolitionists were a small though noisy faction, and that their violent doctrines were condemned by all reasonable people at the North. Nevertheless the rapid increase in the numbers and importance of the agitators soon caused general alarm in the South.[e] The governor of Georgia in 1835 considered the abolitionists few and contemptible, but prophesied the dangerous results, and advised precautionary measures on the part of the South.[f] The legislature reviewed the whole range of the slavery questions and declared its convictions upon each. It stated that it was the duty of the North to crush the abolitionists; that Congress should regulate the postal laws to prevent the circulation of inflammatory matter; that Congress could not constitutionally interfere with slavery in the District of Columbia or in the Territories. The sixth article of the resolutions is

[a] Athenian, Jan. 25, 1828, Feb. 6, 1826, and May 10, 1831.
[b] Law of 1829. Dawson, Compilation, p. 413.
[c] Athenian, Nov. 1, 1831.
[d] Acts of Ga. Gen. Assem. 1831, p. 255.
[e] Georgia Journal, June 30, 1835.
[f] Message of Governor Schley, Nov. 4, 1835; Niles's Register, vol. 49, p. 187.

important in that it pointed the way to the position reached by the South some twenty years later, that the Missouri compromise was unconstitutional in its principle. The article reads:

"*Resolved*, That the District of Columbia and the several Territories of the United States are the common property of the people of these States; that the right of exclusive legislation in the former, and the power to make all needful rules and regulations for the government of the latter, which are vested in the Congress of the United States, are derived from the Constitution, which recognizes and guarantees the rights resulting from domestic slavery; and that any interference by that body with those rights will be unauthorized by and contrary to the spirit of that sacred charter of American liberty." [a]

The contention for the legality of slavery in all of the Territories had not previously been made, because it had not been seen to be necessary in preserving the equilibrium between the slave and free States. It was not taken up by the Southern statesmen for the next fifteen years, because their attention was directed to the annexation of Texas as a better means of attaining the same object.

The slave owners were anxious to increase the area of slaveholding not because of any anticipated benefits to the territory secured, but in order to gain more representative strength for the slave interest, so as to prevent the possibility of the overthrow of the institution by the powerful North against the opposition of the Southern minority. The free States had long controlled the lower House of Congress, but with great effort the South was able to keep the balance in the Senate.

The West was seen to be rapidly developing; several of the organized Territories north of the line of 36° 30′ were ready for statehood, while the available area for the erection of new slaveholding States was very restricted. Antislavery sentiment had become very powerful in the North, showing itself in abolition petitions, in the obstructions to the capture of fugitive slaves, and in efforts to restrict the area of slavery. The South was obliged to take more radical ground if it did not wish the defeat of its contentions.

[a] Acts of Ga. Gen. Assem., 1835, p. 299.

H. Doc. 702, pt. 2——11

When they considered it necessary for the welfare of the section, the Southern leaders did not hesitate to advocate measures which were dangerous to the integrity of the Union. Ex-Governor Lumpkin, in 1847, advocated the organization of the South to resist the aggression of the North. He expressed great love for the Union, but preferred its dissolution to the oppression and destruction which he foretold as a consequence of the Wilmot proviso. He saw the great struggle between free and slave States rapidly approaching, and lamented that the South was not united under resolute leadership.[a]

A complex of disputed measures presented themselves before Congress in 1849, the amicable solution of which promised to tax the powers of the pacificators. The unsettled question of the western boundary of Texas and the assumption of its State debt were made issues between the slave and free States; a recent decision of the Supreme Court denying the obligation of State officials to enforce the laws of the United States necessitated some new legislation for the rendition of fugitive slaves; the application of California for statehood without slavery was an encroachment upon the territory which the South considered as in a measure pledged to slavery; and the attack upon the slave trade in the District of Columbia, at this time becoming very vigorous, was feared by the South as an opening wedge for the overthrow of the system.

Upon all of these questions the two national parties were split into pieces. The turbulence of the Congressional session of 1849–50 was introduced by a bitter struggle over the election of the Speaker of the lower House. The Georgia Whigs were anxious for the Southern wings of both parties to unite and elect a Southern man by the votes chiefly of Southern Representatives, but their plan was not followed. Scores of ballots were taken without a majority being cast for any candidate. The Whigs and the Democrats voted for members of their own parties, but the Northern and Southern wings of either failed to concentrate upon any one man, while the small delegation of the new Free Soil party added to the confusion. At length the proposition was made to choose a Speaker by a mere plurality vote. Mr. Toombs, of Georgia, protested vigorously and violently against the scheme, but in vain.[b] The decisive ballot was at length reached. Howell

[a] Calhoun's Letters, pp. 1102 and 1133.
[b] Stephens's War between the States, vol. 2, pp. 161 to 195.

Cobb, of Georgia, was elected by a plurality vote from the Democrats, while the Georgia Whigs connived at the result by throwing away their votes on a member who was not a candidate for the chair.[a]

The several vexed issues on slavery were introduced into each House and heated debates arose over them. Some of the bills were to the advantage of the South, while others were against the slave interest. The altercation became violent, but Mr. Clay rose to the occasion and brought in the last of his great compromise measures, in the shape of a bill including all of the bills connected with slavery which were then before Congress. This omnibus bill was on the whole of decided advantage to the South. Among the most conspicuous supporters of the compromise were Toombs and Stephens, of Georgia, who foretold disunion and threatened dire calamities if it should fail of passage. Mr. Calhoun, speaking almost from his deathbed, warned the Senate against the consequences of intolerance, while Mr. Webster in his famous 7th of March speech, in advocacy of prudence and moderation, urged tolerance on the part of the North for the contentions of the South. The omnibus bill itself was destroyed by amendments; but at length all of the measures contained in it were adopted by Congress. Restricted limits were fixed for Texas, but a large indemnity was given the State. California was admitted without slavery. New Mexico and Utah were erected as Territories with nothing said as to slavery. The slave trade was abolished for the District of Columbia, and a fugitive slave law was enacted which gave promise of being efficient.

In the fall of 1850 the people of Georgia, through a partial misunderstanding of the compromise, were plainly opposed to it.[b] Earlier in the year the governor and the legislature had provided for the meeting of a State convention which should decide upon the course of action which Georgia should pursue. The attitude of those calling the convention had been one of alarm at the developments and tendencies in Congress and of anxiety for the adoption by the South of some policy for the defense of the section. The Representatives of Georgia had considered the emergency extremely dangerous to the interests of the South, and their speeches in Congress had been

[a] Congressional Globe, Dec. 22, 1849.   [b] Federal Union, Oct. 6, 1850.

highly threatening and inflammatory; but these speeches had been made with the object of controlling the North by fear of disruption, so as to make it possible for the South to remain in the Union.[a] The people of Georgia, however, had not been shown the underlying intention of their Representatives, and taking their fire-eating speeches and their awful prophesyings in dead earnest had grown so much excited as to be almost ready for immediate secession.[b] For more than a year the people had been wrought up over the probable passage of the Wilmot Proviso, the object of which was to exclude slavery from the Southwestern Territories. Although that measure had been defeated, certain other contentions had been won by the Free States, and the passage of the compromise did not put an end to the agitation. Mass meetings of the citizens in the summer of 1850 listened with approval to speeches on the infractions of Southern rights and the advisability of secession from Rhett of South Carolina, McDonald of Georgia, and Yancey of Alabama.[c]

But the Georgia Congressmen returned from Washington in September, and the triumvirate—Toombs, Stephens, and Howell Cobb—set about demonstrating to the populace that the South had won a great victory by the compromise, and that by far the best course of action under the circumstances was to accept it as the basis for continuity of the Union. The trio took the stump in Georgia with great energy, and speedily reversed the tide of public opinion in the causing of which they had been so largely responsible. As the result of their efforts, the delegates to the convention, who were elected in November, were Union men in immense majority, whereas before the arrival of the Congressmen in the State many voices had demanded of the coming convention open resolutions of resistance to the North, and even the moderates wanted the body simply to meet and adjourn without action.[d]

Toombs, Stephens, and Cobb seized upon the convention as a great opportunity for good to their cause. By bringing about the election of Union delegates and defeating the resist-

[a] Johnston and Browne, Life of Stephens, p. 245. Federal Union, Oct. 15, 1850. Cf. J. F. Rhodes' History of the United States, vol. 1, p. 134. Also Coleman, Life of Crittenden, vol. 1, p. 365, and Stovall, Life of Toombs, pp. 76 to 80.

[b] Federal Union, Oct. 8, 1850.

[c] J. C. Butler, Historical Record of Macon, Ga., p. 194.

[d] Federal Union, Oct. 15 and Dec. 3, 1850. Stovall, Life of Toombs, p. 64.

ance men, they prepared the way for the adoption, by the supposedly resistance gathering, of the pacific policy embodied in the celebrated Georgia Platform.[a] The platform set forth that, though the State was not entirely content with the compromise just reached by Congress, still upon the ground of its provisions Georgia was willing and anxious to remain in the United States; but that in case of the slightest further encroachment by the North, the attitude of Georgia would at once be reversed and disruption would most probably ensue. The platform was adopted by the convention with the surprising vote of 237 to 19.[b]

By the action of their delegates the people of Georgia, bringing to a halt the progress of resistance doctrines, caused public opinion throughout the South to set in the opposite direction, and began the revival of the conviction that the necessity for preserving the Union overbalanced the wrongs which the South had suffered up to that time.[c]

The work of the Georgia convention of 1850 was not the result of the efforts of either of the political parties, but of a coalition comprised of nearly all the Whigs in Georgia and a strong section of the Democrats, led by Howell Cobb and located chiefly in the northern counties of the State. The local opposition to the acceptance of the compromise came almost entirely from Democrats. It is apparent, then, that each party had in large measure reversed its position regarding the rights of the States since the nullification controversy. Yet the contentions of the friends and the opponents of the Georgia platform in 1850 were not radically different. Practically all Georgians believed that the rights of the South had been invaded. The point of difference was whether the encroachments made forcible resistance advisable.

Although the platform was adopted in the convention by an overwhelming majority, it was realized that there existed strong popular disapproval of any semblance of a sacrifice of Southern rights. The necessity was felt for an organization which would firmly uphold the principles of the compromise. There was therefore held on the night of December 12, 1850,

[a] Gilmer, Georgians, p. 576.
[b] Journal of the State Convention of 1850. Johnston and Browne, Life of Stephens, p. 259.
[c] Von Holst, Constitutional History of the United States, vol. 4, p. 6.

166

between the sessions of the convention, a meeting of the prominent members of that body, at which it was resolved that party alignments as then existing were illogical and hurtful to the country and should be destroyed.[a]

At that meeting a new political party was organized for Georgia, with Toombs and Stephens responsible for its existence. All friends of the Union were invited to join the Constitutional Union Party, which laid down as the guide for its actions the platform adopted by the Georgia convention, and which nominated Howell Cobb as its candidate for governor in 1851. Cobb, as a Democrat, had always before been opposed by Toombs and Stephens, but of course they were the strongest of his supporters in the newly formed party.

The organization in favor of "Constitutional Union" was opposed by another for "Southern Rights," whose contention was that the compromise involved too much sacrifice on the part of the South, and whose candidate for the governor's chair was ex-Governor McDonald, a former Democratic colleague of Cobb. As was shown by the results of the contest, the Southern Rights party had alone as its constituency the major part of the Democrats. Cobb was elected by the very great majority of 18,000 votes.[b] All of the Whigs entered the Constitutional Union party, and were joined in it by the mass of the population in the mountainous northern counties, who were accustomed to follow Cobb's leadership, and who were glad of an opportunity to support a party which favored the perpetuation of the Government of the United States and to antagonize one which seemed inclined to destroy it.

A few weeks after the gubernatorial contest the legislature was called upon to elect a United States Senator to succeed Judge J. M. Berrien, the old Whig champion, and at that time the ablest constitutional lawyer in Congress. Mr. Berrien did not approve of the Georgia platform, and, in view of the fact that his party had established the platform, was not a candidate for reelection. Mr. Toombs was placed in nomination, but was opposed by a determined group of Berrien's friends.[c] Owing to the high esteem in which the

a Stephens, War Between the States, vol. 2, p. 176. Federal Union, Jan. 21, 1851. Southern Recorder, Feb. 24, 1853, and Dec. 24, 1850.

b Federal Union, Dec. 17, 1850. Stovall, Life of Toombs, pp. 97 to 102; Southern Recorder, Nov. 11, 1851. Savannah Republican, Oct. 24, 1851.

c Stovall, Life of Toombs, p. 95.

platform was held, as much as to Toombs's own popularity, the opposition was readily overthrown by the friends of the platform. Mr. Berrien was the last of the older school of Georgia statesmen to retire from the field of politics. Troup, Gilmer, and Wilson Lumpkin had long been in private life. Each of them saw and dreaded the clouds mounting above the horizon, and none of them had great confidence in the ability of the younger school to meet the coming emergencies.[a] Mr. Lumpkin alone of the four lived through the war which he declared inevitable, to witness the defeat which he dreaded.

The Southern secession movement of 1850 had been defeated by the resolution of the Georgia people, and a desire for peace spread throughout the section. The Constitutional Union party had been organized to meet an emergency, and had met it most successfully. Failing in their contentions, the secessionists ranged themselves under the Georgia platform, as a declaration setting forth the limit of what they would concede.[b] For several years after 1850 Georgia was strongly in favor of maintaining the Union; but, as there was no special need of a party with such a platform, a tendency set in toward the former arrangement of parties.

For the Presidential contest of 1852 both the Whigs and the Democrats in the nation planted themselves upon the compromise of 1850, and, as far as platform was concerned, there was little ground for choice by Southern voters; but the northern wing of the Whigs was more antagonistic to slavery than that of the Democrats, and General Scott, who was nominated by the Whigs for the Presidency, was quite unacceptable to the bulk of the Southern people.

The situation of factions in Georgia during the contest of 1852 was complex. A large portion of the Whig party, led by Toombs and Stephens, decided that it could not support General Scott, and held a convention to nominate Daniel Webster and Charles J. Jenkins as President and Vice-President.[c] Furthermore, the supporters of the Democratic candidate were divided into two sections. The body of the Democrats in the State who had composed the Southern Rights party of the previous year declared in favor of Franklin

a Wilson Lumpkin to J. C. Calhoun, Nov. 18, 1847, Calhoun's Letters, p. 1135.
b J. W. DuBose, Life of W. L. Yancey, p. 295.
c Federal Union, July 20 and Sept. 21, 1852.

Pierce, with a ticket of electors from their own ranks, but most of the Union Democrats who had voted for Cobb in 1851 followed his lead in nominating an independent electoral ticket, which was also pledged to vote for Pierce. There was little excitement, however, in the race. Webster died just before the time of the election, but most of those who had decided to vote for him cast their ballots for him, notwithstanding his death. An effort was made to reconcile and combine the two factions supporting Pierce, but it only resulted in failure.

The vote cast in Georgia was as follows: For Pierce on the regular Democratic ticket, 33,843; for Pierce on the Union ticket, 5,773; for Scott, 15,779; for Webster, 5,289; for Troup and Quitman, on a Southern Rights ticket, 119.[a] The Democratic vote for Pierce was decidedly larger than that for all the other tickets combined. The local vote is interesting. The Whig vote was cast in its usual localities, and was much smaller than customary. In sections especially under the influence of Toombs, Stephens, or Troup, the Whig vote was in favor of Webster, and the Webster ticket obtained pluralities in several counties. The Union vote for Pierce was also concentrated, and was confined to the northern counties, in several of which the ticket received actual majorities. The supporters of Scott were so widely scattered over the State that while he received a considerable vote in every section he obtained hardly any county pluralities. The Democratic ticket received the majority of all votes cast in every section, except in the northern counties and in the neighborhood of Toombs, Stephens, or Troup.

In the quiet period after 1851 the parties in Georgia fell back into their old alignments,[b] for when there was nothing to disturb the usual course of affairs men preferred to vote as they had been accustomed. For the gubernatorial contest of 1853, the party of Stephens and Toombs, calling itself the Union party, and being very nearly the same in personnel and constituency as the former Whig party,[c] put forward C. J. Jenkins, and the Democrats nominated Herschel V. Johnson. Johnson had been a Southern Rights man, and

[a] Savannah Republican, Nov. 6, 1852.

[b] Southern Recorder, Apr. 27, 1852. H. Fielder, Life of Jos. E. Brown, p. 76.

[c] Southern Recorder, Mar. 15, 1853.

was mildly denounced as a fire eater by his opponents in the campaign of 1853. The election, though not exiting, was very close; Johnson was victorious by about 500 votes. His support came from the old Democratic area, but the county votes all over the State were closer than had been usual.

Before the occurrence of the next election the strain between the sections was renewed, and the growth of that sentiment was rapidly increased, which was to result in secession from the Union. The Whig party disastrously failed to meet the emergency in the Kansas-Nebraska struggle. The dissolution of that party had, indeed, begun as early as 1849, when its Northern and Southern wings split asunder upon the Wilmot Proviso, and when the Georgia Whig Congressmen attempted to substitute a distinctly Southern party for the unsatisfactory alignments then existing.[a] The Presidential election of 1852 was far from reuniting the antagonistic wings. There was no plank upon which the Whigs could substantially agree,[b] and no efficient reason for the continued existence of the party.[c] Whiggery died a slow death, and no one can say when it breathed its last in Georgia. Toombs and Stephens finally left the party in 1854, and with a considerable following of their Whig supporters entered the ranks of the Democrats. The remainder of the Whigs were absorbed by the Know-nothing party, and notwithstanding their want of a fixed policy kept up an opposition to the Democrats for some years longer.

The position of Georgia parties was unstable throughout the period of Whig and Democratic rivalry. The parties had reached their respective conditions through a series of opposition policies. The Whigs were at first organized to oppose Andrew Jackson, and it happened that the Georgia State Rights party, in opposition to the Union party, which adhered to the President, was driven to join the Whigs. The State Rights leaders when joining the national organization modified their former tenets of State sovereignty, and upon their adoption of moderate consolidation principles the Union or local Democratic party took up the doctrines which their rivals had let fall.

[a] Stephens, War between the States, vol. 2, p. 178.
[b] Federal Union, Sept. 21, 1852. (Statement of Toombs.)
[c] Southern Recorder, Feb. 24, 1852. (Letter of Stephens.)

In the election of delegates to the Georgia convention of 1850, and in the actions of the delegates during the deliberations of that body, principle and conviction were strongly exhibited. The people at the time were nerved to meet a crisis, and when they were led in the proper course of action by Toombs and Stephens and Cobb, the great majority were convinced that the course was the right one, and were eager to follow it; while the minority, also from conviction, took the opposite view, attempting to lead the South to demand greater concessions than the compromise had secured.

As soon as the crisis had passed the sentiment was almost the same throughout the State—peace for the present with the compromise as the basis; resistance in future to any further aggressions of the North. When nearly all were agreed upon general policy the only contests which could arise were those of an unimportant and personal character, such as the Presidential election of 1852 and the election of governor in the year following.

When the struggle for slavery extension broke forth in 1854 the logical development would have been for the whole of Georgia to combine in one organization. That this did not actually occur was due to the fundamental classification of the people upon economic and social lines and to the personal antagonisms which we have noticed as being so influential in antebellum Georgia politics. The actual result was that the local Whig party degenerated into a mere opposition party, adopting inconsistent positions from time to time as the best chances of victory seemed to advise.[a]

[a] Cf. Speech of Toombs at Augusta, Sept. 8, 1859; Federal Union, Oct. 4, 1859.

CHAPTER VII.—THE KANSAS-NEBRASKA STRUGGLE AND ITS RESULTS.

The great question of the perpetuation of slavery was opened afresh and in a new phase early in 1854 by the introduction into the United States Senate of a bill drawn up by Stephen A. Douglas, of Illinois, for the organization of Kansas and Nebraska as Territories. The bill was accompanied by a committee report stating that the compromise measures of 1850, inasmuch as they had given territorial government to Utah and New Mexico with a reference of the question of the existence of slavery to the local courts, had established the principle of non-intervention by Congress with slavery in the States and Territories. The conclusion of the report was that "all questions pertaining to slavery in the Territories and the new States to be formed therefrom are to be left to the decision of the people residing therein, by their appropriate representatives to be chosen by them for the purpose;" and that "all cases involving title to slaves and questions of personal freedom are to be referred to the jurisdiction of the local tribunals, with the right of appeal to the Supreme Court of the United States." The bill itself provided for the creation of the two Territories of Kansas and Nebraska, which when admitted as States should be received into the Union with or without slavery, as their constitutions might prescribe at the time of their admission. Section 8 of the law of 1820, known as the Missouri Compromise Act, was declared inoperative and void by the Douglas bill, as being "inconsistent with the principle of nonintervention by Congress with slavery in the States and Territories." The act of 1820 had forbidden the establishment or existence of slavery in the Territories as then possessed by the United States lying north of the line of 36° 30′ north latitude. The effect of the act of 1854, when passed, was to remove the question of the establishment of slavery in a Territory entirely out of the sphere of Congressional legislation and to establish the possibility of indefinite slavery extension. Congressional restriction was abandoned in favor of popular sovereignty.

Nearly every Southern Senator hastened to give his support to the Kansas-Nebraska bill. Most of the Northern Democrats also favored the measure. With the opposition chiefly of the Northern Whigs, the bill passed the Senate by a vote of 37 to 14. A stronger opposition was encountered in the House, where the South had much less strength. Popular sentiment was being aroused in the Northern States in condemnation of the bill, and it was necessary to hurry it to a final vote. A bit of parliamentary strategy on the part of Alexander H. Stephens shut off the debate, and the bill passed the House with a vote of 113 to 100. The success of the bill in the House, as well as in the Senate, was due to the fact that the majority of the Northern Democrats voted for it, though the Northern Whigs were unanimous against it.

The theories of Mr. Douglas immediately found strong approval with the government and the people of Georgia. We have already noticed a resolution of the Georgia legislature in 1835 which declared the inability of Congress to interfere with slavery in any of the Territories and which anticipated the repeal of the Missouri Compromise, or rather ignored any binding effect which the compromise may have had.[a] There is no doubt that public opinion in Georgia in 1835 was in consonance with the declaration of the general assembly, and it is further true that at no subsequent period was sentiment in the State less radical on the slavery question. The Georgia platform of 1850 declared that the State would not withdraw from the Union on account of the infractions of Southern rights theretofore made. On the other hand, it by no means pledged the State against attempting to secure any further advantages for the South.

The Kansas bill was introduced into the Senate on January 4, 1854. As soon as the news of it reached Georgia the Democrats accepted it with enthusiasm as a just yet magnanimous concession to the South by the lovers of the Union at the North, and they loudly praised Douglas for his broad-minded statesmanship. The Georgia Whigs at first held aloof, but soon became quite demonstrative in support of the principle of the Kansas bill, and declared that the Democrats had stolen their thunder.[b]

[a] Infra, p. 161.   [b] Federal Union, Feb. 21 and 28, 1854.

The Georgia legislature lost no time in stating that the commonwealth had firmly fixed itself upon the principles of the compromise of 1850 as a final settlement of the agitation upon the question in point, distinctly recognizing that Congress could not impose upon the Territories any restrictions as to the existence of slavery in them, and providing that such matters must be determined by their citizens alone. The legislature stated its approval of the Douglas bill for Kansas and Nebraska as showing the determination of the people of the North to carry out the principles of the compromise of 1850. It instructed the Georgia Senators and requested the Representatives to support the bill in Congress.[a]

The editorial condemnation of the bill in the North soon showed to the people of Georgia that the mass of the Northern people would make no voluntary concession to the slave-holding interest. By the time of the signing of the act by the President on May 30, 1854, it was realized that if any substantial benefit was to be gained from its passage, the struggle in Congress was only the prelude to a contest within the debatable land itself.

The Georgians were grateful to the Northern Democrats for the assistance which they had rendered, but they soon became anxious on account of the great excitement which the passage of the bill aroused in the North.[b] The emigrant aid societies in the free States made necessary some counter move from the South. Companies of emigrants were formed in the cotton States with the purpose of increasing the number of voters in Kansas who would vote and work for the establishment of a pro-slavery constitution. The company organized and conducted by Major Buford, of Alabama, was the most conspicuous of these; but among the smaller squads, several were composed wholly of Georgians.[c] Large private subscriptions of money were raised for the furtherance of the project. The Georgia legislature directed the superintendent of the Western and Atlantic Railroad, which was owned and operated by the State, to give free passage to Major Buford's company on their route, and to any other emigrants to Kansas of like character.[d]

[a] Approved Feb. 20, 1854; Acts of Georgia Gen. Assem. 1853–1854, p. 590. U. S. Senate Misc. Doc. No. 48, 33d Cong., 1st sess., vol. 1.

[b] Federal Union, June 19, 1855.

[c] Federal Union, Oct. 6, 1855, and Aug. 26, 1856.

[d] Acts of Ga. Gen. Assem. 1855–1856, p. 553.

The pro-slavery and ant-islavery factions in Kansas carried on a harassing struggle for the supremacy through 1855, 1856, and 1857. Each erected a government which it declared to be the only legitimate one. Three successive territorial governors, appointed from Washington, wrestled with the problems only to fail in mastering them. The Georgia politicians at first expected Kansas to apply for admission in the near future as a slave State.[a] The immigrants from the South were the more numerous for two or three years after the passage of the Kansas act, and at that time the chief fear of the South was that the anti-slavery power would bring about the rejection of the application of Kansas when it should ask for admission with a pro-slavery constitution.[b] The general conviction was that such an event would render a dissolution of the Union justifiable and very probable. Governor Johnson actually advised the legislature, in accordance with the fourth resolution in the Georgia platform of 1850, to provide for the calling of a convention of the people to determine the time and method of resistance in the expected contingency.[c] But as time wore on the contingency grew less probable, and the wave of excitement on that score died away.

Notwithstanding the widespread hostility in the North to the principle of the Kansas-Nebraska act, the Democratic party, in its national convention at Cincinnati in June, 1856, adopted that principle as one of the planks in its platform, and Mr. Buchanan, as the candidate of the party, accepted the plank. The party thus declared for non-interference with slavery in the Territories, but such a declaration was capable of two constructions, and in fact the Northern and Southern Democrats placed different interpretations upon it. After the party had won the election the misunderstanding became more apparent.

According to the Southern view, there were two methods of restricting slavery in the Territories, both of which were illegal and unconstitutional. The first was by direct Congressional legislation against slavery, such as had been contained in the Missouri Compromise, which was now sometimes spoken of in the South as an odious piece of legislation; the

a Federal Union, June 19, 1855; Mr. Howell Cobb's opinion.
b Resolutions of the Georgia Democratic convention, June 10, 1855, Federal Union June 12, 1855.
c Federal Union, Nov. 6, 1855.

second was by the application of the squatter sovereignty doctrine before the Territory was ready for statehood. The Northern or Douglas Democrats condemned the first method, but approved of squatter sovereignty. The newly organized Republican party, in its various elements, favored almost any means which would secure the restriction and the weakening of the institution of slavery.

A large portion of the Southern delegates to the Democratic convention at Cincinnati were instructed to vote for no candidate for the nomination who would not unequivocally avow himself to be opposed to either form of restricting slavery.[a] In his letter of acceptance Mr. Buchanan seemed to say what the South demanded, but there was some vagueness in his language. An emergency was required before his exact policy would be revealed. In June, 1857, he sent Robert J. Walker to Kansas as Territorial governor. Walker delivered an inaugural address in which he expressed his opinion that Kansas must become a free State, and showed an inclination to interfere with the recent acts of the legislature in prescribing the method of ratification of the constitution which was about to be formulated.

The attitude of Walker was objectionable to the Southern interest. The convention of the Democratic party in Georgia, June 24, resolved that Walker's inaugural address was a presumptuous interference in matters over which he had no legitimate control; that it was a gross departure from the principle of non-intervention established by the Kansas bill; and that it was the President's duty to remove Walker at once. These resolutions were too mild to suit some of the Georgia Democrats,[b] while by others they were thought to be radical and out of place. This led to a division of the Democrats of Georgia into "National" and "Southern" factions.[c] The whole matter was simplified for the local politicians by the decision of the United States Supreme Court rendered in March, 1857, in the Dred Scott case; but for the country at large the dictum of the court had the effect of aggravating the dispute which it was expected to settle.

The circumstances of the famous case of Dred Scott v.

a J. W. DuBose, Life of Yancey, p. 320.

b T. W. Thomas, in Southern Recorder, Nov. 7, 1857. See also Federal Union, June 30, 1857.

c Southern Recorder, Sept. 8, 1857.

Sandford are too well known to make a review advisable in this connection. The decision of the court was entirely in accord with the extreme Southern view on slavery extension. The chief question before the court was whether Dred Scott was constitutionally a citizen with any rightful standing in the courts of the United States. The court decided that he, a negro and the descendant of slave parents, was not a citizen of any State or of the United States, and therefore could not be a party to any suit in the courts; and that, further, the residence of his master in Illinois and Minnesota did not change the negro's status as a slave. The court then proceeded to pronounce its opinion on a matter which was not necessarily involved in any degree in the case before it. It stated that, slaves being regarded as property and not as persons by the Constitution, Congress had no right to legislate slavery out of any territory of the United States, and therefore the legislation of 1820, known as the Missouri Compromise, was unconstitutional.[a]

Though the infallibility of the Supreme Court had in former times been questioned by the people of Georgia, the universal opinion in the State was that for the Dred Scott case the court had had a remarkably clear insight into revealed law.[b] The Northern Democrats also accepted the decision. Mr. Douglas in some way reconciled the opinions of the court with the doctrine of popular sovereignty, and joined in the general Democratic rejoicing. But the anti-slavery men were far from acquiescing in any such settlement.

Developments connected with Kansas soon afterwards disturbed the harmony in the only remaining national party. The Lecompton convention, for which arrangements had been made by the pro-slavery legislature before the inauguration of Walker as governor, drew up a constitution which placed numerous safeguards around the institution of slavery, and refused to submit most of these articles for popular ratification. Before the close of 1857 it was clear that the majority of settlers in Kansas were anti-slavery men.

Mr. Douglas refused to abandon the principle of popular sovereignty. He was therefore driven to act with the Republicans in their hostility to the Lecompton constitution. The

---

[a] For report of the case see Howard, U. S. Supreme Court Reports, vol. 19, p 293.
[b] Cf. Federal Union, Mar. 31, 1857.

Southern Democrats then read him out of the Democratic party, branding him with treason to the South and to the Democracy.[a]

The South wished to secure the admission of Kansas under the Lecompton constitution, but when conditions in the Territory had been used as a text for numerous tirades against slavery in general, the section grew anxious to put an end by any feasible means to the agitation over "bleeding Kansas." The Republicans were accused of being so eager to keep open the irritating question that they were ready to oppose the admission of the State even with an anti-slavery constitution.[b] The whole matter was finally closed by the submission of the Lecompton constitution to a popular vote in Kansas, and its rejection by the majority on August 2, 1858. It was thus decided that slavery should not exist in Kansas. But this settlement was not reached until the rift in the Democratic ranks had become so serious as to render the Republican triumph almost inevitable in 1860.

At this period the whole American people expected a crisis to arrive at the end of Buchanan's administration; and the conviction grew the stronger as the Presidential election drew nearer. In Georgia there was considerable difference of opinion as to the best course of action for the State to pursue in the dreaded emergency of a Republican accession to power. To appreciate the positions of the respective leaders in Georgia, we must take a short review to cover the more recent developments in State politics.

The first rumor of the existence of the American or Know-nothing organization reached Georgia in May or June, 1854. Shortly afterwards the first lodges were established in Georgia. By the end of the year the American Party had become an important factor in Georgia politics.[c] A large portion of the Whig party at the North had gone openly into the anti-slavery camp after 1852. Another portion entered the American party with the object, professedly, of causing America to be ruled by Americans and not by foreign immigrants or by Catholics. The ends of the organization were to be secured through the work of secret lodges spread over the country.

a Federal Union, Apr. 6, 1858.
b Ibid., Mar. 30, 1858.
c Ibid., Sept. 12, Dec. 26, 1854, and Mar. 13, 1855.

Most of the Georgia Whigs joined the order, not because they considered nativism to be a pressing issue, but because by so doing they could best oppose their old enemies, the Democrats.

The Know-nothing movement was popular with the rank and file of the Georgia Whigs, but most of the prominent men in the party declined to join it. Toombs voted with the Democrats throughout the Congressional session of 1853–54, and in 1855 he condemned the Know-nothings, urging the whole South to unite for the safety of Southern rights and to support the band of patriotic Democrats at the North who were fighting for the observence of the Constitution. Stephens was prevented by his extreme regard for consistency from abandoning his Whig colleagues quite so readily. In May, 1855, he announced that since so many of his former supporters had entered the Know-nothing organization, of which he could not approve, he would not be a candidate for reelection to Congress. But shortly afterwards, having decided to defy the Know-nothings, he declared himself a candidate independent of all parties. He showed that one of the pledges of Know-nothingism was to uphold the Union, while nothing was said about the Constitution; therefore it was against the Georgia platform and supportive of abolitionism.[a] Stephens, like Toombs, was welcomed by the Democrats, whose ranks he entered, and was at once returned to Congress.

For the gubernatorial race of 1855 three candidates entered the field. The Democrats nominated Herschel V. Johnson for a second term; the Know-nothings selected Garnett Andrews as their champion, and the Temperance party supported B. H. Overby, a Methodist preacher who had been a fire-eating Whig. All three candidates stumped the State, but there was never any doubt of Johnson's election. The vote as cast in October was, for Johnson 53,478, for Andrews 43,222, for Overby 6,284.[b]

It soon became evident that the Northern and Southern wings of the American party were out of sympathy. The Georgia Know-nothings seem not to have been distressed over the fact, for their State convention declared in its platform in December, "The Territories of the United States we regard as the common property of all the States as coequal

[a] Cleveland, Life of Stephens, p. 472. Federal Union, May 22, June 5, and July 17, 1855.
[b] Federal Union, July 31, Mar. 13, and Oct. 16, 1855.

sovereignties, and as such open to settlement by the citizens of the several States with their property as matter of right. We repudiate, therefore, the doctrine commonly called squatter sovereignty."[a] This resolution was clearly a bait to catch local support, for all of the leaders knew that the Northern wing of the party could never be brought to approve it.

The national convention of the Know-nothings which met at Philadelphia in March, 1856, nominated Fillmore and Donelson as its candidates, and adopted a platform containing nothing but platitudes. The nomination was not a popular one at the South, but caused numerous desertions from the party.[b] E. A. Nisbet, a leader of the Know-nothings, and C. J. Jenkins, an anti-Know-nothing Whig, decided to vote for Buchanan, because Fillmore had no chance of election, while in order to preserve the rights of the South,[c] it was necessary to defeat Fremont, the candidate of the newly formed Republican party. The death of J. M. Berrien, on January 1, left the brilliant young orator, Benjamin H. Hill, as the only noteworthy leader of the Fillmore party in Georgia.[d] He, nothing daunted by his isolation, vigorously stumped the State for his candidate, occasionally having a brush with Toombs or Stephens, both of whom he accused of base desertion from the Whig party.

The result of the contest in Georgia was a victory for Buchanan of 14,000 votes. The only counties carried by Fillmore were in those parts of middle Georgia where the Whigs had formerly been especially strong. The veterans Troup and Lumpkin both wrote public letters from their retirement in support of the Democratic party.[e] The men who voted for Fillmore did so in order merely to prevent their party from falling to pieces, and because there was no urgent reason to the contrary. In many parts of the North the American party abandoned its own candidate, preferring to assist in the advancement of the anti-slavery cause by joining the Republican party.[f] Fillmore accordingly received the electoral vote of the State of Maryland alone.

[a] Federal Union, Dec. 25, 1855.
[b] Ibid., Mar. 11 and July 8, 1856.
[c] Ibid., Sept. 9 and 16, 1856.
[d] Fielder, Life of Brown, p. 81. Federal Union, Aug. 5, 1856.
[e] Federal Union, July 31, 1855, and Apr. 29, 1856.
[f] Speech of Toombs, Federal Union, Oct. 4, 1859.

The crushing defeat of 1856 came near destroying the Georgia Know-nothing party, but during the spring of 1857 its leaders and its editors urged that the organization be not abandoned.[a] Accordingly, a convention of the party met in July to prepare for the gubernatorial contest. It adopted a platform opposing squatter sovereignty, upholding the Georgia platform, condemning further agitation upon the right of property in slaves, and declaring that the Dred Scott decision was but a judicial indorsement of the position theretofore held by the American party of Georgia. As its candidate for the governorship the convention nominated B. H. Hill by acclamation.[b] The platform ably expressed the popular sentiments of the time. The candidate was by far the strongest man in the party, but the Know-nothings knew from the first that they had no chance of success, because the Democrats had lived up to all that they themselves could promise, and furthermore because nearly all the strong politicians in the State were among their opponents.

The Democratic State convention, meeting on June 24, adopted the two-thirds rule for nominations. The drafting of a platform was not necessary, for the past record of the party showed where it stood on all vital issues. The prominent men in the party were so numerous that a choice was very difficult. Nineteen ballots were cast without a majority for any candidate. A large committee was then appointed to report some method of harmonious action by the convention. The committee reported the name of Joseph E. Brown for the nomination; the names of all other candidates were withdrawn, and Brown was given a unanimous vote.[c]

The personality of the Democratic candidate is important, in that it throws strong light upon the attitude of the poorer class of white citizens in the State. Brown was born in Pickens District, S. C., in 1821, but in early youth moved with his parents to Union County, Ga., to a valley shut in by the ranges of the Blue Ridge, remote from all centers of culture, and out of touch with the current of politics. The slender resources of the family rendered it necessary for the future governor and senator to help his father and brothers

a Southern Recorder, April, May, and June, 1857.

b Ibid., July 14, 1857. Federal Union, July 14, 1857.

c Avery, History of Georgia, p. 37. Federal Union, June 30, 1857.

in the farm work. At an early age he began to plow behind oxen, which were then and are now the chief motive power in the mountain region. With only the rudiments of education, young Brown set out at the age of 19 for Dr. Waddell's well-known school in South Carolina, carrying with him a yoke of steers to pay in part for tuition and board. Proving himself an excellent student, he afterwards was able to borrow money to take a course in law at Yale College. He then returned, in 1846, to enter the practice of law in Cherokee County, in another part of the mountain district of Georgia.

Joseph E. Brown always remained a representative of a horny-handed constituency. Born and raised without the personal service of slaves, he was, like many others in the same circumstances, strong in support of the institution and firm in the belief that the non-slaveholding Southerners derived much benefit from the existence of slavery in their country. His sojourn in Connecticut not changing these views, he soon had occasion to express them in part, as a member of the Georgia legislature. Speaking on February 1, 1850, upon the subject of the legislation upon slavery then in contemplation by Congress, he defended the justice of slavery, showing that its hardships had been greatly lightened since the colonial period, when the system was in existence throughout the colonies. He declared that the Constitution gave Congress no right to abolish slavery in the Territories, and stated that in his opinion the South had surrendered valuable rights when the Missouri Compromise line was established. He was in favor of calling a State convention in order that firm ground might be taken for the protection of the rights of the South.[a]

For some years before 1857, Brown held the office of judge of the superior court in the northern district, at the same time managing his farm near Canton, Ga. There is a tradition that the committee sent to inform him of his nomination for the governorship found the judge hard at work in the field gathering his crop of wheat.

The nomination of such a man by the Democratic party, and his subsequent election as governor with a large majority of votes,[b] was in its moral effect similar to the accession of Andrew Jackson to the Presidency in 1828. A shock to the

[a] Federal Union, July 14, 1857.
[b] The vote cast was, for Brown, 57,568; for Hill, 46,826; Federal Union, Oct. 20, 1857.

aristocratic régime in Georgia,[a] it placed at the helm of the State a man who was in the closest touch with the sturdy yeomen, and it added to the group of official leaders a strong thinker, with a new point of view and with valuable fresh ideas. By his arguments in the campaign and his subsequent able discharge of his executive duties, Governor Brown quickly gained for his utterances such attention throughout the State as was accorded very few other politicians.

The inaugural address of the new governor showed what might be expected of him in case any attack should be made upon slavery during his term of office. He stated his conviction that the State of Georgia would not remain in the Union if the Constitution were tampered with, and he declared his unalterable determination to maintain her rights and vindicate her honor at every hazard and with every means in his power.[b]

The year 1858 was devoid of excitement in Georgia. It was a period of reflection; and reflection brought determination. While there was difference of opinion in unimportant matters, the people were of only one mind on the vital issues of slavery and State rights. If there were more than one side to either question the people of Georgia could not appreciate the fact.

The great slavery issue was of course one which concerned the sections of the country rather than the individual States, and it had chiefly been so considered down to the time when the comparative weakness of the South in Congress became manifest. After that point had been reached, and after the abolitionists began their agitation, more and more emphasis came to be placed by the Southern people upon the limitations which the Constitution had laid upon the central Government in regard to slavery. The first direct and conscious connection between slavery and State rights by a prominent Georgian was probably in the inaugural address of Governor Gilmer, delivered in November 1837. In it he said that on account of slavery and its products, "our true position is to stand by the powers of the States and the people as the surest safeguards of our rights, of liberty, and of property."[c] Among the people this conviction grew stronger year by year. The slavery question was acknowledged to be a sec-

a Avery, History of Georgia, p. 47.   b Federal Union, Nov. 10, 1857.
c Niles's Register, vol. 58, p. 181.

tional one, but the section had no constitutional standing or rights, as did the States which composed it.

The sectional feeling grew very strong. The antagonism between the North and the South was partially smothered by the compromise of 1850, but flared out afresh when the Kansas question arose, and was thereafter steadily aggravated by the course of events. The enactment of laws by certain Northern States to prevent the operation of the fugitive-slave law led to the unanimous adoption by a convention of the Democratic party of Georgia, in 1855, of resolutions requesting the legislature to pass efficient retaliatory measures. [a] Senator Toombs gave his support to the plan, advising the levy by each Southern State of an ad valorem tax on all articles offered for sale which had come from other States. This would foster home production and direct importation from abroad, and at the same time it would hurt New England.[b] The plan was kept under popular consideration for some time, and though the contemplated laws were not enacted, the citizens were guided in many cases by the principle involved. The purchase of commodities from the North, and even the subscription to the Northern newspapers came to be condemned by many as a form of paying tribute to the North at the expense of the South. [c] A business depression in New England in 1858 was partly accounted for by the stopping of orders by Southern merchants. Some of the Bostonians thought of retaliation in kind upon the South, but came to realize that the section had a monopoly upon all of its export products, and therefore could not be hurt by nonintercourse. [d]

The development of the Free Soil organization into the more powerful Republican party and the strengthening of the anti-slavery cause had the effect in the South of making radical policies the more popular. Even conservative Southerners did not condemn Mr. Brooks for chastising Mr. Sumner. They regretted that the Senate Chamber had been selected as the place of punishment, but the general sentiment was that "while Massachusetts chooses to be represented in the United

a Federal Union, June 12, 1855.

b Letter of Toombs, Federal Union, Dec. 23, 1856. See also editorial in Federal Union, Apr. 13, 1858.

c Federal Union, Feb. 9, 1858.

d Editorial of Boston Herald, reprinted in Federal Union, Sept. 21, 1858.

States Senate by blackguards, she ought not to complain if they receive a blackguard's reward." [a]

From the Southern standpoint the institution of domestic servitude was more firmly established in 1858 than ever before. The suggestion that slavery was not ethically right was frowned down and denied utterance.[b] The number of slaves in Georgia was almost equal to the number of white persons, and their value as property was considerably greater than that of all the land in the State, with town and city property included.[c] The market value of slaves increased rapidly in the years just preceding secession. Throughout the preceding decade or two the rule for pricing slaves had been to multiply the price of a pound of cotton by 10,000—e. g., if cotton sold at 12 cents, an able-bodied negro would be worth $1,200. But that rule was now abandoned. The price of slaves rose 25 per cent in three years.[d] Well-grown negro boys were sold in Milledgeville in 1860 for $2,000 each.[e]

The project of emancipation, even with compensation to the masters, found very little favor in Georgia.[f] Several plans were brought forward to strengthen the local support of the institution which might have been adopted had they been thought necessary for the purpose. One of these was that one slave should be included in the homestead legally exempt from levy or sale, in order to encourage every family to have one slave.[g] But even without such legislation the poorer whites were rightly thought to be, in thousands of cases, as sturdy defenders of the institution as those who owned slaves.[h] A few individuals favored the reopening of the slave trade;[i] but, as a Georgia editor very aptly said, "the Southern people have no more idea of reviving the slave trade than they have of admitting their slaves to the rights and privileges of citizenship."[j]

[a] Editorial in Federal Union, June 3, 1856.

[b] Federal Union, Aug. 14, 1855.

[c] Georgia tax returns, 1856: Total value of slaves, $210,538,634; total value of land, $157,899,600; Federal Union, Feb. 17, 1857.

[d] Federal Union, Jan. 17, 1860.

[e] Ibid., June 12, 1860.

[f] Ibid., Feb. 1, 1859.

[g] Ibid., Dec. 30, 1856.

[h] Editorial, Federal Union, Aug. 28, 1860. Speech of Senator Iverson, Federal Union, July 26, 1859. Letter of Governor Brown, Federal Union, Dec. 11, 1865.

[i] Message of Governor Adams to legislature of South Carolina, Federal Union, Dec. 2, 1856. Letters of Dr. Lee, of Athens, Ga., Federal Union, Mar. 1, 1859.

[j] Federal Union, Dec. 2, 1856.

The people of the South of course realized that a very strong campaign was being made against slavery, but they were convinced that it could never be peacefully successful. A work on slavery, showing much thought and research, was published by T. R. R. Cobb, in 1858, which may be taken as authoritative upon the Southern side. His conclusion as to emancipation was that, "until the white race is exterminated or driven off, it can never be forcibly effected. Amalgamation to any great extent is a moral impossibility. Colonization on the coast of Africa could be effected only at immense cost, and at the sacrifice of the lives of at least one-fourth of the emigrants. So long as climate and disease and the profitable planting of cotton, rice, tobacco, and cane make the negro the only laborer inhabiting safely our Southern savannas and prairies, just so long will he be a slave to the white man. Whenever the white laborer can successfully compete with him in these productions and occupy this soil, the negro will either be driven through the Isthmus to become amalgamated with the races of South America, or he will fall a victim to disease and neglect, begging bread at the white man's door."[a] Mr. Cobb's attempt to foretell the future of the negro was, as he himself said, only a conjecture. He could not foresee the abolition of slavery within the next decade, but from his study of the characteristics and the condition of the race he could have assured the North that sweeping emancipation would rather complicate than simplify the negro question.

The period of quiet which preceded the storm extended beyond the middle of the year 1859. Mr. Stephens, in a speech to his constituents on July 2, called attention to the lack of political agitation and to the general prosperity of the State and of the whole country, and stated that he was no longer a candidate for Congressional honors.[b] Mr. Stephens, however, appreciated the numerous indications which foreboded the early arrival of evil times, and his conviction of his own inability to avert them was so strong as to be the true cause of his retirement from Congress.[c]

The first renewed rumbling of the coming storm burst upon Georgia in a speech of Senator Alfred Iverson, at Griffin,

[a] Cobb on Slavery, p. CCXXI.
[b] Cleveland, Life of Stephens, p. 637.   Federal Union, July 19, 1859.
[c] Letter of Stephens to Dr. Z. P. Landrum; Cleveland, Life of Stephens, p. 668.

Ga., on July 14, 1859. He proclaimed the powerlessness of the Northern Democracy, and the extreme probability of the election of a free-soil President in 1860, declaring that in such an emergency he would favor an independent confederacy of the Southern States. He urged the South at once to repudiate all compromises, and to hurl square defiance at the abolitionists in every possible way.[a] This speech caused great controversy in the State, which lasted through several months. The prevailing opinion seemed to be that Mr. Iverson had exaggerated the evils, but the news of John Brown's raid led to a very general acceptance of the truth of what he had said.

A slave insurrection was the one thing most dreaded by the Southern people. The improbability of its occurrence did not lessen its theoretical horrors. Information concerning plots which were sometimes unearthed was spread abroad as carefully as possible, so as to encourage vigilance without arousing excitement. The newspapers generally avoided the subject, but occasionally referred to it in order to prevent the complete decay of the patrol system,[b] toward which there was a very strong tendency, due to the indulgent and easy-going disposition of the Southern people.

The details of John Brown's exploit were quickly made known to everyone in Georgia by the electric telegraph, the local press, and word of mouth. The news was of an intensely exciting character, but it was necessary to avoid all manifestations of frenzy. As soon as the insane folly of Brown's scheme became apparent, as well as its hideously criminal character, the fierce hatred in the South toward its perpetrators and abettors gave place to a widespread and more resolute hatred than had existed before toward all antislavery men at the North. It was recognized by conservative men that the whole of the North was by no means abolitionist, but the numerous demonstrations on the day of Brown's execution and the popular canonization of the fanatic criminal overshadowed in the Southern vision the Union meetings which were held in the chief Northern cities.[c]

A substantial result of the John Brown incident was the strengthening of the conviction that the South must achieve

---

[a] Avery, History of Georgia, p. 104. Federal Union, July 26, 1859.
[b] Federal Union, Dec. 23, 1856.
[c] Ibid., Dec. 27, 1859.

unity. If the non-slaveholders in Georgia had at any former time been lukewarm in support of slavery, their strenuous hostility to forcible abolition was no longer a matter of doubt.

The non-slaveholding class continued to repose their chief trust in Joseph E. Brown, who, from the ability shown in his discharge of the executive duties, had won great popularity with all people who appreciated efficient government.[a] As the Democratic nominee for reelection in 1859 he was opposed by a candidate put forth by the traditional enemies of the Democratic party, but was elected governor by a very large majority of votes. In his inaugural address for the second term he took much the same position that Senator Iverson had adopted in his speech of four months previous.

He voiced the opinion, which had then become very general, that the great contest of 1860, which might decide the fate of the Union of the States, would be fought between "the Black Republican and the National Democratic parties." He regarded the Democratic party as the last hope of the Union. Should it be broken down, the rights of the South denied, and her equality in the Union destroyed, he declared his conviction that the section should strike for independence.[b] As mere words this address was nothing unusual. What gave it importance was the well-known character of the governor as a man absolutely serious and determined in any policy once undertaken. His annual message, also delivered in November, 1859, was squarely in line with the inaugural address.

In former messages Brown, like his predecessors, had advised the legislature to take steps to improve the State militia,[c] but the legislature had paid no attention to the matter. The militia in Georgia, as in other Southern States, had fallen sadly into neglect. The old-fashioned public drills and musters had so long been discontinued as to be known from the tales of the old citizens only as a farcical and valueless relic of colonial and revolutionary times.[d] The governor now advised a tax upon all citizens not members of military companies, the proceeds of the tax to be devoted to the erection of a foundry for arms, so that Georgia would be inde-

[a] Southern Recorder, July 12, 1859.

[b] Federal Union, Nov. 8, 1859.

[c] Federal Union, Nov. 6, 1855 (Governor Johnson). Federal Union, Nov. 9, 1858 (Governor Brown).

[d] Fielder, Life of Brown, p. 163.

pendent should an emergency arise.[a] The legislature was still not ready to act upon all of the governor's advice, but Brown was able through his influence to develop much enthusiasm in the State for the military service, and to prepare the people for swift action when the crisis should arrive.

The general outlines of the Presidential contest of 1860 were as follows: The Democratic national convention met at Charleston April 20, 1860. Its committee on platform made two reports, the one of the majority declaring that the United States Government was bound to protect in the Territories all the property of every citizen immigrating from any State of the Union, and that slavery must legally exist in every territory until the organization of a State government. The minority report set forth that, whereas differences existed in the Democratic party as to the powers and duties of Congress over slavery in the Territories, resolved, that the party would stand by the Supreme Court in the matter. The Northern delegations secured the adoption of the minority report, whereupon most of the Southerners, in view of the disagreement in the party, and with the determination to establish the principle of the Dred Scot decision, followed William L. Yancey and the Alabama delegation in a secession from the convention. Soon afterwards the remaining delegates, failing to nominate a candidate, adjourned to meet again at Baltimore. In the adjourned session Mr. Douglas, of Illinois, was nominated for the Presidency, and, Mr. Fitzpatrick declining, Mr. H. V. Johnson of Georgia was selected as his companion on the ticket. A second secession of Southern delegations occurred at Baltimore, leading to the nomination by the combined seceders in their conventions at Baltimore and at Richmond of J. C. Breckenridge, of Kentucky, and Joseph Lane, of Oregon as President and Vice-President.

Meanwhile the Republican convention had nominated Lincoln and Hamlin, and had declared not only that slavery did not exist in the Territories, but that Congress could not legalize it in them. Still a fourth ticket, bearing the names of Bell and Everett, was put in the field by the "Constitutional Union" party, with the Federal Constitution as the only plank in its platform.

The split in the Democratic party was deeply regretted in

a Federal Union, Nov. 8, 1859; Fielder, Life of Brown, p. 164.

Georgia, but the responsibility for it was laid at the door of the Douglas Democrats. All of the local leaders were interrogated for their approval or disapproval of the bolting of the Georgia delegation at Charleston and for advice to the party in its dilemma. Their replies were published for the guidance of the people.[a]

Mr. Stephens, lamenting the disruption of the convention, thought that the South had done wrong in abandoning its former position favoring non-intervention with slavery in the Territories. He relied upon sober second thought to determine whether Georgia should be represented at Baltimore and what course of action the delegation should follow.

Mr. Herschel V. Johnson wrote that though the Union was not an object to be idolized, it should be preserved as long as the interests of the South did not distinctly require its abandonment. Since the overthrow of the Democratic party would be a long stride toward dissolution, that contingency should be avoided. The South should therefore adhere to its policy favoring non-intervention, for insistence in its new demand would bring no special advantage, but would antagonize many Northern Democrats. He urged that delegates be sent to Baltimore instructed to preserve the integrity of the party.[b]

Governor Brown was of the opinion that the masses North and South were willing to have mutual justice done, and he hoped for harmony at Baltimore. He held that the people of the South had the right to demand of Congress the enactment of laws for the protection of slave property in the Territories, but the expediency of such a demand was questionable. He advised that Georgia send delegates to Baltimore, where it still might be possible to agree upon a compromise plank and an acceptable candidate.

Mr. Howell Cobb explained that there were two points of difference at Charleston—the platform and the candidate. The fifteen Southern States, together with the two Democratic States on the Pacific coast, agreed upon a platform which recognized the equality of the Southern States, claiming for their citizens with their property the same protection which the laws of the land extended to the citizens of the non-

a Most of these letters were printed in the Federal Union May 22, 1860.
b Federal Union, May 29, 1860.

slave-holding States and their property; the remaining sixteen States, with their superior numbers in the convention, refused to recognize these principles, but adopted an ambiguous platform with the intention of nominating a candidate known to be hostile to the Southern contention.

The letter of Mr. Toombs was the most radical of the series. He said that the proceedings of the convention had been very interesting, but had caused him no apprehension. In the developments at Charleston he saw positive evidence of the advance of sound constitutional principles; it might not have been prudent to present so much truth on the slavery issue as was contained in the majority platform, but since it had been so presented it ought to be firmly supported. While he approved the secession of the Georgia delegation, he thought that, in view of the overtures of the New York delegation, the State should be represented at Baltimore. Such action would involve no sacrifice of principle, since the convention of seceders could still be held at Richmond. Mr. Toombs was not frightened at the prospect of disunion. "Our greatest danger to-day," he wrote in conclusion, "is that the Union will survive the Constitution."

The State Democratic convention, which met at Milledgeville on June 4, approved the Charleston secession by a vote of two-thirds, and reappointed the original Georgia delegation to attend the session at Baltimore, with instructions to secede if the adjourned convention should refuse to protect slavery in the Territories. But Ex-Governor Johnson led a body of bolters from the Milledgeville convention, which appointed a different delegation to Baltimore with more moderate instructions.[a] The Baltimore convention resolved to recognize both delegations from Georgia, giving to each one-half of the full vote of the State. The regular delegation refused to accept this, and withdrew to join the conventions of the bolters in Baltimore and in Richmond.[b] The Johnson delegation accordingly cast the full vote of Georgia in the regular convention at Baltimore.

The remnant in Georgia of the American party, calling itself the Constitutional Union party, held its convention in Milledgeville on May 2 to select and instruct a delegation to

[a] Butler, History of Macon, Ga., p. 228.
[b] Letter of the regular Georgia delegation, Federal Union, July 10, 1860.

the general convention of their party at Baltimore. Resolutions were adopted for the guidance of the delegates, or more probably for local effect, which declared the right of property in slaves, the obligation on the part of the Federal Government to protect slave property in the Territories, and the unconstitutionality of any State legislation against the fugitive slave law.[a]

The general convention refused to adopt a vigorous platform of any kind, but hoped by the example of its own placidness to relieve the country from the turbulence and strain of the times. Bell and Everett were very suitable candidates to make the campaign upon the spiritless platform of the party.

Of course, Lincoln received no support whatever in Georgia. He was considered a negligible factor in the local campaign. The strongest argument in favor of any one of the other candidates was that he was the most likely to defeat the Republican party. Aside from Yancey, of Alabama, the favorite campaign orators of the South were Toombs in support of Breckinridge, Stephens for Douglas, and Benjamin H. Hill for Bell.[b] All of the hotspur leaders in the State were strongly in favor of Breckinridge because of his outspoken platform. Very many were so irritated by the long-continued uncertainty that they were determined to have a satisfactory President or dissolve the Union forthwith.

The Douglas and the Bell partisans were very much akin in their policies. Anxious to preserve the rights of the South in the Union, and to remove slavery from politics, each faction struggled on independently, hoping against hope that the Republicans would be defeated. Several efforts were made to fuse the two parties in Georgia without entire success, though many Douglas men probably decided at the eleventh hour to vote for the Bell electors.[c]

Early in October it became known to be practically certain that Lincoln would be elected.[d] From that time began the agitation, led at first by Breckinridge men, looking to the secession of Georgia at an early date. The popular vote cast in Georgia was for Breckinridge 51,893, for Bell 42,855, for Douglas 11,580. The result of the contest at large became known very quickly after the ballot boxes were closed. The

a Federal Union, May 15, 1860.   c Federal Union, Oct. 30, 1860.
b Du Bose, Life of Yancey, p. 512.   d Ibid., Oct. 2, 1860.

news that their worst fears were realized caused depression for a time in Georgia, but dread quickly gave way to defiance, and hesitation was replaced by resolution.[a] Georgians of every faction had the fellow feeling of a common defeat, and they determined to waste their strength no more in fruitless dissensions, but to work, and if need be fight, together in the patriotic cause.[b] The hearts of thousands upon thousands of men, women, and children were thrilled with the motto, "Georgia expects all of her sons to do their duty."

[a] Fielder, Life of Brown, p. 171.   [b] Federal Union, Nov. 13, 1860, ff.

CHAPTER VIII.—THE SECESSION OF THE STATE OF GEORGIA.

The idea of secession from the Union of the States is practically as old as the Federal Constitution itself. It was occasionally alluded to as a possibility in the early years under the present frame of government; but the first occasion upon which the question of the advisability of secession was seriously discussed by any important body was the meeting of the Hartford convention, composed of delegates from the New England States, at the close of 1814.

Secession as a remedy for the ills of the South was first mooted in Georgia about the year 1849. The compromise of 1850 tended to check the discussion, but the theoretical privilege of secession was one of the contentions of the local Southern Rights party in 1851. Early in 1854 Gen. James N. Bethune established the "Corner Stone" at Columbus, Ga., which for some length of time had the distinction of being the only newspaper in the South which advised the immediate dissolution of the Union.[a] From the beginning of the Kansas struggle, secession as a last resort for the protection of Southern rights was never completely out of the contemplation of Southern statesmen. Hiram Warner, in accepting a Democratic nomination to Congress in 1855, expressed his approbation of withdrawal from the Union should it become necessary in defending the rights of the State of Georgia.[b] Herschel V. Johnson, while governor of Georgia, wrote in 1856 that the election of Fremont as President would drive the Southern States to dissolve the Union, while Howell Cobb, in discussing the same contingency, declared that he would hasten home, in the event, to take the stump for immediate secession.[c]

William L. Yancey, of Alabama, was first and last the most

[a] Federal Union, Feb. 8, 1854. [b] Federal Union, July 3, 1855.
[c] Du Bose, Life of Yancey, p. 333.

determined advocate of secession, and was of great importance in directing sentiment in Georgia. He was in the lead
of the radical movement in 1850, and was among the last to be
reconciled to the Georgia platform. In the following years
he laid aside his secession arguments to join in the struggle
for Southern rights in the Union, yet he continued to look to
a refuge in case of tyranny on the part of the North, and we
find him in 1858 organizing the "League of United Southerners," the members of which, while keeping up their old party
relations on all other questions, were to hold the Southern
issue paramount.[a]

The rapid growth of the Republican party led all Southerners to become familiar with the idea of secession as a last
recourse in case the antislavery party should ever gain control of the Government. We have already seen that for several years the Presidential contest of 1860 was expected to
bring on a crisis which would necessitate heroic measures.
Immediately after Lincoln's election preparations were set on
foot to meet the emergency.

The chief magistrate of Georgia was in the very forefront
of the aggressively defensive Southern movement. On
November 7, 1860, Governor Brown sent a special message
to the legislature advising against the projected convention of the slaveholding States on the ground that very few
States would be represented in it, but urging effective measures
on the part of Georgia without the delay which a Southern
conferer ce would make necessary. He condemned the duplic-
ity of the Northern people in bringing the slaves to America
and afterwards demanding that the Southern people liberate
them, make them citizens, and intermarry with them. He
stated that the Constitution was a compact, and that one of
the conditions of its adoption had been the agreement by each
State to deliver up fugitive slaves. Showing the breach of
this agreement, he advised that the governor be empowered
to use the military in making reprisals on the public or private property of the offending States, and further, that the
citizens of such States be excluded from the protection of the
laws of Georgia. He recommended the calling of a convention of the State and the appropriation of $1,000,000 as a
military fund for the ensuing year, to be used in putting the

---

[a] Letter of W. L. Yancey to James Slaughter, June 15, 1858; Federal Union, Aug. 3, 1858.

State in a defensive condition as swiftly as it could be done.[a]
While deliberating upon the advice in the governor's special
message, the legislature requested several of the most distinguished men of the State to speak before the assembly upon
the condition of the Republic.   Accordingly, on the night of
November 13, Mr. Toombs made a very powerful address
before the two houses in favor of immediate secession.[b]   On
the following night Mr. Stephens replied to Mr. Toombs in
a speech which, on account of the very great respect in which
the people of every section held the speaker, as well as for
the merits of the address itself, attracted great attention
throughout the country.[c]

In beginning his address, Mr. Stephens expressed his opinion that the South as well as the North was to be blamed for
the existing state of the Union.   Discussing the actual predicament, he said that the election of no man, however hostile
to the South, would justify the disruption of the Republic,
since the constitutional checks upon the President must prevent his doing any great mischief.   If there should be any
distinct attempt to carry out the Republican policy of excluding slave property by act of Congress from the Territories,
and so to destroy the perfect equality of all the States, Mr.
Stephens declared he would be second to no one in advocacy
of resistance to the last extremity; but meanwhile he urged
sober deliberation and solemn remonstrance, followed where
necessary by reprisals against the States which had broken
the fugitive-slave compact.   He therefore advised the sum-
mons of a convention of the people of Georgia and a conference with the neighboring States to secure conservative
action on the part of the whole South.   If these means should
fail to check and remedy the evils of the South, then, and
only then, should a united appeal be made to the god of battles.   "My position, then, in conclusion," he said, "is for
the maintenance of the honor, the rights, the equality, the
security, and the glory of my native State in the Union, if
possible; but if these can not be maintained in the Union,
then I am for their maintenance at all hazards out of it.

a Federal Union, Nov. 13, 1860.

b A. H. Stephens, Constitutional View of the War Between the States, vol. 2, p. 234.

c Rhodes, History of the United States, vol. 3, p. 210.   For correspondence between
Lincoln and Stephens arising from this speech, see Cleveland, Life of Stephens, pp. 151
to 155.

196

Next to the honor and glory of Georgia, the land of my birth, I hold the honor and glory of our common country."[a]

The convictions of the most conservative Southerners were ably expressed in this speech, but it failed to sway the multitude because the most favorable result from the pursuance of the policy outlined would probably be the continuance of the unsettled and objectionable state of affairs. Every outspoken man in Georgia was in favor of resistance,[b] and most of them thought the sooner it was made the better it would be for the interests of the South. Toombs, Brown, and the two Cobbs were the spokesmen for the policy which was clearly destined to carry the State. Farmers prepared to plant larger grain crops than usual in the spring because of the warlike outlook.[c] Homespun clothing was worn at social gatherings to show a patriotic independence of the manufacturing States.[d] A wave of military ardor led to the spontaneous organization of infantry and cavalry companies in all sections of Georgia.

The legislature was far from lukewarm. Its members were gratified at the tenor of the governor's special message; they listened with enthusiasm to the arguments of Toombs, T. R. R. Cobb, H. R. Harris, and others for immediate secession, and they applauded to the echo the declaration of Mr. Stephens that any policy which the sovereign people of the State should adopt in the emergency would command his own hearty support.

The most important of the recommendations of the special message were speedily embodied in legislative enactments. A million dollars was appropriated to be used by the governor in the preparation of the State for defense, the outlay to be met by the issue of bonds to run for twenty years, at 6 per cent.[e] After listening, on November 17, to an address from Hon. W. L. Harris, who, as commissioner from the State of Mississippi, appealed to the State rights actions in the history of Georgia and asked that the State should join his own in taking efficient measures for the safety of the South, the legislature directed the call of a convention of the sovereign people of Georgia, since the right was theirs to determine the

a Stephens, War Between the States, vol. 2, p. 279. Cleveland, Life of Stephens, p. 694.
b Southern Recorder, Dec. 4, 1860.
c Federal Union, Dec. 11, 1860.
d Ibid., Jan. 1, 1860.
e Approved Nov. 16, 1860; Acts of Ga. Gen. Assem., 1860, p. 49.

mode, measure, and time of the resistance which in the general opinion had manifestly become necessary.[a] The act required the governor to order the election on January 2, 1861, of delegates, who should assemble on January 16 in the State capitol. Each county entitled to two members in the house of representatives should elect three delegates to the convention, and each county entitled to one member should send two delegates. Full powers were given the convention to redress all the grievances of the State as a member of the Union. In order to insure the presence in the convention of the ablest men of the State, a subsequent act ordered the adjournment, during its deliberations, of all the State courts.[b] A further defensive measure authorized the governor to accept the services of not more than 10,000 troops of the three arms, and to equip and discipline them for service as infantry, cavalry, and artillery, and also to furnish arms to volunteer companies in the State and to encourage their formation.[c]

A set of resolutions approved December 19 described the state of things which was responsible for the steps already taken by the legislature and for those expected to be taken by the convention. A large portion of the non-slaveholding States, they declared, had for many years shown a fanatical spirit bitterly hostile to the Southern States, and had finally organized a political party for the avowed purpose of destroying the institution of slavery, and consequently spreading ruin and desolation in every portion of the country where it existed. This spirit of fanaticism had become allied with a long-harbored design to wield the taxing power of the Government in a way to protect the interests of the North, and also to appropriate the common Territories of the United States to the exclusive use of Northern immigration, so as to render the power of the section irresistible. These designs had attained such ascendency as to combine a large majority of the Northern people in a sectional party, which had just elected to the Presidency and Vice-Presidency candidates pledged in the most solemn manner to wield all the power and influence of the Government to accomplish its purposes. In order that these reprehensible designs might be counter-

a Approved Nov. 21, 1860; Acts of Ga. Gen. Assem., 1860, p. 26.
b Approved Dec. 19, 1860; Acts of Ga. Gen. Assem., 1860, p. 240.
c Approved Dec. 18, 1860; Acts of Ga. Gen. Assem., 1860, pp. 50, 52.

198

acted to the best effect, the legislature advised that should any or all of the Southern States withdraw from the Union and resume their sovereignty, such States should form a confederacy and adopt as a frame of government the Constitution of the United States so altered and amended as to suit the new state of affairs.[a]

The spirit of the messages of Governor Brown was exactly that with which most Georgians agreed. After the call of a convention had been enjoined upon the executive, the personal opinions of the governor were requested by a group of citizens. The letter of advice to electors of delegates, which accordingly appeared on December 7, was considered to be a complete reply to Mr. Stephens's speech of November 14. In Mr. Brown's view, Mr. Lincoln was a mere instrument in the hands of the great fanatical abolitionist party, under the control of which the whole Government would soon be brought. He said that the triumph of the Northern section upon a platform of avowed hostility to Southern rights afforded ample justification for withdrawal; submission to the inauguration of Lincoln he firmly believed would result in the total abolition of slavery and the utter ruin of the South within twenty-five years. Branching into a special plea to the poorer class of whites, he prophesied that the abolition of slavery would effect their complete misery and degradation. Emancipation would necessarily be accomplished by the purchase of the slaves by the Government. The cost of the four and a half million slaves in the South would amount to two and a quarter billion dollars, to raise which the taxation must be extremely severe. The colonization of the free negroes would also be enormously expensive, but if they were to remain in the South the condition of the poor white would be dreadful. The former slaveowners would soon acquire possession of all the land; the poor white must become a tenant or a day laborer, and, in competition with the negro, must descend to the lowest standard of living; there would be legal, economic, and social equality of the races, with the prospect of intermarriage. The people of the mountains also, the governor continued, had a vital interest in the question. Thousands of freed negroes would remove from the seacoast, and would soon be plundering and stealing in

[a] Acts of Ga. Gen. Assem., 1860, p. 238.

North Georgia as elsewhere. Probably one-fourth of the negro population would have to be kept in jail all the time. Returning to the general issue, Mr. Brown continued: "My honest convictions are that we can never again live in peace with the Northern abolitionists, unless we can have new constitutional guaranties, which I do not believe the people of the Northern States will ever give while we remain together in the Union. Their opinion is that the cotton States will always compromise away their rights, and submit for the sake of peace." The secession of the cotton States before Lincoln's inauguration might lead to Northern concessions and to reunion. Secession would probably not bring on a war, he concluded, for President Buchanan had recently declared that the General Government had no power to coerce a seceding State. On the other hand, the submission to wrongs might necessitate a war to redress those wrongs in the future. [a]

Another document which had influence in the cause of independence was a letter of Mr. Howell Cobb, dated at Washington, December 6. It reached the people of Georgia, together with the news of Mr. Cobb's resignation from Buchanan's Cabinet, soon after the publication of Mr. Brown's letter of advice. It proclaimed that the Union established by the fathers, which was one of equality, justice, and fraternity, would be supplanted on the 4th of March by a Union of sectionalism and hatred—the one worthy of the support and devotion of freemen, the other only possible at the cost of Southern honor, safety, and independence.[b] Mr. Cobb soon afterwards arrived in person to stump the northeastern part of the State for secession.

In order to rally the opposition party, Mr. Stephens arranged a meeting of the members of the general assembly, fifty-two in number, who were opposed to immediate secession. Resolutions were adopted asking for a convention of the Southern States, and advising voters to require pledges from the candidates for the Georgia convention that they would oppose secession unless all other measures of safety should have failed. These "cooperationists" proceeded to make a campaign for a demand on the part of the united South for a guarantee of its rights, which failing, would be followed with

[a] Federal Union, Dec. 11, 1860.
[b] S. Boykin, Memorial Volume of Howell Cobb, p. 31, referring to New York Tribune, Dec. 21, 1860.

a formal dissolution of the Union and a division of the common property.[a]

Mr. Stephens, saw that his following was of considerable strength, but felt that the odds were against him.[b] The current against which he fought was further strengthened by a letter addressed by the Southern Congressmen to their constituents, stating that all hope of saving the Union by legislation was gone and that the honor, safety, and independence of the Southern people required the organization of a Southern Confederacy after the separate withdrawal of the States from the Union.[c]

Even more powerful was a ringing dispatch of Senator Toombs, who had returned to Washington after making his plea for immediate secession at Milledgeville on November 13. The anxiety which Congress showed at the recent startling events had led him to write a public letter to the effect that there was still a possibility of an agreement between the sections, and therefore immediate secession was not imperative.[d] But he quickly reverted to his former position. On December 23 he telegraphed to the Savannah Morning News a dispatch to the people of Georgia. Giving a brief account of the refusal of the Republicans in the Senate committee of thirteen to agree to Crittenden's resolutions or to any others of a similar kind, he proclaimed as if from a rostrum within the hearing of every citizen of the State: "I tell you upon the faith of a true man that all further looking to the North for security for your constitutional rights in the Union ought to be instantly abandoned. It is fraught with nothing but ruin to yourselves and to posterity. Secession by the 4th of March next should be thundered from the ballot box by the unanimous voice of Georgia on the 2d of January next. Such a voice will be your best guaranty for liberty, security, tranquillity, and glory."[e]

Veterans in statecraft and novices in the political arena added their persuasions to swell the triumph of the sectional cause. T. R. R. Cobb, in his maiden political speech, pleaded with the legislature to carry the State out of the Union with-

[a] Southern Recorder. Dec. 25, 1860.
[b] Letter of Stephens to G. T. Curtis, Nov. 30, 1860; Cleveland, Life of Stephens, p. 159.
[c] Federal Union, Dec. 25, 1860.
[d] Letter of Toombs, dated Dec. 13, 1860; Southern Recorder, Dce. 25, 1860.
[e] Federal Union, Jan. 1, 1861.

out waiting for a convention;[a] Wilson Lumpkin wrote from his retirement advising separate State secession and the formation of a Southern Confederacy. "The idea of forcing a State back in the Union," he said, "is quite too preposterous to merit refutation."[b]

When the second day of January arrived, the voters of Georgia had been fully instructed as to the emergency. In most of the counties there were two sets of candidates—the one in favor of immediate secession, the other opposed to immediate secession. The opposition was further divided into those who favored secession after the failure of a last united effort for Southern rights in the Union—the "cooperationists"—and those who did not consider secession at any time to be the best remedy for the grievances felt. There were practically none who denied the right of the State to secede if it should see fit to do so.

In every county the foremost citizens stood as candidates for the convention, and among the candidates those who were held in greatest esteem for strength of judgment were, as a rule, elected, for the people knew that party lines were at last destroyed, and in many cases they thought it better to delegate a strong man, without requiring pledges, than to rely upon their own weaker judgments without the benefit of the debates in the convention.

After the middle of December the secession of all the cotton States was held as certain. On the first of January Mr. Toombs telegraphed from Washington that the vacancies in Buchanan's Cabinet, resulting from the withdrawal of the Southern members, had been filled by the appointment of enemies of the South, which meant that the policy of coercion was already adopted by the Administration. He warned the State that Fort Pulaski, at the mouth of the Savannah River, would very soon be fully manned by Federal troops.[c]

On the very next day Governor Brown issued orders to the colonel of the First Regiment of Georgia Volunteers, directing him to descend the river from Savannah, to occupy the fort, and hold it until the convention should decide concerning its disposal. Accordingly, on January 3, Colonel Lawton took possession of Fort Pulaski in the name of the

a Butler, History of Macon, Ga., p. 235.
b Federal Union, Jan. 1, 1861.
c Savannah Morning News, Jan. 3, 1861.

State of Georgia.[a] There may have been some Georgians who disapproved of this proceeding, but the citizens of Savannah considered the seizure of the fort so necessary that the failure of prompt action by the governor would have been remedied by a spontaneous movement of the people.[b] The United States arsenal at Augusta was not seized before the actual secession of the State, because although, unlike Fort Pulaski, it had a garrison, it was not in ready access from the North, but must continue to be at the mercy of the State forces.

The convention of the people of Georgia was called to order on January 16, 1861, in accordance with the governor's proclamation of November 21. With the exception of one man, who was then on his deathbed, every delegate was in attendance. It was without doubt the most distinguished body of men which had ever assembled in Georgia. Every Georgian of political prominence was a member, with the exception of Jos. E. Brown, Howell Cobb, and C. J. Jenkins, while these gentlemen were invited to seats on the floor of the convention. Of the 297 delegates, there were not four whose names were not of pure English, Scotch, or Irish origin. It would not have been possible to assemble in one hall, by any method of selection, a more truly representative body of the best intelligence of Georgia.

The first two days were devoted to the organization of the convention and to the reading of communications from the already independent States of South Carolina and Alabama. In a secret session of January 18 Mr. Nisbet offered the following resolutions as a test in the matter of secession:

"1. *Resolved*, That in the opinion of this Convention it is the right and duty of Georgia to secede from the present Union, and to cooperate with such of the other States as have or shall do the same, for the purpose of forming a Southern Confederacy upon the basis of the Constitution of the United States. 2. *Resolved*, That a committee of ——— be appointed by the Chair to report an ordinance to assert the right and fulfill the obligation of the State of Georgia to secede from the Union."[c]

[a] Fielder, Life of Brown, p. 178.

[b] Savannah Morning News, Jan. 3, 1861.

[c] Journal of the Convention of the People of Georgia held in 1861, p. 15. Fielder, Life of Brown, p. 177.

Mr. H. V. Johnson offered as a substitute a resolution stating the affection of Georgia for the Union and her desire to preserve it if possible without injury to her own rights and safety, and an ordinance calling a convention of delegates from the States south of Pennsylvania and from the independent republics of South Carolina, Florida, Alabama, and Mississippi, to meet on February 16 to consider the existing state of affairs, and declaring that if the efforts of such convention should fail to secure the rights of the South in the Union the State of Georgia would secede and unite with the other Southern States.[a]

After an elaborate discussion, in which Messrs. Nisbet, H. V. Johnson, T. R. R. Cobb, A. H. Stephens, Toombs, Means, Reese, B. H. Hill, and F. S. Bartow participated, a call was made for the previous question, which brought the convention to a direct vote on Nisbet's resolution to secede. The vote, taken by yeas and nays, showed the adoption of the resolution by a majority of 166 to 130.

On the following day Mr. Nisbet, as chairman of the committee, reported an ordinance for secession, in the form of a repeal and abrogation of the ordinance adopted by the people of Georgia in convention on January 2, 1788, ratifying the Constitution of the United States, and the several acts of the general assembly adopting amendments to that instrument, together with a declaration of the resumption by the State of Georgia of the full exercise of all rights of sovereignty which belong to a free and independent State.[b]

Benjamin H. Hill at once moved the adoption of Mr. Johnson's resolution of the day before as a substitute for the secession ordinance. His motion was lost by a vote of 133 yeas to 164 nays. This vote and the one of the day before were considered as the definite test. The delegates who subsequently voted against secession did so with the object of recording their firm opposition to the precipitate measure. The ordinance was soon afterwards adopted by a vote of 208 to 89, and thereupon the president of the convention declared that it was his pleasure to announce that Georgia was a State, free, sovereign, and independent.[c]

[a] Journal of the Convention, pp. 15 to 20. Stephens, War Between the States, vol. 2, p. 301.

[b] Ibid., p. 31.

[c] Ibid., p. 39.

Just before the final vote on the ordinance Mr. N. M. Crawford rose to explain the grounds of his preceding votes against secession and of his intended vote on the pending motion.   He said that he had consistently voted against the proposition to secede, but in view of the question having been settled by the test votes, he considered it his duty to acquiesce in the declared policy of the State and had decided to strengthen the moral effect of the State's action by voting for the ordinance.[a] Forty-three delegates adopted the same plan to show a similar attitude.   In order to establish complete harmony, the convention ordained that, whereas the lack of unanimity on secession was due not so much to difference of opinion on the rights of Georgia and her wrongs as to the remedy and its application before a resort to other means of redress, resolved that all who voted against the ordinance, as well as those who supported it, would sign the document in order to show unanimous determination to sustain the State in her chosen remedy. All of the delegates signed the ordinance but six, who protested against the immediate secession of Georgia, but who pledged their lives, if necessary, to defend the State from hostile invasion from any source whatever.[b]

It is to be regretted that, owing to the exclusion of reporters, the speeches made in the convention, except that of Mr. Stephens,[c] were never put into a durable form; but they were probably little more than repetitions of what had already been said or written.   Mr. A. H. Stephens records that the most powerful argument in the whole campaign was that of Mr. T. R. R. Cobb, "We can make better terms out of the Union than in it."   Mr. Stephens says, probably with much truth, that two-thirds of those who voted for the ordinance of secession did so expecting a subsequent re-formation of the Union with constitutional guaranties for slavery on the general line of those set forth in the substitute resolutions of Mr. Johnson.[d]

After the decision upon the main question before the convention there were numerous matters which demanded and received attention.   A unanimous vote of thanks was tendered the governor for his prompt action in seizing Fort Pulaski.

[a] Southern Recorder, Jan. 22, 1861.
[b] Journal of the Convention, p. 51.
[c] For which see Stephens, War Between the States, vol. 2, p. 305 ff.
[d] Stephens, War Between the States, vol. 2, p. 381.

All Federal civil officers in Georgia were instructed to continue in the discharge of their duties until otherwise ordered by the convention. Provision was made for the equipment of a small army and navy for the temporary defense of Georgia and the neighboring States. Commissioners were sent to those Southern States which had not yet decided to secede, and delegates were appointed to attend the convention of the seceded States, which was expected to establish a Southern Confederacy.

An ordinance was unanimously adopted by the convention on January 23 establishing in full force for Georgia all laws of the United States in reference to the African slave trade, except the fifth section of the act of May 10, 1800, and with a modification of the act of May 10, 1820, so that instead of being piracy the slave trade should be punishable by confinement in the penitentiary for from five to twenty years.

On January 29 a report by Mr. Toombs was adopted as being suitable for publication to accompany the ordinance of secession and to justify it in the popular mind, [a] after which the convention adjourned to meet again in Savannah at the call of the president. It convened, accordingly, on March 7, adopted the constitution of the Confederate States by a unanimous vote, directed the governor to turn over the military and naval forces to the Confederate Government, formulated and adopted a new constitution for the State of Georgia, and finally adjourned on the 23d of March.

The record of the yeas and nays upon every important measure taken by the convention renders easy the task of tracing the votes of each delegate to the county which he represented. When the vote upon the question to secede is plotted in this way upon the map of the State, several interesting comparisons may be instituted regarding the attitude of different localities toward secession and toward the former political parties, and concerning the local distribution of slaves.

The local vote in the Presidential election of 1860 was not essentially different from the usual party votes in the preceding years. On the eastern edge of the State most of the Democratic votes, together with a number of Whig votes, were cast for Douglas, but elsewhere the Democrats voted for

Breckinridge. The support of the Constitutional Union candidates came from the old Whig sections, though there was some diminution from the usual Whig vote on the seaboard, with a counterbalancing gain in the mountains. We have said that all the hot-heads were for Breckinridge, but it must be noted that just at this time there were very few radical hot-heads in the State. Everyone was awed by the impending calamity. In the general consideration it mattered little whether Bell, Breckinridge, or Douglas carried Georgia. If Lincoln were not elected by the Electoral College, the choice would fall to the United States House of Representatives, where all of Lincoln's enemies would unite in support of one of his opponents. The light vote which was cast in Georgia showed the popular indifference to the result within the State.

The strongholds of the Democratic party in Georgia, in a typical contest with the old Whig party, coincided, as a rule, with the districts in which the white people were more numerous than the slaves. In the contest of 1860 this was still true, except on the seaboard, and with the proviso that the supporters of Douglas be not classed with the Georgia Democrats. Regarding the vote for secession, no such generalization can be made. In fact, party lines were not in any way preserved in the convention of 1861. The only general tendency to be stated is that delegates sent by the Whig or Constitutional Union counties were inclined to vote for secession, and those from counties which had given Breckinridge majorities tended to vote against immediate secession.

This was exactly the reverse of what might have been expected if Georgia politics had been quite logical in the preceding period. As a rule, the Whigs in the South were the moderates, opposing the Democratic fire eaters, and in Georgia the case in all appearances was not an exception; but an historical development had been temporarily reversed in 1840, when the Georgia State Rights party had joined the Whigs, and an anomalous state of things had resulted. There had been no great disruption of parties in 1840, because the existing economic and social bonds were stronger than those of strictly political character. The State Rights men became moderate Unionists in the Whig party and the members of the Union party, as Democrats, took up the advocacy of State rights. This double somersault decided the policy which each party was to advocate for the next twenty years: The election of 1860 was the last one before the destruction of the false arrangement. In it the slave-owning Whigs voted for the conciliatory Bell and the anti-secessionist Douglas, while the Unionist, nonslaveholding Democrats supported the radical Breckinridge. It was inevitable that the crisis of 1861 should bring about a counter somersault in some degree.

It is not easy to determine whether the policy of secession was radical or conservative. Its advocates as well as its opponents claimed the quality of conservatism for their respective causes, and each party had some ground for their contention. A study of the courses of the individual party leaders between 1850 and 1860 will throw light on the question, though it will not give a solution.

Messrs. Toombs, Stephens, and Howell Cobb were, in 1850, responsible for the adoption of the Georgia platform, supportive of the national compromise of that year. Of these, Mr. Toombs was from first to last the most pronounced for Southern rights, and for State rights as a means to an end. In 1850, though a Whig, he stood upon the Georgia platform as an ultimatum to the North. In 1853 he abandoned the Whig party because it favored the restriction of slavery. In 1861 he stood for secession, because of the refusal of the Republicans to give guaranties against their anticipated attack upon Southern rights.

Mr. Cobb, a Democrat throughout the decade, favored the compromise in 1850 because it was conservative and promised peace; but after the triumph of the Republicans became a certainty he took up the advocacy of secession, because he thought that any other course would in the near future bring about a war between the two sections as a result of the aggressive Republican policy.

Mr. Stephens was always eminently conservative. When the Georgia Whigs joined the sectional Southern Know-nothings, he became a member of the Democratic party. In the contest of 1860 he supported Douglas as the candidate of the only remaining national party. In the convention of 1861 he advocated delay and remonstrance instead of immediate withdrawal from the Union.

Mr. Johnson was dissatisfied with the Georgia platform in the early part of the decade,[a] and in 1853 he was elected gov-

[a] Letter of Mr. Johnson, expressing disunion sentiments, dated Aug. 30, 1851; Federal Union, Sept. 11, 1860.

ernor by the Democrats as an advocate of Southern rights
and in opposition to Mr. Jenkins as the Union candidate.
Finding reason in later years to change his attitude, he
joined Mr. Stephens in the leadership of the peace faction of
the Democrats and accepted a nomination to the Vice-Presidency on the ticket with Mr. Douglas. In the Georgia convention, with Mr. Stephens and Mr. Hill as his colleagues, he was
a champion of the project for a Southern convention which
should precede and might obviate the necessity for secession.

Mr. Nisbet had been in touch with Georgia politics for
thirty-five years or more. An admirer of Troup in his youth,
he had followed the general tendency, becoming successively
a member of the State Rights, Whig, and Know-Nothing parties. He was a warm supporter of the compromise in 1850,
but was in the forefront of the secessionists in 1861.

Mr. Hill, though a much younger man, had been the colleague of Mr. Nisbet in the Whig and American parties.
From a comparison of his utterances it may be seen that Mr.
Hill wavered between the antagonistic policies before 1860,
but from the beginning of the Presidential campaign he decided
against secession unless it were by the advice of a Southern
convention.

Mr. T. R. R. Cobb had never felt any strong interest in politics until the capture of the Government by the anti-slavery
party inspired him to lead Georgia out of the Union, the better to secure stronger guarantees for the peculiar institution
upon her reentrance into the sisterhood.

As for Mr. Brown, we have seen that he was a progressive
Southern Rights Democrat in 1849; that, though he acquiesced
in the compromise of 1850, he was not convinced of its finality,
and that as governor he urged the State to secession, and, indeed,
anticipated the action of the convention by seizing Fort
Pulaski.

We thus demonstrate that, with the exception of Mr. Jenkins and Mr. Stephens, whose courses had been very similar,
there were no two leaders of political thought in Georgia in
1861 who had been in complete agreement throughout the
decade. Most of those above named were conservative in disposition, yet they could not agree upon a policy.

The institution of domestic servitude had naturally a conservative influence upon those who were interested in its

maintenance. Slaves were capital, and capital is always conservative in its tendency. Moreover, slavery was generally on the defensive against attack, and thus in a conservative position. It was a long-established institution, and for that reason its maintenance was conservative. Secession was advocated by its supporters as a means to the more certain preservation of slavery, and in that light the policy seems itself to have been conservative.

But, on the other hand, the opposition to secession in Georgia was not opposition to the principle but to the advisability of applying the drastic remedy without first taking milder measures which might render it unnecessary. Secession appears from this point of view to have been radical. When we consider, however, that from the practical certainty of the refusal of the North to yield the constitutional guaranties which were demanded for the permanent advantage of slavery, the only result from a Southern convention would probably have been a concerted secession at a later period. The question as to conservatism is again unsettled.

The plot of the vote in the secession convention, when traced to the counties, shows that there was a general, though by no means universal, tendency in favor of secession among delegates from the sections where slaves were numerous, and an opposite, but no more universal, tendency from the districts where the whites preponderated. The personal influence of Stephens, Johnson, and Hill carried their home sections against immediate secession; while Brown, Toombs, Nisbet, Bartow, and the two Cobbs were powerful in their districts for withdrawal from the Union. It is interesting to note that every county in which a city or large town was located had in 1860 a comparatively small slave population. Yet every delegate from such counties voted for secession when the test question was upon its passage.

We see, then, that the progressive townspeople as well as the great conservative slaveholders, of whom Howell Cobb was a type, were strong in the advocacy of immediate secession; and that the people of the mountains and of the barren parts of the southern pine region, who were so conservative as to be almost retrogressive, tended to combine in opposition to immediate withdrawal; but that all Georgians were agreed in the opinion that their State had a constitutional right to

H. Doc. 702, pt. 2——14

secede whenever its sovereign people should see fit to exercise that right.

It has been our object in large part in the preceding pages to set forth the history of the doctrine of State rights in Georgia. We have noted the influence of such matters as Indian affairs and the protective tariff in developing opposition to a highly centralized government, and we have explained the cumulative effect of the slavery struggle in bringing about actual secession. In our pursuit of historical truth we have at length reached the culmination of the whole movement in the adoption of an ordinance by the people of Georgia to secede from the United States and to resume on the part of the commonwealth all rights of sovereignty which had been delegated to the Federal government. We have not attempted to settle constitutional questions which were involved, but have usually confined ourselves in such matters to the statement of the interpretations of history and the Constitution which were advanced by prominent Georgians. It only remains to state that after so many years of political disagreement between the various successive parties, the people of Georgia at length achieved unanimity, when each citizen excelled his neighbor in the support of the ordinance by which Georgia had declared herself again sovereign and in the defense of Southern rights and Southern independence.[a]

a Cf. Editorial in Southern Recorder, Jan. 29, 1861.

BIBLIOGRAPHY.

HISTORIES OF GEORGIA.

ARTHUR, T. S., and CARPENTER, W. H.   History of Georgia from its earliest settlement to the present time.   Philadelphia, 1882.
>   Of little value as an authoritative work.

AVERY, I. W.   History of the State of Georgia from 1850 to 1881.   New York, 1881.
>   Notwithstanding his extravagance in the use of adjectives, the facts stated by Mr. Avery are reliable.   The work is in large part a biography and eulogy of Joseph E. Brown.

EVANS, LAWTON B.   A student's history of Georgia.   New York, 1898.
>   An excellent school history.   Indeed, though meager, it is the fullest in detail of any work covering the whole field of the history of the State.

JONES, C. C., Jr.   History of Georgia.   2 vols.   Boston, 1883.
>   One of the very best of American colonial histories.   The work as published only reaches the end of the American Revolution.   The author did not carry out his design of covering the history of Georgia as a State in later volumes.

M'CALL, HUGH.   History of Georgia.   2 vols.   Savannah, 1811–1816.
>   The contents of the first volume are taken almost bodily from Hewitt's Historical Collections of South Carolina.   The second volume contains valuable material relating to Georgia in the Revolutionary war.

MITCHELL, FRANCES L.   Georgia land and people.   Atlanta, 1900.
>   Considerable research is shown, but little constructive ability.   This work, in common with nearly all others on Georgia history, has the fault of giving no references to sources of information.

SMITH, CHARLES H.   A school history of Georgia.   Boston, 1896.
>   In addition to an outline of the history of Georgia to 1893, this little book contains chapters upon social and political institutions in ante-bellum Georgia, which are worthy of note as being written by one who has lived observingly in the period of which he writes.

SMITH, G. G.   Story of Georgia and the Georgia people.   1732 to 1860.   Macon, 1900.
>   Contains noteworthy material upon the process of settlement.   For the general history of the State the author relies mainly upon secondary authorities.   County histories fill a large part of the volume.

STEVENS, W. B.   History of Georgia to 1798.   2 vols.
>   A very satisfactory history of colonial Georgia.   The treatment of the period after the Revolution is somewhat fragmentary.

WHITE, GEORGE.   Historical Collections of Georgia.   New York, 1854.
>   Contains much valuable material in the shape of original documents, biographical sketches, and local history.   According to a statement of Governor Wilson Lumpkin, White's account of Cherokee affairs is faulty.

212

WHITE, GEORGE. Statistics of Georgia, its natural, civil, and ecclesiastical history, description of each county, accounts of the aboriginees. Savannah, 1849.

Most of the valuable material in this volume, which itself is quite good, is incorporated in the later work by the same author—Historical Collections of Georgia.

LOCAL AND SPECIAL HISTORIES.

BUTLER, J. C. Historical record of Macon and central Georgia. Macon, 1879.

The best local history in the Georgia field.

BOWEN, ELIZA A. Story of Wilkes County. Washington, Ga., circ., 1882.

CHAPPELL, ABSALOM H. Miscellanies of Georgia, historical, biographical, descriptive, etc. Columbus, Ga., 1874.

Contains sketches of Alexander McGillivray, Elijah Clarke, Benjamin Hawkins, James Jackson, of the Georgia land lottery, and of the Yazoo fraud. Possesses value for the general reader; it deals too much in eulogies and generalities to have great value as an authority.

DUTCHER, SALEM (and JONES, C. C., Jr.). Memorial history of Augusta, Georgia . . . Syracuse, N. Y., 1890.

GEORGIA HISTORICAL SOCIETY COLLECTIONS. Savannah, vol. 1, 1840; vol. 2, 1842; vol. 3, 1873; vol. 4, 1878.

Contains valuable material, largely in the shape of reprints of documents for the colonial period. "A Sketch of the Creek Country in 1798 and 1799" was printed in 1848 as part of vol. 3, but was never published.

In addition to its "collections," the society has published a considerable number of pamphlets, devoted chiefly to the annual addresses before the society. Some of these are of considerable value.

HASKINS, CHARLES H. The Yazoo Land Companies. 1891. Reprinted from American Historical Association Papers, vol. 4, No. 4.

This excellent little monograph was printed as a doctor's dissertation at Johns Hopkins University. It is the final authority in its field. Fully equipped with references.

JONES, C. C. The Dead Towns of Georgia. Savannah, 1878.

In explaining the reasons for the decay of such towns as Frederica and Ebenezer the author throws light upon the economic history of Georgia. This was also published as vol. 4 of Georgia Historical Society Collections.

LEE, F. D., and AGNEW, J. L. Historical record of the city of Savannah. Savannah, 1869.

MEMOIRS OF GEORGIA, containing historical accounts of the State's civil, military, industrial and professional interests and personal sketches of many of its people. 2 vols. Atlanta, 1895.

PICKETT, ALBERT J. History of Alabama, and incidentally of Georgia and Mississippi, from the earliest period. Third edition. Charleston, 1851.

This excellent history of Alabama contains much authoritative material on Georgia history. It concludes its view with the year 1819.

REED, WALLACE P., editor. History of Atlanta, Georgia. Syracuse, N. Y., 1889.

SCOMP, H. A.   King alcohol in the realm of king cotton, or a history of
of the liquor traffic and of the prohibition movement in Georgia from
1733 to 1887.   1888.
> Incidentally to the main theme, the history of Georgia receives some treat-
> ment in its political, economic, and social aspects.

STROBEL, P. A.   The Salzburgers and their descendants,   Baltimore, 1855.
> In relating the history of the German colony at Ebenezer, near Savannah, the
> author describes to some extent the economic and social conditions in Georgia as
> a colony and as a young State.

SHERWOOD, ADIEL.   A gazeteer of the State of Georgia.   Charleston, 1827.
Second edition, Philadelphia, 1829.   Third edition, enlarged, Washington, 1837.   Fourth edition, 1860.
> Of some value as containing data showing the condition of the State at the
> various dates of publication.   The later editions have maps of indifferent quality.
> The issue of 1860 gives a list of the literary productions of Georgia to that date.

STACY, JAMES.   History of Midway Church, Liberty County, Ga.   New-
nan, Ga., 1899.
> The history of the community at Midway, which included a large number
> of leading Georgia men and families, is an important contribution to Georgia
> history.

VEDDER, O. F., and WELDON, FRANK (and JONES, C. C., Jr.).   History of
Savannah . . .   Syracuse, N. Y., 1890.

WILSON, ADELAIDE.   Historic and picturesque Savannah.   Boston, 1889.

WOOLLEY, E. C.   The Reconstruction of Georgia.   New York, 1901.
> A painstaking monograph in a field for which there is little material generally
> accessible.   Full bibliographical apparatus.

BIOGRAPHIES AND MEMOIRS.

ANDREWS, GARNET.   Reminiscences of an old Georgia lawyer.   Atlanta,
1870.

BOYKIN, S.   Memorial volume of Howell Cobb.   Atlanta, 1870.
> Contains a biographical sketch by W. H. Browne.

CALHOUN, JOHN C.   The correspondence of J. C. Calhoun, edited by J. F.
Jameson.   Printed in the Report of the American Historical Association for 1899, vol. 2, Washington, 1901.
> Contains much material of great value for Southern history.   The letters to
> and from Wilson Lumpkin are to be noted as relating to Georgia.

CHARLTON, THOS. U. P.   The life of Maj. Gen. James Jackson.   Augusta,
1809.   Reprinted, Atlanta, no date.
> The reprint contains accounts of Jackson by several writers, and also contains
> a valuable set of letters from Jackson to John Milledge and others.

CLEVELAND, H.   Alexander H. Stephens in public and private.   Philadelphia, 1866.
> The collection of letters and speeches is valuable.

CRAWFORD, W. H.   Correspondence.   MSS.
> A small collection is in private possession in Athens, Ga.   There are also a few
> letters of Crawford in the library of the Department of State at Washington, in
> the New York Public Library, and in the Boston Public Library.   Scattering let-
> ters of Crawford are to be found in the printed correspondence of Clay and of
> Gallatin.   On the whole, very few Crawford letters have been preserved.

DRAPER, LYMAN C. Collection of MSS. in the Wisconsin Historical Society Library.

> The volume of documents relating to Georgia is chiefly concerned with Elijah Clarke.

DU BOSE, J. W. Life and times of W. L. Yancey. Birmingham, Ala., 1892.

> A painstaking work, which is useful in the study of the secession movement.

FIELDER, H. Life, times, and speeches of Joseph E. Brown. Springfield, Mass., 1883.

> The shortcomings of the biography are offset by the collection of documents and the sketches of Brown's contemporaries.

GILMER, GEORGE R. Sketches of some of the first settlers of upper Georgia, of the Cherokees, and of the author. New York, 1855.

> A noteworthy book of remarkable frankness; contains biographical and genealogical sketches of the Gilmers and the neighboring families, an account of the settlement of upper Georgia, and an autobiography, including documents chiefly concerning the Cherokees.

——. The literary progress of Georgia. The semi-centennial address of the University of Georgia. Athens, Ga., 1851. pm.

> A rambling discussion of conditions in early Georgia. Little attention given to the literary progress. Much of the material was afterwards used by the author in writing the work listed above.

HARDEN, E. J. Life of George M. Troup. Savannah, 1840.

> A satisfactory work. Numerous documents are given in connection with the account of the Creek controversy.

HILLIARD, HENRY W. Politics and pen pictures at home and abroad. New York, 1892.

> Valuable chiefly for its authoritative account of Southern and national politics. Contains notices of Georgia history prior to 1860.

JONES, C. C., Jr. Biographical sketches of the delegates from Georgia to the Continental Congress. New York, 1891.

> All of Colonel Jones's work is of an accurate and valuable character. In addition to his works listed herein, he wrote a large number of pamphlets, addresses, etc. In a brief memorial of his father (Augusta, Ga., 1893), Mr. C. E. Jones gives a bibliography of eighty titles, mostly relating to Georgia history.

HAWKINS, BENJAMIN. Journals and papers. MSS.

> There are ten small MSS. volumes of the Hawkins papers in the library of the Georgia Historical Society at Savannah. The society has printed the most valuable of these, "A sketch of the Creek country in the years 1798 and 1799," as an extra part to the third volume of its "collections." The remaining Hawkins papers are journals of routine work among the Creeks and correspondence which is of a kind useful only in very minute research in Creek affairs.

JOHNSTON, R. M., and BROWNE, W. H. Life of Alexander H. Stephens. Philadelphia, 1878.

> A most excellent biography, giving a good view of political history and containing a full and well-selected collection of letters and the shorter speeches.

LUMPKIN, WILSON. Incidents connected with the life of. 2 vols. MSS.

> A valuable autobiography covering the period of the author's active political life from about 1810 to about 1840. It contains a large number of letters, speeches, and executive messages dealing largely with internal improvements and Cherokee Indian affairs. The manuscript, if printed, would fill some 1,500 octavo pages. It is now in private possession in Athens, Ga.

MAYES, EDWARD. Lucius Q. C. Lamar: his life, times, and speeches, 1825–1893. Nashville, 1896.

> The early chapters contain some treatment of conditions in Georgia in Lamar's youth.

MILLER, S. F.   Bench and bar of Georgia: memoirs and sketches.   Philadelphia, 1858.   2 vols.

> A collection of mediocre biographical sketches.   Contains valuable documents and some other material of value which is not readily accessible elsewhere. The sketches of J. M. Berrien and A. S. Clayton are the most valuable in the collection.

MEIGS, W. H.   Life of Josiah Meigs.   Philadelphia, 1887.

> Josiah Meigs was president of the University of Georgia from 1801 to 1811. This short biography gives some account of the primitive conditions in upper Georgia at that time.

STOVALL, P. A.   Robert Toombs: statesman, speaker, soldier, sage.   New York, 1892.

> One of the best biographies in the Georgia field.   It gives a good view of political affairs in the lifetime of Toombs.

SPARKS, W. H.   The memories of fifty years.   Philadelphia, 1870.

> While not reliable for strict accuracy, this volume of reminiscence contains in its early chapters good accounts of men and conditions in Georgia in the first decades of the nineteenth century.

WADDELL, JAMES D.   Biographical sketch of Linton Stephens.   Atlanta, 1877.

> Linton Stephens was the younger brother of A. H. Stephens.   This work has little value except as simple biography.

THE LAWS OF GEORGIA.

GEORGIA GENERAL ASSEMBLY, acts passed by, from 1778 to the present time, except 1777–1799, 1805–1810, etc.   MSS. in the office of the secretary of state, Atlanta.

> The text or substance of all laws of general application may be found in the compilations and digests.   The acts and resolutions of each session were printed from about 1812.

GEORGIA COLONIAL ASSEMBLY.   Acts passed by the Georgia assembly, 1755–1774.   Wormsloe, 1881.

> Contains such colonial acts of Georgia as are not to be found in the regular compilations of laws.   Privately printed.   The edition was limited to 49 copies.

MARBURY, H., and CRAWFORD, W. H.   A compilation of the laws of Georgia from 1755 to 1800.   Containing also the constitutions of Georgia of 1777, 1789, and 1798.   Savannah, 1802.

WATKINS, GEORGE.   A compilation of the laws of Georgia.   1802.

> This compilation failed to obtain recognition by the State authorities, because it contained the Yazoo act, which had been ordered expunged from the records.

CLAYTON, A. S.   A compilation of the laws of Georgia passed between 1800 and 1810.   Augusta, 1813.

PRINCE, O. H.   Digest of the laws of Georgia enacted previous to 1820.   Milledgeville, 1822.

DAWSON, W. C.   A compilation of the laws of Georgia passed between 1819 and 1829.   Milledgeville, 1831.

FOSTER, ARTHUR.   A digest of the laws of Georgia passed between 1820 and 1829.   Philadelphia, 1831.

PRINCE, O. H.   Digest of the laws of Georgia enacted previous to 1837.   Athens, 1837.

HOTCHKISS, W. A.   Codification of the statute law of Georgia.   Savannah, 1845.

COBB, T. R. R.   Digest of the statute laws of Georgia in force prior to 1851. 2 vols.   Athens, 1851.

CLARK, R. H., COBB, T. R. R., and IRWIN, D.   Code of Georgia.   Atlanta, 1861.

GEORGIA PUBLIC DOCUMENTS.

GEORGIA EXECUTIVE COUNCIL.   Journals for 1783–84 and 1789–1792.   MSS. in the office of the secretary of state, Atlanta.   Continued in the senate journal.

GEORGIA SENATE.   Journal from 1790 to the present time, except 1792–1799, 1805–1810, etc.   MSS. in the office of the secretary of state, Atlanta. The journals of the senate were printed from about 1808.

GEORGIA HOUSE OF REPRESENTATIVES.   Journal from 1781 to the present time, except 1789–1795, 1798–1800, 1801–2, 1805, 1811, etc.   MSS. in the office of the secretary of state, Atlanta.   The journals of the house were printed from about 1808.

CONVENTION OF 1839.   Journal of the convention to reduce and equalize the representation of the general assembly of Georgia.   Milledgeville, 1839.

CONVENTION OF 1850.   Journal of the Georgia convention held in Milledgeville in 1850.   Milledgeville, 1850.

CONVENTION OF 1861.   Journal of the public and secret proceedings of the convention of the people of Georgia, held in Milledgeville and Savannah in 1861.   Milledgeville, 1861.

DELEGATES OF GEORGIA in the Continental Congress.   Observations upon the effects of late political suggestions.   Wormsloe, 1847.
See infra, p. 26.

LEGISLATURE OF GEORGIA.   Address and remonstrance (1801).
For numerous Georgia documents see American State Papers, Indian Affairs, to 19th Congress, 1827, 2 vols., and Public Lands, to 24th Congress, 1837, 8 vols., Washington.   Also H. Niles, Political Register, 1811 to 1849, Baltimore.

CHARLTON, T. U. P.   Reports of cases argued and determined in the superior courts of the eastern district of the State of Georgia. N. Y., 1824.

DUDLEY, G. M.   Reports of decisions made by the judges of the superior courts of law and chancery of the State of Georgia.   N. Y., 1837.

CHARLTON, ROBERT M.   Reports of decisions made in the superior courts of the eastern district of Georgia.   Savannah, 1838.

DECISIONS OF THE SUPERIOR COURTS OF THE STATE OF GEORGIA.   Part 1, containing decisions rendered during the year 1842.   Augusta, 1843.

REPORTS OF CASES IN LAW AND EQUITY, argued and determined in the supreme court of Georgia.   110 + vols. (1846 to the present).   Various reporters and places of publication.

WORKS ON STATE RIGHTS AND SECESSION.

POWELL, EDWARD PAYSON. Nullification and Secession in the United States. A history of the six attempts during the first century of the Republic. N. Y., 1897.

HOUSTON, D. F. Nullification in South Carolina. N. Y., 1896.
A careful history of the movement, from the original documents.

CALHOUN, JOHN C. A discourse on the Constitution and Government of the United States. Columbia, S. C., 1851.
An exposition of the extreme particularist, or State sovereignty, view of the federal constitution.

HODGSON, JOSEPH. Cradle of the Confederacy, or the times of Troup, Quitman, and Yancey. Mobile, 1876.

STEPHENS, ALEXANDER H. Constitutional view of the late war between the States. 2 vols., Phila., 1868–1870.
The ablest defense extant of the Southern policy leading to secession. Gives special attention, in parts of the second volume, to occurrences in Georgia.

CURRY, J. L. M. Civil history of the government of the Confederate States. Richmond, 1901.
A large part of the volume is devoted to a legal and constitutional defense of secession.

DAVIS, JEFFERSON. Rise and fall of the Confederate Government. 3 vols., N. Y., 1881.

WORKS ON SLAVERY.

ADAMS, NEHEMIAH. A South-side view of slavery. Second edition. Boston, 1855.
A rose-colored account of conditions in Savannah, by a Boston clergyman who made a trip to the South and experienced a shattering of his preconceived opinions.

BURKE, EMILY P. Reminiscences of Georgia. Oberlin, Ohio, 1850.
A fairly satisfactory account of social and economic conditions.

COBB, THOS. R. R. An historical sketch of slavery. Phila., 1858.
Chapters IX to XVIII treat of negro slavery, chiefly in the United States, of abolition, and of colonization.

COBB, THOS. R. R. An inquiry into the law of negro slavery in the United States of America. Vol. I, Phila., 1858.
This volume treats of the legal status of the slaves as persons. The volume on slaves as property was never published.

KEMBLE, FRANCES A. Journal of a residence on a Georgia plantation in 1838–39. N. Y., 1863.
A dark picture of conditions in the sea-island district of Georgia, where the evils of slavery existed in intensified form. The bad features are over-emphasized, and the inference is made that everywhere else slavery was worse than where the author saw it.

MALLARD, R. Q. Plantation life before emancipation. Richmond, 1897.
A description of the status of slaves in Liberty County, Georgia, by a former slaveholder. Shows the ameliorations, which the author of Kemble's Journal could not appreciate.

OLMSTED, F. L. A journey in the seaboard slave States, with remarks on their economy. N. Y., 1856.
Hardly so prejudiced as the account of slavery given by Miss Kemble (Mrs. Butler).

218

ROYCE, C. C.   The Cherokee Nation of Indians: A narrative of their official relations with the Colonial and Federal governments.   In report of the United States Bureau of Ethnology.   1833–84, pp. 121–378.   Washington, 1887.
A meritorious work, with excellent maps of the Cherokee lands.

WEIL, ROBERT.   Legal status of the Indian.   N. Y., 1888.
Doctor's dissertation at Columbia College.

MAPS OF GEORGIA.

1750.   "A new and accurate map of the province of Georgia in North America."   (British Museum.)

1780.   Sketch of the northern frontiers of Georgia, extending from the mouth of the river Savannah to the town of Augusta, by Archibald Campbell.   Engraved by Wm. Faden, Charing Cross, 1780.
Shows plantations, fortifications, roads, forests, and swamps between Savannah and Augusta.   Nearly all the farms and plantations above Savannah front upon the river, while the highroad is a mile or two distant from the river.   Frequent plantation roads branch off the highroad.   Mills and taverns are very few.   The names of many planters are laid down.   The map is apparently accurate and certainly valuable.   Reprinted herewith.

1781.   The seaboard region of Georgia, in the "Atlantic Neptune," vol. 2, part 3, plate 9.   (British Museum.)
An excellent map.

1794.   "A new and general map of the Southern dominions belonging to the United States of America."   (British Museum.)

1818.   Early, Eleazer.   Map of the State of Georgia, prepared from actual surveys and other documents.
A fine large wall map, of which numerous copies are extant.

1826.   Map of North Carolina, South Carolina, and Georgia, showing an extensive scheme of proposed canals.   (British Museum.)

1827.   Tanner, H. S.   Map of Georgia and Alabama.   Phila., 1827.   (British Museum.)

1830.   Map of the State of Georgia, drawn by Carlton Wellborn and Orange Green.   Savannah, 1830, fold 12mo.   (Georgia Historical Society.)

1835.   Tanner, H. S.   Map of Georgia and Alabama.   Phila., 1835.

1835.   Mitchell, S. A.   Map of North Carolina, South Carolina, and Georgia.   Phila., 1835.   (British Museum.)
Gives stage routes and their schedules.

1846.   Tanner, H. S.   Map of Georgia and Alabama.
Shows railroads and highways.

1861.   Bonner, W. G.   Map of Georgia by direction of the general assembly.   Published at Milledgeville.
A large wall map.

1864.   Lloyd, J. T.   Topographical map of Georgia.   N. Y., 1864.
A large map.   Accurate in details.

ATLASES CONTAINING MAPS OF GEORGIA.

1796. Reid, John. The American Atlas. N. Y., 1796. To accompany Winterbotham's History. (Congressional Library.)
1823. Carey, H. C., and Lea, I. Atlas. Phila., 1823.
1830. 'Finley, Anthony. Atlas. Phila., 1830.
1853. Thomas, Copperthwaite & Co. Atlas. Phila., 1853.
1861. Colton. General Atlas. N. Y., 1861.
1862. Mitchell. New General Atlas. Phila., 1862.

GEORGIA NEWSPAPERS, ANTE BELLUM.

Files in the University of Georgia Library, Athens, Ga.

ATHENS: Georgia Express, 1808 to 1813. Athens Gazette, 1814 to 1817. Athenian, 1827 to 1833. Southern Banner, 1833 to 1846.
AUGUSTA: Augusta Chronicle, 1786 to 1841, except 1793 and 1800 to 1804. Augusta Herald, 1799 to 1806, 1812, 1815, 1817–18, 1821. Columbian Sentinel, 1807. Augusta Courier, 1827–28. Constitutionalist, 1825 to 1841.
COLUMBUS: Columbus Enquirer, 1832 to 1841. Sentinel and Herald, 1838.
MACON: Georgia Messenger, 1831 to 1841. Macon Telegraph, 1832 to 1835.
MILLEDGEVILLE: Georgia Journal, 1810 to 1837. Southern Recorder, 1820 to 1836.
SAVANNAH: Georgia Gazette, 1798 to 1802. Columbian Museum, 1804 and 1813–14. Savannah Republican, 1802 and 1833, except 1816 and 1831. Georgian, 1819 to 1823, and 1829 to 1841.

Files in the library of the Georgia Historical Society, Savannah, Ga.

SAVANNAH: Georgia Gazette, 1774, 1775, 1783 to 1802, 1817 to 1820. Columbian Museum, 1796 to 1802, 1804, 1806 to 1808. Patriot, 1806–7. Public Intelligencer, 1807–8. Savannah Republican, 1807 to 1813. Georgian, 1819, 1822 to 1850. Savannah Journal, 1852, 1853, 1855.

AUGUSTA: Augusta Chronicle, 1790 to 1800. Southern Centinel, 1793 to 1799.

MILLEDGEVILLE: Southern Recorder, 1829 to 1840, 1845 to 1847.

CASSVILLE: Standard, 1855.

Files in the Congressional Library, Washington.

ATHENS: Southern Whig, 1849.

AUGUSTA: Augusta Chronicle, 1819 to 1830, 1849 to 1854, 1858 to 1860. Constitutionalist, 1856, 1858 to 1860.

COLUMBUS: Columbus Enquirer, 1841 to 1847. Columbus Times, 1845 to 1849.

MILLEDGEVILLE: Georgia Journal, 1819 to 1828, 1830, 1841 to 1843, 1845. Patriot, 1823–4. Southern Recorder, 1822 to 1825, 1843, 1851, 1852. Statesman, 1826. Standard of Union, 1841. Federal Union, 1843 to 1845, 1847 to 1849.

Savannah: Georgia Gazette, 1775, 1779 to 1799 fragmentary. Georgian, 1823 to 1826, 1829–30, 1833 to 1841, 1846 to 1849, 1832 to 1856. Georgia Republican and State Intelligencer, 1803 to 1805. Savannah Republican, 1807 to 1812, 1814 to 1872.

Files in the Library of the Wisconsin Historical Society, Madison, Wis.

ew Echota: Cherokee Phoenix, 1828 to 1834. Also fragmentary files of other Georgia newspapers.

Files in the office of the Union and Recorder, Milledgeville, Ga.

Milledgeville: Statesman and Patriot, 1826–7. Southern Recorder, 1836 to 1847, 1857 to 1860. Federal Union, 1830 to 1874. Union and Recorder, 1874 to the present.
Augusta: Courier, 1827–8.

File in private possession, Milledgeville, Ga.

Milledgeville: Southern Recorder, 1820 to 1868.

Files in the office of the Savannah Morning News, Savannah, Ga.

Savannah: Georgia Gazette, 1794 to 1796. Columbian Museum, 1803. Savannah Morning News, 1850 to the present.

File in the office of the Augusta Chronicle, Augusta, Ga.

Augusta: Augusta Chronicle, 1800 to the present. Also a partial file before 1800.

Files in the office of the Macon Telegraph, Macon, Ga.

Milledgeville: Georgia Journal, 1819 to 1825, 1826–7, 1829 to 1835, 1837 to 1841, 1843 to 1845, 1847 to 1849.
Penfield: Christian Index, 1850–51, 1856–7, 1859.
Macon: Georgia Messenger, 1825, 1829, 1833 to 1842, 1845 to 1847. Journal and Messenger, 1851 to 1857, 1860–61. Georgia Telegraph, 1847 to 1853. Telegraph and Messenger, continued as Macon Telegraph, 1863 to the present.

File in the office of the Columbus Enquirer, Columbus, Ga.

Columbus: Enquirer, 1828 to the present.

Files in the State Capitol, the Carnegie Library, and the office of the Atlanta Constitution, Atlanta, Ga.

None antedating 1861.

INDEX TO GEORGIA AND STATE RIGHTS.

221